EVALU
INFORM

A GUIDE FOR USERS
OF SOCIAL SCIENCE RESEARCH

EVALUATING INFORMATION

A GUIDE FOR USERS OF SOCIAL SCIENCE RESEARCH

FOURTH EDITION

Jeffrey Katzer
Syracuse University

Kenneth H. Cook
3Com Corporation

Wayne W. Crouch
Crouch Associates

Boston, Massachusetts   Burr Ridge, Illinois   Dubuque, Iowa
Madison, Wisconsin   New York, New York   San Francisco, California   St. Louis, Missouri

McGraw-Hill

*A Division of The **McGraw·Hill** Companies*

EVALUATING INFORMATION: A GUIDE FOR USERS OF SOCIAL SCIENCE RESEARCH

Copyright © 1998, by The McGraw-Hill Companies, Inc. All rights reserved. Previous editions © 1978, 1982, and 1991. Printed in the United States of America. Except as permitted under the United States Copyright Act of 1976, no part of this publication may be reproduced or distributed in any form or by any means, or stored in a database or retrieval system, without the prior written permission of the publisher.

This book is printed on acid-free paper.

1 2 3 4 5 7 8 9 0 QF/QF 9 0 9 8 7

ISBN 0-07-034309-8

Editorial director: *Phillip A. Butcher*
Sponsoring editor: *Jill Gordon*
Developmental editor: *Katherine Blake*
Marketing manager: *Sally Constable*
Project manager: *Paula M. Buschman*
Production supervisor: *Heather D. Burbridge*
Typeface: *10/12 Times Roman*
Printer: *Quebecor Printing Book Group/Fairfield*

Library of Congress Cataloging-in-Publication Data

Katzer, Jeffrey
    Evaluating information: a guide for users of social science
research / Jeffrey Katzer, Kenneth H. Cook, Wayne W. Crouch—4th
ed.
      p. cm.
    Includes bibliographical references and index.
    ISBN 0-07-034309-8
    1. Social sciences—Research—Methodology. 2. Social sciences—
Methodology. I. Cook, Kenneth H. II. Crouch, Wayne W.
III. Title.
H62.K378   1997
300'. 72—dc21   97–5646

http://www.mhcollege.com

PREFACE TO
FOURTH EDITION

This book was originally written to help offset an error we had been making as teachers. We had been giving our undergraduate students, our master's students (in a professional program), and our doctoral students (in a research program) the same type of introduction to social science research. All were taught from the researcher's point of view. Such a perspective is appropriate for those few students who will actually do research, but we had become convinced that it was not the best perspective for the many who will rarely, if ever, conduct a research investigation.

We are pleased that so many others found our approach from the user's point of view valuable. The previous editions were adopted at several hundred colleges and universities in diverse fields of the social sciences. Thus, there is no reason to alter the major focus of the book in this edition. We still have in mind undergraduate and graduate students in all the social sciences and related professional areas, such as the following:

advertising	education	nursing
anthropology	geography	political science
broadcasting	journalism	psychology
communication	labor relations	public relations
counseling	library science	social work
criminal justice	management	sociology

What all these students need is a research course with a consumer's point of view. In their coursework and in their professional careers these students will be called on to read and make use of social research findings, yet a researcher-oriented methods course of one or two semesters is not well-suited to their needs.

One approach is to develop a separate course for these students, a course in which the primary aim is to teach students how to understand and evaluate published research reports. This book can serve as the major textbook for such a course. However, we did not expect, and have not found, that many such courses exist.

A more viable approach is to add to existing courses some training and practice in research evaluation. Thus, we wrote this book primarily as a supplementary textbook. It can be used in courses on research methods and statistics and in courses that review research findings or make use of the original journal articles.

The wide applicability of the book is due in part to our approach. Our presentation is thematic, focusing on the broad concerns common to all forms of social research. Psychologists, for example, have traditionally relied on methods that are different from those of sociologists. Similarly, journalists have favored particular methods, while therapists have favored others. Common to all these methods, however, are the same concerns, the same norms and values arising out of much of contemporary Western scientific practice and philosophy.

Most consumers of research will need to evaluate various types of research: experimental, survey, case study, and so on. Unlike researchers, consumers will not have much opportunity to become specialists in one or a few research methods. Consequently, they need a general orientation to what social research is about and a set of criteria that applies in most situations.

Our major objectives in writing this book are to give the reader a framework for understanding how to evaluate research reports, and to translate that framework into a practical set of criteria—stated as questions—that the reader should ask of the research.

The framework is presented in the form of what we call an "error model." That model assumes that research, by its very nature, cannot guarantee to be free of error. Therefore readers of research must search for potential errors that the researcher may have missed. The error model assumes that if a research study has controlled for or minimized all important potential errors, its findings will be considered to be correct unless subsequent research shows otherwise. This view of research reflects an approach toward social-science research that developed out of logical empiricism. Though there are several alternative paradigms used in social science, it is impossible for this book to incorporate more than one of them. We have, therefore, remained reasonably faithful to a modern version of logical empiricism at the expense of what can be usefully learned from hermeneutics, critical theory, or other paradigms of social-science research. Our choice reflects to some degree the fact that we are more comfortable with logical empiricism. But, much more importantly, our choice was based on what we believe to be the needs of consumers of research throughout the social and behavioral sciences and the related professions where most of the literature is still strongly steeped in the traditions of logical empiricism.

The bulk of the book is devoted to translating the error model into specific evaluation criteria a reader can apply. Each chapter provides a rationale that leads to a few specific questions that a reader must ask of a research report. At the end of the book we put these questions together into a framework and a set of steps for conducting an evaluation (Chapters 16 and 17); we then apply this framework to the evaluation of two journal articles (Chapters 18 and 19).

Because this book is aimed at non-researchers, we were able to omit many of the technical terms, most of the fine distinctions, and all the formulas that are often important ingredients in a research-methods textbook. In this fourth edition, we have gone even further to make the book more readable. We added illustrations to help present the main theme of each section of the book. We moved the footnotes that contained the more technical details of the research process to a separate "Notes" section at the back of the book. We updated much of the end-of-chapter material. And, we fixed errors of fact or misleading oversimplifications that we were aware of.

We also strengthened the linkages between the chapter content, the Questions to Ask, and the practice exercises at the back of the book. In response to several suggestions, we added two additional articles that do not have our evaluations attached. Our hope is that instructors can use these new materials to take students on a guided series of discussions from,

- the concepts in a given chapter, to
- the Questions to Ask at the end of that chapter, to
- an evaluation framework based on those questions in Chapters 16–18, to
- our use of that framework to evaluate the articles in Chapter 19, to
- their use of that framework in the sample articles in Chapter 20.

Not only is this a nontechnical book but it may even be fun to read. We think that looking for clues as to whether information is correct and usable is a challenging and rewarding pursuit, and if it doesn't qualify as a pleasure, it can at least be palatable and understandable.

Since its original publication in 1978, many friends and colleagues have made suggestions, supplied citations, pointed out errors, and in many other ways have been very helpful. Although we did not implement every suggestion, we always gave their ideas serious consideration. The book is clearly better than it would have been if we had not received their input. To some, we must apologize: we have not added the many technical topics that were suggested. Unfortunately, there were almost as many additional technical topics to consider as there were people suggesting them—each reviewer had a pet topic. Other reviewers suggested that we resist the temptation to make the text much longer; we listened to them. We could not possibly add all the technical topics suggested and still maintain the flavor of the earlier editions.

To the many who have given us their comments and reactions, we say "thank you." We especially want to acknowledge the assistance, whether direct or indirect, of a few specific individuals:

Susan Banducci	Donald P. Ely	Brenda Manning
Rosemarie Bertran	Richard V. Farace	Alan C. Mazur
Burton Blatt	William Frakes	Gerald R. Miller
Harold Borko	Herbert Goldhor	John Olsgaard
Walter Carroll	Arnold Goldstein	David Ralph
Richard Clark	Randy Harrison	Janet Ruane
Pauline Cochrane	Allan F. Hershfield	John Simpkins
Michael Cody	Michael Hennessy	James Sodt
William D. Coplin	Dean E. Hewes	Albert Talbott
Cathy Covert	David R. Krathwohl	James A. Taylor
David Davidson	Nan Lin	Robert S. Taylor
Clive Davis	Craig B. Little	Douglas Zweizig
Brenda Dervin	Donald MacDonald	

Two research articles are evaluated in Chapter 19, using the criteria developed throughout the book. Two additional articles are provided in Chapter 20 for practicing evaluation, but without our guidance. We are grateful to the publishers and authors of those articles (Robert S. Sobel and Nancy Lillith; Horace E. Johns; Stephen Ansolabehere, Shanto Iyengar, Adam Simon, and Nicholas Valentino; Amy Jordan) for granting us permission to reprint them here. And, lastly we want to express our genuine appreciation to Theresa Gilliard-Cook, whose able and thorough assistance in preparing this edition, reminds us (in this age of information technology) of the special value that competent and caring people can provide.

Jeffrey Katzer

Kenneth H. Cook

Wayne W. Crouch

CONTENTS

INTRODUCTION

How does anybody know anything?

The social sciences have made great strides in advancing our understanding of people and social institutions. Yet with these advances also came some false starts, anomalous results, bad luck, and just plain mistakes. Unfortunately, there is no guaranteed way to prevent these errors from reaching print—for it is only with the certainty of hindsight that one can identify those studies which did not contribute to (or that even hindered) progress.

But how about the thousands of studies published each year that are too recent to be tested by time—how can they be evaluated? The approach we advocate in making this assessment is captured in what we call an "error model" of research. That model can not only be used by researchers to conduct their investigations, but it can be used equally well by readers of research to evaluate the published findings. We introduce this model in the first two chapters. The subsequent organization of the book as well as the particular criteria suggested for evaluation are based on this error model.

Thus, this first section of the book, though introductory, is essential. For unless you appreciate the need for evaluating the published research in the social sciences, you will not have much motivation to read the remaining sections. And unless you accept our beliefs about how a researcher learns about the world, you will probably not accept our advice about how to evaluate what a researcher claims to have learned.

1

PURPOSE: WHAT WE ARE TRYING TO DO

Much information reported by scientists, published in reputable journals, and used by students, practicing professionals, and the general public is misleading. Some of it is just plain wrong. The purpose of this book is to help you detect such misinformation. It will help you become a more critical consumer of research published in the social sciences and in the related professional areas.

Students

Students need to know how to evaluate research. More and more undergraduate courses include original research reports and journal articles as required readings. Course projects and term papers also often make use of published studies. Yet rarely are students taught how to evaluate what they need to read. Research courses exist, but they typically are introductions to how to *do* research, not how to independently *evaluate* it.

Professionals

Professionals also need to know how to evaluate research. Included in this category are graduate students in those professional schools which make use of the theories, principles, and research findings of the social sciences. If you are, or are preparing to be, a social worker, educator, journalist, librarian, or manager, you will not be conducting research very often during your career. Training in a profession requires time and coursework devoted to job preparation and practices; relatively little, if any, coursework is in research methods. But as a practicing professional you will be expected to keep up to date, to continually improve your skills and the knowledge by which you make decisions. Most new information will come from the ideas, suggestions, and research findings presented at professional meetings or published in professional journals. You must evaluate this new information and decide whether or not to act on the basis of it.

General Public

People, in general, need to evaluate information. Television bombards us with advertising claims. Popular magazines tout new diets and give tests to determine whether you are really happy. Politicians and administrators want our support so they can change things for the better. Many times these appeals seem to be supported by research. But are they? In order to make sensible decisions, viewers, readers, and constituents must be able to evaluate the information presented.

The dilemma is clear. Whether you are a student trying to learn, a professional trying to do a better job, or a citizen trying to act intelligently, you need to read the published literature. Yet there is little in your training that will help you evaluate that literature.

THE LITERATURE IS PROBABLY WORSE THAN YOU THINK

Why should you have to evaluate research reports? Scientists have good reputations, and the editor must have reviewed what was printed. It was published, so why not assume that it probably will be correct and applicable to current problems? There are many reasons why each article must be carefully read and evaluated. The various chapters of this book explore those reasons. But for the moment let us just consider the general accuracy or truthfulness of the published literature.

With a little thought it should become obvious that mistakes do happen, even to researchers, and that not all researchers or editors are equally knowledgeable or competent. Some errors will occur in published reports. Many people, however, would underestimate the seriousness of the errors, assuming that small mistakes in arithmetic or use of bibliographic citations or scientific equipment may be the problem: This book was written not because of such minor errors but because of the prevalence of errors that invalidate the major findings or conclusions of many studies. We will be concerned not with small errors, but with those poor research practices that leave the conclusions unsupported by the evidence or the arguments of the researcher. Some examples may help.

1 In a study of the quality of educational research, expert researchers evaluated a random sample of 81 articles published in 31 different educational journals. Acting as if they were editors, they judged that only 7 percent of the articles were worthy of publication as written, 41 percent needed revision if they were to be published, and the remaining 52 percent of the published articles should not have been published at all.

2 In a carefully reasoned examination of the work of many contemporary and famous historians, one critic identified no fewer than 100 different fallacies common and sometimes prevalent in their writings. These fallacies were often of such a nature as to seriously weaken the conclusions drawn.

3 In one small-scale study an attempt was made to obtain the actual data upon which some published articles were based. The original data for seven articles published in psychology journals were obtained. These data were reanalyzed and compared with the findings presented in the published articles. In three of the seven articles the second analysis found major mistakes that were not apparent in the published version. The mistakes, if known, would have altered the conclusions originally presented.

4 In a book devoted to examining errors in various economic fields, the author found large and apparently unacknowledged errors in foreign trade statistics, prices, mining and agricultural production figures, employment statistics, national income statistics, and economic growth rate indexes. Use of these figures could be misleading to policymakers as well as to the casual reader.

5 Several other investigators found that practicing researchers in psychology, education, sociology, and communication believe things to be true about the process of research that are clearly not true.

6 "Dr. Richard W. Roberts, director of the National Bureau of Standards, estimates that half or more of the numerical data published by scientists in their journal articles are unusable because there is no evidence that the researcher accurately measured what he thought he was measuring or no evidence that possible sources of error were eliminated or accounted for."

7 A review of 24 different studies of the accuracy of data in 40 real spreadsheets from 22 different companies found that between 21 and 80 percent of the spreadsheets had some kind of error, and that between 1 and 5 percent of the cells in each spreadsheet had errors.

8 One of the consequences of the rapid growth in the number of journals is a decrease in the standards for accepting research reports for publication, especially in the less established journals. A senior editor of a major medical journal recently asserted that "there seems to be no study too fragmented, no hypothesis too trivial, no literature citation too biased or too egotistical, no design too warped, no methodology too bungled, no presentation of results too inaccurate, too obscure, and too contradictory, no analysis too self-serving, no argument too circular, no conclusions too trifling or too unjustified, and no grammar and syntax too offensive for a paper to end up in print."

Other examples can be given, but we think the point is clear. In all of the social sciences the literature contains more errors and erroneous conclusions than the average nonresearcher is usually led to believe. If the journals in the scientific fields where the better-trained researchers publish their findings are not 100 percent accurate, what is the situation in the more applied journals and in the magazines that popularize social research? An insidious possibility is that poorly conducted research will be published in these journals precisely because they do not meet the standards of the other ones. Furthermore, readers of popularized or applied social science may find these articles more believable because they are more understandable or because the article looks "scientific" and "statistical." In the 1940s, Ralph A. Beals characterized the literature in library science as "glad tidings and testimony, with precious little research." The increase in research-based literature has grown since that time in all professions. It does not always, however, offer anything more than glad tidings and testimony.

We do not mean through these examples and comments to condemn the various fields and professions cited. All journals in all fields publish articles that contain errors or are at some later time shown to be in error. We cite the fields that we do because the number and seriousness of errors have been studied. When we consider the findings of these studies along with the inadequate training in evaluating research that many nonresearchers in these fields receive, we believe there is ample reason to broadcast a warning: All readers in their own best interests need to be able to identify poorly conducted research. And, unfortunately, they cannot avoid that responsibility by relying on the prestige of the journal or the status of the author—neither is a guarantee, and in some areas it may not even be a good rule of thumb. Readers must also not assume that an editor will successfully weed out all major errors and poorly conducted studies. The explosion of information, the reward structure in higher education, the increasing number of new journals being published, the evaluation procedures used by editors, and a variety of other factors make it necessary that each reader judge each article on its own merits.

WHAT THIS BOOK CAN DO FOR YOU AND HOW WE DO IT

The purpose of this book is to help you become a more critical consumer of research. We will focus on the published literature in the social and behavioral sciences and

---

DISCOVERING THE RIGHT CLUES

Reading just the text of this book provides only half its value. The other half comes from discovering and learning how to use clues that help you evaluate research. The clues we provide take the form of questions.

Becoming a critical consumer of research requires first an understanding of why these questions are asked; the body of each chapter provides that material. The critical clues, the questions, are described at the end of each chapter.

These questions that this book provides are detection devices that help you identify factors that can increase error and counterbalancing factors that can decrease error.

The researcher's responsibility is to identify all potential sources of error that could have an important impact on the results. It is the reader's responsibility—that's you—to determine if the researcher dealt with these errors appropriately and to search for any sources of error the researcher might have missed.

The most challenging but rewarding task for you is discovering how to use those clues. To get you started, we've provided Section Six, "Applications: How to Do Evaluations," at the end of the book. We provide you with a "Step by Step Guide for Evaluation" that explains how to actually conduct an evaluation. We also give you two annotated sample evaluations and some guidance so you can practice doing your own evaluations. Two additional sample articles are included that let you do your own evaluations with no assistance.

You may not want to read all of Section Six until after you have read the earlier sections. However, one chapter—Chapter 18, Practicing—is valuable because it provides you with an active way to participate in the evaluation process after reading any one of the 14 chapters in the preceding sections. If you want to practice as you read, do not pass GO, go directly to Chapter 18 now.

---

related professional areas, although evaluation of any purported factual information is subject to the same considerations. For instance, friends and colleagues cite facts in conversations, advertisers use the results of studies to promote their products, and textbooks and newspaper articles provide secondhand reports of the results of research. What you learn from this book can be applied to those situations as well.

This book is for readers of research, not researchers. In its preparation we wanted to omit all technical aspects or procedural details that would be important to a researcher, but we didn't want to sacrifice the principles upon which these methods are based. Moreover, we wanted to describe these principles in a nontechnical way. This is a very fine line to draw, and we may have occasionally missed the mark. Because we do omit some more technical concerns, you will not be able to detect all errors in the literature. In our experience, however, poor research often clearly demonstrates itself through a variety of errors, and most major errors can be detected by readers who understand the material in the remaining chapters of this book.

The Error Model

Our view of research is based on an "error model," and our approach to evaluation reflects that point of view. We believe that the researcher's job is first to identify, and then to remove or reduce, sources of potential error so that findings can be trusted. Consequently, it is the job of an evaluator to challenge a research report by searching for possible errors missed by the author. Since we will focus on various sources of

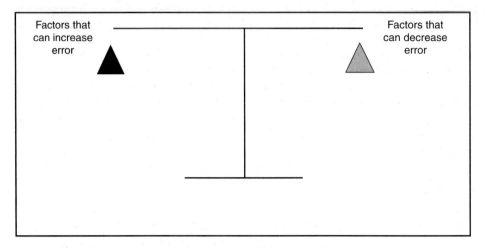

THE ERROR MODEL: IDENTIFYING, CONTROLLING, AND REMOVING ERROR

error throughout the book and often use examples of poorly conducted research, you might get the idea that we do not believe in research. That would be a false impression. Not only do we do research ourselves, but we also put a lot of faith in research as a very good method for obtaining accurate information.

We do find, however, that poor research practices serve as more interesting and more useful examples than do good practices. To interpret our concern with error as a reflection of our view of the usefulness of research would be a most unfortunate case of guilt by association—when in fact we associate with error only to eliminate it.

Thus, the major focus of this book will be on how well the researchers have identified, removed, and controlled the potential errors in their study. To evaluate information means to weigh those factors in a study that have the potential to add error with those factors a researcher uses to decrease error.

The figure above is our way of representing the error model; you, a reader of research, need to decide if the researchers' actions "balanced" the potential errors. You'll see this basic graphic used in the introduction to each section of this book as a way to describe what that section is about in terms of error.

We will try to provide the basis for you to understand and apply criteria for evaluating information in each new chapter by focusing on specific factors that will affect error. However, we cannot provide all the criteria you will need. As we pointed out, this is a nontechnical (and, by the way, short) book, but a more fundamental reason is that journal articles can be evaluated on both external and internal criteria.

External Criteria

"External criteria" are all those which are based on comparisons of what is in the article with what is already known about the topic. You would want, for instance, to compare new findings with everything else you know about the subject. Do they agree with the results of previous research? Do they correspond with, or at least not contradict, first-hand experiences you have had? External factors are important in assessing the usefulness and credibility of a journal article, but this book can be of little help. Your own personal experiences and training in the subject matter are your primary tools.

Internal Criteria

"Internal criteria," on the other hand, are those which are relatively independent of the specific subject matter and are mainly concerned with the adequacy of the methods used in the study itself. Most of this book is devoted to an examination of internal criteria. We will focus on how the authors discovered, supported, or proved their findings, conclusions, and recommendations. We will point out specific clues to look for.

Notice that we used the word "clues." Our students frequently want to know if an article is correct. Unfortunately, there is nothing an author can write in an article or say in an oral presentation that will prove something to be correct unequivocally. The best of methods, meticulously carried out, sometimes lead to false findings. And the worst methods will sometimes produce correct results. Thus, finding clues of bad methodology is only the start. You must go beyond the identification of errors and estimate the consequences of those errors on the findings, conclusions, and recommendations presented. You can never be absolutely sure of your evaluation, but a reasonable estimate is far better than blind acceptance or rejection.

We are all tempted to damn the perpetrators of bad methodology, but we must be careful not to fall victim to what David Hackett Fischer calls the "fallacist's fallacy," which consists of any of the following *false* statements.

1 *An argument which is structurally fallacious in some respect is therefore structurally false in all respects.*

2 *An argument which is structurally false in some respect, or even in every respect, is therefore substantively false in its conclusion.*

3 *The appearance of a fallacy in an argument is an external sign of its author's depravity.*

4 *Sound thinking is merely thinking which is not fallacious.*

5 *Fallacies exist independent of particular purpose and assumptions.*

This may not be the worst fallacy, but it is the most difficult for the new critic to avoid.

Thus, we contend that you need to evaluate research because much published work is in error. This book will give you an understanding of the concepts and principles that help competent researchers discover accurate information about the world. Most importantly, we will help you use this understanding to evaluate their work by identifying specific clues to look for. These clues are presented as questions at the end of each chapter.

Resist the temptation to read only these questions. This book is not mainly a step-by-step guide for evaluating research or merely a collection of the essential questions to ask. It is a presentation of concepts, of a way of thinking, and of an attitude to take as you approach a published report. Evaluators must know how to choose criteria appropriately and apply them knowledgeably. That is what this book is about.

QUESTIONS TO ASK

At the end of each chapter we will summarize by giving you specific questions to ask about research and your reactions to it. Here are the first ones.

---

1 Are you too optimistic about the accuracy of this research report?
Most nonresearchers are. There are many reasons why each article you use must be carefully read and evaluated. Studies have shown that much published research is not completely accurate.

2 What do you already know about this topic—firsthand knowledge as well as the results of other research?
This book deals primarily with internal criteria—those which are relatively independent of the specific subject matter and are for the most part concerned with the methods used in a study. You must also be concerned about external criteria, which are all those based on comparisons of what is in the report with what is already known about the topic.

3 Are you too quick to condemn all aspects of the report because of some detected shortcomings?
Most studies, including those which were competently done, have some weaknesses. But the mere presence of a weakness does not invalidate an entire study. Judgment is needed; the baby shouldn't be thrown out with the bath water.

PRACTICE EVALUATIONS

Reminder: Answering the questions on the facing page yourself is good practice. Chapter 18 provides guidelines for you to follow in doing that. Chapter 19 provides two articles along with our evaluations of them. Chapter 20 provides two additional articles for you to practice on.

FOR FURTHER THOUGHT

1 When, if ever, can you rely on the reputation of a journal or author instead of evaluating the research itself? What is the trade-off in terms of your time and effort versus the danger of acting on the basis of erroneous information?

2 How would the literature of your field compare with the quality of published research cited in this chapter?

3 Were you surprised by the poor quality of much social science research literature? Why?

4 It is possible for scientific research (including social science research) never to produce results that will later be proven to be mistaken? Why do you think so?

5 Interpret the following quotations in terms of the material in this chapter.

  (a) "An educated person is one who has learned that information almost always turns out to be at best incomplete and very often false, misleading, fictitious, mendacious—just dead wrong." (R. Baker)

  (b) "The positions for which social science students are likely to be preparing themselves— teaching, administration in government or business, community consultations, social work—increasingly call for the ability to evaluate and to use research results: to judge whether a study has been carried out in such a way that one can have reasonable confidence in its findings and whether its findings are applicable to the specific situation at hand." (C. Selltiz, L. S. Wrightsman, and S. Cook)

  (c) "Mistakes are at the very base of human thought, embedded there, feeding the structure like root nodules. If we were not provided with the knack of being wrong, we could never get anything useful done. We think our way along by choosing between right and wrong alternatives, and the wrong choices have to be made as frequently as the right ones. We get along in life this way. We are built to make mistakes, coded for error." (L. Thomas)

  (d) It's not what we don't know that gives us trouble. It's what we know that ain't so." (Will Rogers)

FOR FURTHER READING

Other fascinating examples of misinformation can be found in:

1 T. Burnham. *Dictionary of Misinformation.* New York: Crowell, 1975.

2 _____. *More Misinformation.* New York: McKay, 1980.

3 R. Shenkman. *Legends, Lies, and Cherished Myths of American History.* New York: William Morrow and Company, 1988.

4 A. Kohn. *You Know What They Say. . . : The Truth about Popular Beliefs.* New York: Harper & Row, 1990.

2

ASSUMPTIONS:
WHAT WE BELIEVE
ABOUT HOW WE KNOW

Consider the following situation.

You are in charge of the Student Psychological Counseling and Guidance Office at a large university. The majority of students who come to your office come on their own initiative. All a student needs to do is to call or come in and make an appointment to meet with a professional counselor or psychologist. Most of the students who come to the first counseling session continue to come to as many sessions as needed.

Your problem is that about 25 percent of the students who make an initial appointment never show up at all. You suspect that these students may be the ones most in need of help, and you wonder if the appointment secretary could in some way be affecting the "no-shows" adversely.

The current appointment secretary is a clerk-typist with twenty years of experience working for the university. There doesn't seem to be anything unusual about the way she treats students, but you could hire a student instead, or one of your professional counselors could handle the job.

A student appointment secretary would be approximately the same age as the students seeking counseling. Moreover, an appointment secretary who was also a college student would presumably be more understanding and empathic than would a career typist. The extra empathy and understanding might help reduce the percentage of students who do not attend their first counseling session.

The professional counselor, on the other hand, would have extensive training in interpersonal relations. Thus, he or she could conceivably be very effective in influencing students who make appointments to actually show up.

Your problem, then, is to choose among the three possible appointment secretaries: the clerk-typist, a student, or a professional counselor.

How can you get the information you need to decide which will produce the fewest no-shows? Notice that we do *not* immediately ask what is the correct decision. Rather we are first interested in how you would go about gathering the information on which to base your decision.

WAYS OF KNOWING

Common Sense

Common sense is one way to answer this question. Of course, common sense has many shortcomings, and one is particularly apparent here. There seems to be a commonsensical argument supporting all three possibilities. It might make sense to some people to use a student appointment secretary because of the greater empathy and understanding that a peer might offer. It also may make sense to use a professional counselor because of a background of extensive training. And finally, it might also be argued that the clerk-typist is the best of the possible appointment secretaries. As compared with a student, the clerk would be less well known, older, and more mature. These characteristics might make students feel more comfortable because their privacy would be preserved and the fact that they are seeking help would be respected. As compared with a professional counselor the clerk-typist might have the advantage of not being viewed by the students as someone who is trained to judge them. Students wouldn't need to worry about what they were saying and how they were saying it when they called for an appointment.

Maybe these arguments don't all make sense to you, but we hope they contain enough common sense to make our point. For some people, each alone would sound quite plausible. Only when they are juxtaposed do we see that each may or may not be correct. We clearly need better information in this case than our common sense supplies.

Advice of Colleagues

A second way to answer the question is to seek the advice of colleagues and acknowledged leaders in your profession. Experience and expertise often are helpful, but as a general method of knowing they also have some severe weaknesses.

A major weakness is the haphazard way in which experience is obtained by experts as well as by everyone else. Over a long period of time different professionals get quite different experiences. Some stay on the same job over that period, others change jobs every couple of years. On-the-job people are bombarded with all sorts of impressions and insights. Some of these are promptly forgotten, and others are remembered inaccurately. Furthermore, each vivid experience, each lesson learned the hard way, is probably overgeneralized.

In the appointment-secretary problem, whom would you query? Suppose you asked the director of student counseling at another university, an experienced and acknowledged authority in the profession. What are the limits of his experience? That director might recommend using a professional counselor because he has always used them and is satisfied with the results. In this case the expert's experience was limited to many years with one type of appointment secretary. It is conceivable that another colleague of yours, a director of a third university counseling center, has always used clerk-typists and was satisfied with the result. Which expert should you believe?

Or suppose that an expert you consult has tried different appointment secretaries. Should you follow her recommendation? Over a period of time things change, and it is likely that the changing social environment for college students has affected the kinds of problems counseling centers are dealing with. Changing patterns of dating, sexual relationships, drug usage, career goals, and individual value systems may make one kind of appointment secretary more appropriate in one time period than another. If this is true, is it wise to accept the recommendation of someone who has used one type of secretary five years ago, but a different one now?

Or how about an expert who manages an outpatient counseling clinic at a nearby hospital. Are the differences between the type of people seeking help (students in your case, the general public in his) important here? Should his advice be followed?

We can continue describing various experts, but the same possibility will exist for each. Since all the experts have had different experiences and since none of them are currently working at your institution with your staff and students, how can you know if their experience, however vast, is applicable?

Equally important is that the lessons of experience are not learned in a controlled situation. One should not attribute a successful guidance center to any one thing. Your colleagues probably did not control other influences on whether or not students showed up for the first appointment. Thus they cannot be sure that it was the kind of appointment secretary they used that produced the better results. An article in the student newspaper, an interactive advising program, or many other events or experiences may have influenced the results. Even if you judge your colleague's experience applicable to your situation, how do you know that the effect reported (a low percentage of no-shows) is due to the kind of secretary used?

Do Your Own Research

Doing your own research is a third way to attempt to answer the question. There are various ways to go about this—for starters, suppose you decide to ask students how they feel about various types of appointment secretaries. What are some of the sources of error that are possible?

The first problem arises when you try to determine which students to ask. Of those students who failed to meet their first appointment in the past, many will be impossible to locate. You may have only their names, and besides, old appointment books are probably destroyed. So you can either ask the students you are currently working with, or you can ask a sample of the general university population. The first group of students, since they came to their first appointment, are probably not representative of those who failed to appear. They may not be sensitive to the secretary issue at all. Their answers may not be useful to you.

If you try a general student survey you have to contend with the fact that most of these students cope with the stresses of college life somewhat better than the students who request counseling. Consequently, the general university student may not react differently to the different types of secretaries.

Another problem has to do with the questioning process. Asking students about the kind of appointment secretary they would prefer may alert them to an issue they never thought about before. Thus, the responses you get are no longer like those of unquestioned college students, who are the ones you are really interested in.

Other possible problems abound in this study. When should the students be questioned, how should they be questioned, what questions should be used—each of these has one or more sources of possible error.

Searching the published literature is still another way to go about answering the question. Researchers, of course, are trained to overcome many of the difficulties noted above. If the problem has been studied, you may be able to get valuable information from the literature. For instance, is anything known in general about clients' reactions to the first person they contact in a counseling or guidance office? You might turn to your professional journals to find out. If you have read Chapter 1, you know that there are many sources of error in this kind of information as well. But researchers have attacked many important problems, and you would be negligent if you ignored their contribution.

We could probably think of some other ways to find an answer to this question. For each way, it would not be difficult to identify at least one possible source of trouble—something that could distort the correct answer or produce a less than accurate finding. Some methods are more prone to certain kinds of errors than are other methods. But *every* method of knowing about the world is subject to some sort of error. This is true regardless of the question asked and the expertise of the person attempting to answer it. We don't know, of course, if a possible source of distortion will actually occur in a given situation, but the fact that such a possibility exists should cause us some concern.

It is important to reassure ourselves, however, that we know quite a bit about the world. Though our knowledge can never be 100 percent certain, we can act as if it were in many cases, and we frequently will be right. What we need to understand and recognize are the conditions necessary for us to consider something true: what are the characteristics of accurate information?

SCIENCE AS A WAY OF KNOWING

This book is our answer to the preceding question, and our answer depends entirely on certain beliefs we hold about the nature of accurate information. To oversimplify, we believe that science offers the best guidance for determining the accuracy of information. When we speak of science we are not referring to any particular discipline but to the overlap among the norms, practices, and values of many areas in science. It is the scientist's job to learn about the world. As a group, scientists have had, we believe, the most fruitful experience in trying to make accurate observations and conclusions. Over the years they have identified the major sources of error and have been successful in continually developing techniques to decrease the size of those errors.

The criteria used by scientists to plan, control, and carry out their investigations can be adopted by nonscientists to evaluate research. These criteria will also be useful in the evaluation of all types of reports that claim to contain factual statements—that is, that attempt to describe a part of the world accurately. Included are reports based on common sense, expert opinion, your own research, and the research of others. The criteria can also be applied to information presented in essays, editorials, advertisements, and lectures, as well as research studies.

However, all that is important to you cannot be evaluated by scientific criteria. Beliefs cannot, and questions of value, of esthetics, of logic, and of law cannot either. Likewise, questions from philosophy, the arts, and religion are outside their domain. Or as May Brodbeck put it, "the questions science can answer are not the only questions worth asking." Even when we limit the power of science to establishing and evaluating facts, it is important to remember that the criteria, norms, and practices in science are not always followed by all scientists. We are interested in learning from science at its best, science in the ideal, rather than how it is occasionally mispracticed.

The ideals of science are incorporated into the practice of research through a reliance on evidence, a need for controlling error, and a standard of publicness. We believe that readers need to consider each of these when they evaluate published research reports. Throughout the book you will find that the specific criteria we suggest are based on one or more of these concerns.

Reliance on Evidence

The first is a reliance on evidence. Experts, as Bertrand Russell observed, can be wrong, even if they all agree. The history of any field, including scientific ones, has many examples of renowned experts being wrong. The opinions of authorities and the strength of their arguments should help formulate the beginnings of a research study and help interpret the results of one, but they should not be used instead of one to determine the outcome of the study. Evidence is paramount. If the results of well-conducted studies disagree with the authorities, then the authorities may very well be wrong. The proper method for an expert to use in appealing this verdict is to conduct another study. Or, if two research reports disagree, then additional studies need to be conducted to resolve the issue. The point is that knowledge about the world is best obtained by carefully looking at the world, not by looking at someone's idea of the world. The great tragedy of science, to paraphrase Huxley, is the slaying of a beautiful idea by an ugly fact.

Need for Controlling Error

Next is the need for controlling error. Since every conclusion about the world can be in error, it is important to know if the researcher took steps to control error, what those steps were, and how much error might still be present—that is, how wrong can the conclusions be. One of the distinguishing characteristics of scientific communication is that it attempts to include some measure of how reliable the observations or results are. This measure can take the form of a confidence statement (e.g., there is a 95 percent chance that it will rain today), or of a range of correctness (e.g., the number of people who will vote in Tuesday's election is between 4.6 and 4.9 million), or it can take some other form. But it is usually there.

As we noted in Chapter 1, readers cannot assume that all errors were identified and removed or reduced by the researcher. In order for these errors to be discovered, the norms of science require a researcher to publish, or make available in some other way, information about the study. Publicness means that you should be assisted by the author in your attempt to evaluate a research report.

Standard of Publicness

The standard of publicness applies to the methods employed in a study, to the evidence or data obtained by those methods, and to the overall conclusions of the study. Publicness means that the methods used in the study must be completely described. Since each method has its own particular strengths and weaknesses, it is only by understanding the method and seeing how it was employed in a given study that you can determine whether the possible weaknesses were adequately controlled for. Publicness also means that the evidence collected needs to be presented—at least in some summary form. By making the evidence available, a researcher allows you as a reader to independently analyze it to see if you think the conclusions given were warranted. It decreases your need to trust the researcher. And lastly, publicness means that the researcher's conclusions need to be tempered by the knowledge that (or the possibility that) error was not controlled completely.

ARGUMENTS SUPPORTING RESEARCH CONCLUSIONS

There are two fundamental concerns regarding the conclusions of a scientific investigation: are the reported results or findings correct? And if they are, to whom or to what do these results apply? We call the first of these a concern for factual accuracy, and the second a concern for generality.

The results of the appointment-secretary problem, for example, are said to be factually accurate if the researcher's conclusions (whatever they might be) are actually right for that particular counseling service. And the conclusions are said to be more generalizable if they can be shown to apply to a broader range of cases, people, situations, organizations, and times than the single investigation actually dealt with. Now there isn't any way for the researcher or for the reader to know with absolute certainty that the results are correct and broadly generalizable. Rather, the researcher and the reader need to independently assess the available evidence and "make a case" for factual accuracy and for generality. That is, the researcher and the reader need to evaluate and synthesize all that is known—from the observations made, from the data collected, from the relevant theories, from the related studies, and especially from the known limitations and uncontrolled errors in the study—in order to come to an overall assessment of the research conclusions: to what extent are they factually accurate and to what extent are they generalizable.

Researchers "make a case" for factual accuracy and generality by presenting supporting arguments. As a reader, your first line of defense is to identify the presence or absence of arguments. But a more important consideration is the type of argument. Basically, there are three types of arguments that can be used, and some are intrinsically stronger than others.

Reasoning and Plausibility

The weakest argument is based solely on reasoning and plausibility, and depends only upon what researchers say, not on what they do. When reasoning is used as a form of argument, researchers need to explain why certain uncontrolled errors, which could have weakened factual accuracy or possibly generality, did not occur. Clearly this is a risky business. The researchers may not have identified all uncontrolled errors, or their communication style may hamper your ability to discern weaknesses in their reasoning.

Replications

The strongest argument is based on replication, on other studies that investigated the same topic. If numerous other researchers, working in different environments, using different groups of people, employing slightly different procedures—if all, or most, of these various attempts come up with similar results, you can be quite confident that these findings are both factually accurate and general. Naturally, the more replications, the more your confidence is justified. This type of argument is possible only in those fields which have a well-developed research history. Unfortunately, many areas in the social sciences do not have enough previously completed research to use replications as a major argument for factual accuracy and generality.

Research Methods

Research methods are the third type of argument used. Proper methodology, which is discussed in more detail in Chapters 8 to 14, presents a stronger case than reasoning alone, but not as strong as many successful replications. However, in the absence of copious replications, factual accuracy and generality must be judged on the basis of a combination of reasoning, research procedures, and the available replications.

As a reader, you need to independently assess the strength of the arguments presented by the researcher; you need to actively challenge their validity; you need to invent counterarguments as well as additional supporting arguments; and most importantly you need to supplement what is reported with your own knowledge of the subject matter. You need to apply external as well as internal criteria. Much of what we've said is outlined in the Table 2–1.

TABLE 2–1
ARGUMENTS FOR FACTUAL ACCURACY AND GENERALITY

Type of argument	Strength of argument if used alone	Main location of argument in journal article	Readers should judge the argument by . . .	Typical study using this argument
Reasoning— what the researcher said	Weak	In introduction and discussion sections	• asking how good was the reasoning given • inventing own reasons • using own knowledge of subject matter	Case studies or first-person accounts of unique experiences
Methods—what the researcher did	Stronger	In procedures section	• asking how good were the methods used • inventing own reasons • using own knowledge of subject matter	Surveys
Replications— what other researchers said or did	Strongest	In literature review section	• asking how good and encompassing were the studies reported • inventing own reasons • using own knowledge of subject matter	Laboratory experiments
Some combination of reasoning, methods, and replications	Depends	In all of the above sections	• all of the above	Most social science studies

Much more needs to be said about the norms, values, and practices of science before you are ready to apply them as an evaluator of research. Meeting this need is the primary objective of the remaining chapters in this book. We must also break down the broad concerns of science into more manageable evaluation criteria. These criteria are presented as questions and are summarized at the end of each chapter. Altogether there are 78 such questions. Obviously you cannot ask all of them every time you read an article. In fact, they aren't meant to be used in that way; many overlap and subsume others. They are meant to review each chapter and to suggest a questioning attitude toward evaluation that, we think, will serve you well.

QUESTIONS TO ASK

1 **What additional sources of knowledge should you consider?**
All methods of gaining knowledge permit error, but different methods have different types of errors. Using several methods allows you to cross-check new information. Do not become so "scientific" that you fail to see if research findings make (common) sense and agree with your experience.

2 **What errors are most likely to occur with each source of knowledge?**
This cannot be answered specifically at this point. The next two sections of the book discuss error in more general terms; the final sections identify serious errors in detail.

3 **Do the methods used meet the norms of science?**
The norms are based on a reliance on evidence, a need for controlling error, and a standard of publicness. In Sections Four and Five we present the major criteria for evaluating information based on these norms.

4 **How strong are the arguments used to support the researcher's claim for factual accuracy and generality?**
There are three general types of arguments; from weakest to strongest they are reasoning, methods, and replication. Combine those arguments given by the author with your own assessment of them and your knowledge of the subject matter. The remaining chapters in the book (especially Chapters 8 to 14) will help you assess the strength of arguments based on methods and replication.

5 **Is this one of the many questions that does *not* have to be asked?**
Not all questions will be helpful in evaluating all research reports. The best questions to use depend on your knowledge of the study and your understanding of the ideals of science.

PRACTICE EVALUATIONS

Reminder: Answering the above questions yourself is good practice. Chapter 18 provides guidelines for you to follow in doing that. Chapter 19 provides two articles along with our evaluations of them. Chapter 20 provides two additional articles for you to practice on.

FOR FURTHER THOUGHT

1 Review the hypothetical appointment-secretary problem presented at the beginning of the chapter.

    (a) What other sources of possible distortion are there in the various methods considered to answer the question?

    (b) Can you suggest other ways to answer the question? What are the possible weaknesses in each of these methods?

    (c) Choose any plausible answer to the question. Then write a short paragraph "justifying" your answer with an argument based primarily on reasoning. Repeat this twice again but use hypothetical arguments based on methodology and on replications.

2 Much wisdom gained through experience and common sense is handed down through the generations in the form of aphorisms or maxims. Can you think of some pairs of sayings that are possibly contradictory in their advice? For example,

> The early bird catches the worm
> Marry in haste, repent in leisure

3 Interpret the following quotations in terms of the material in the chapter.

    (a) "Cynicism is a disease of the old. Skepticism is a hallmark of the scientific process . . . One is an emotion, the other an intellectual activity." (G. Lynch)

    (b) "There is no absolute knowledge, and those who claim it, whether they are scientists or dogmatists, open the door to tragedy." (J. Bronowski)

    (c) "Science is one area of communication where the motivation to deceive can be said to be practically eliminated, not necessarily because scientists are extraordinarily virtuous people, but because the nature of scientific activity is such that deception can be easily detected by other scientists. Therefore, we can at least trust the scientists' sincerity whenever they tell us something about the results of their studies." (A. Rapoport)

    (d) The road to wisdom?
Well, it's plain
And simple to express:
Err
And err
And err again,
But less
And less
And less. (Piet Hein)*

    (e) "We still spend endless time in discussions and debate on issues where questions of fact are involved. A few years back, there was endless controversy over why little Johnny could not learn to read, until it occurred to a Swedish educational psychologist to conduct some research on the problem. A great deal of argumentation goes on over drugs where assumptions rather than facts are debated. Scientific research, of course, will not furnish all the answers, but neither should its role be ignored where factual questions are relevant to problem solution." (D. Katz)

    (f) "Science may well be the most sustained critical enterprise in the history of culture, refusing again and again to take nature at face value." (P. C. Ritterbush)

    (g) "Science is the great antidote to the poison of enthusiasm and superstition." (Adam Smith)

FOR FURTHER READING

1 E. Nagel. "Science and Common Sense." In E. Nagel, *The Structure of Science*. New York: Harcourt, 1961, pp. 1–14.

A short chapter examining six different weaknesses of common sense explanations and how scientific explanations attempt to eliminate these weaknesses.

2 J. D. Watson. *The Double Helix.* New York: Atheneum, 1968.

A first-person account of the discovery of DNA. The book is refreshingly honest. It describes the mistakes, the personality clashes, and the role of luck in the discovery that earned him and his colleague the Nobel prize. You can also see how the criteria and norms of his discipline directed his inquiry and helped him make the discovery.

3 M. Rogers. *Contradictory Quotations.* Essex, England: Longman Group Limited, 1983.

A compilation of quotations. The quotes are arranged in pairs that offer contradictory advice.

4 M. Sidman. *Tactics of Scientific Research.* New York: Basic Books, 1960.

A nonnumerical, but thorough, introduction to scientific research with an emphasis on psychology. The author takes a thematic approach similar to the organization of this book. He suggests three major concerns: the importance of the question asked, the realiability of the evidence, and the generality of the findings.

5 G. McCain and E. M. Segal. *The Game of Science,* 5th ed. Pacific Grove, CA: Brooks/Cole Publishing, 1988.

A light-hearted and more personal look at scientists and what they do. The book focuses more on the physical sciences than the social sciences, but it is still useful for understanding the reality of how any of us know things from a scientific perspective.

6 R. Rosenthal and R. L. Rosnow. *Essentials of Behavioral Research*, 2nd ed. New York: McGraw-Hill, 1991.

A researcher's perspective on how social scientists gain knowledge. Especially relevant are Chapter 1, "The Nature of Behavioral Research," and Chapter 2, "Development and Testing of Research Ideas."

7 C. J. Drew, M. L. Hardman, and A. W. Hart. *Designing and Conducting Research: Inquiry in Education and Social Science,* 2nd ed. Boston, MA: Allyn and Bacon, 1996.

Another researcher's perspective. See Chapter 1, "Introduction and Background," and Chapter 2, "Different Research Approaches."

TWO

DISCOVERY AND COMMUNICATION OF RESEARCH FINDINGS

Where do errors come from?

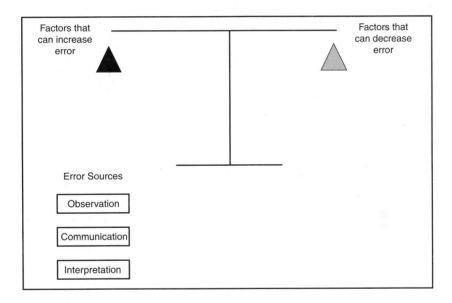

THE ERROR MODEL: IDENTIFYING, CONTROLLING, AND REMOVING ERROR

The error model requires consumers and researchers alike to focus on error in order to deal with it. In this section we discuss three sources of error. They are not the only sources of error, but they tend to be overlooked even though they exist every time a person reads a research report. The first is the process of observation, which is the basic activity, in some form or another, of all empirical research. The second is the process of communication, which is the only way you can learn about the research that other people do. And the third is the process of interpretation, which goes on within you as you think about the research you read.

These three general sources of error are just as important in your evaluation of research as are the more detailed and technical sources of error presented later in the book; do not forget them.

3

OBSERVATION: SEEING IS NOT BELIEVING

The Princeton-Dartmouth football game some years ago was expected to be quite a battle. Earlier games between these teams were always spirited and highly competitive, but this particular year the stakes were higher. It was the final game of the season, and Dartmouth had a chance to spoil Princeton's undefeated record and tarnish the image of their star player, who was being mentioned for All-American honors and had just appeared on the cover of *Time* magazine.

The game was rough. Tempers flared. In the second quarter, Princeton's star left the game with a broken nose. In the third quarter, a Dartmouth player was taken off the field with a broken leg. Princeton won, but there were many penalties against both sides, with Dartmouth collecting about three times as many as Princeton. Controversy over the roughness of the game raged in the public press and especially in the student papers at the two schools.

About a month later, samples of students in both schools were shown a film of the game and asked to check on the questionnaire, as they watched the film, any infraction of the rules they saw. Here is a summary of what students at the two schools saw on the same film.

Princeton students	*Dartmouth students*
Saw Dartmouth make twice as many infractions as Princeton.	Saw both teams make about the same number of infractions.
Judged the game as "rough and	Most judged it "rough and dirty,"

dirty." Not one student thought it was "clean and fair."

but about 10 percent thought it was "clean and fair." And over a third of the students invented their own description of the game—"rough and fair."

About 90 percent thought it was Dartmouth that started the rough play.

About a third thought Dartmouth was to blame for starting the rough play. The majority of viewers thought both sides were equally to blame.

Whether or not the students had been spectators at the game itself made little difference in their responses.

Dartmouth and Princeton students saw the same film, but they saw different games. The discrepancies between the groups were accentuated by one extraordinary Dartmouth alumnus, not in the study, who had obtained the film for showing to an alumni group in the Midwest. He was so unable to "see" the infractions that he wired the school saying: "Preview of Princeton movies indicates considerable cutting of important parts please wire explanation and possibly air mail missing part before showing scheduled for January 25 we have splicing equipment."

Why are there such great discrepancies in these reports of the same event? It is easy to suggest that partisanship was the cause, but the reasons are more complex than that. And they affect researchers as well as football fans and the rest of us.

Seeing the world accurately is not easy. This is true of everyone, including researchers, whose instruments and training help but do not completely solve the problems inherent in observation. One of these problems is that researchers can't see it all even if they want to. A second problem is that they need to interpret what they do see, and a third problem is that they interact with what they see, sometimes distorting it in the process. We've stated these three problems in terms of researchers, even though they apply to all of us, because our source objective in this chapter is to view the process of observation as a major source of potential errors. Many of the procedures used by researchers to ensure factually accurate information and many of the questions we advocate as criteria for evaluation only make sense when observation is considered from this perspective.

This book is intended to help you evaluate findings and conclusions that are based on observation. If the observations are inaccurate, the findings will be distorted. Accordingly, the first line of defense you have as readers is to question the accuracy of the original observations.

YOU COULDN'T SEE IT ALL EVEN IF YOU WANTED TO

Problems in observation begin before we even open our eyes. We have to take into account the enormous mass of potential objects, events, and people that are subject to our sensory awareness at any one time. How can we describe all of what we see? If you look at a person, do you notice each hair, each pore, each fiber in the clothing? If we had to try and record everything, we would drown in the information. We could observe any particular detail if we wanted to, but we would have to ignore something else.

Once at a scientific meeting, a man suddenly rushed into the midst of one of the sessions. He was being chased by another man with a revolver. They scuffled in plain view of the assembled researchers, a shot was fired, and they rushed out. About twenty seconds had elapsed. The chairperson of the session immediately asked all present to write down an account of what they had seen. The observers did not know that the ruckus had been planned, rehearsed, and photographed. Of the forty reports turned in, only one was less than 20 percent mistaken about the principal facts, and most were more than 40 percent mistaken. The event surely drew the undivided attention of the observers, was in full view at close range, and lasted only twenty seconds. But the observers could not observe all that happened. Some readers chuckle because these observers were researchers, but similar experiments have been repeated numerous times. They are alike for all kinds of people.

The Instruments We Use to Observe

One of the reasons for our inability to "see it like it is" lies in the instruments or devices used to observe. If our own senses are the "instruments," we must keep in mind that we cannot perceive some aspects of what goes on around us. For instance, unless a fluorescent bulb starts to go bad, and "flickers" annoyingly in our eyes, we aren't generally aware that the way this bulb works is by constantly "flickering." Fluorescent bulbs produce what appears to be a steady light by a series of on and off sequences that our eyes simply aren't equipped to handle and perceive under normal circumstances. We may understand the principle, but the mechanisms in our image-producing system aren't able to detect such rapid changes.

Similarly, when you use a specially designed dog whistle that produces an extremely high number of cycles per second, you can't hear the sound produced. But your dog can because a dog's ear, unlike ours, can respond to frequencies over 20,000 cycles per second.

Numerous other examples are possible. All our sensory receptors have physiological limits. Our eyes cannot see x-rays, our senses of smell and taste do not respond well to continual inputs—after a while we get used to odors or tastes and they don't seem as strong. Our hands have a hard time distinguishing between something wet and something dry but cold. Each of the senses acts as a filter to those objects around us. The strength of these filters varies from one person to another and of course is influenced by other factors, which will be discussed later in the chapter.

Scientists have developed a variety of sophisticated "mechanisms of perception" that extend our ability to observe. The physical scientists' instruments include the thermometer, the x-ray machine, and the microscope. The social scientists' instruments include questionnaires, coding schemes, trained observers, and carefully developed paper and pencil tests. When used properly, they allow researchers to gather information often unavailable to our unaided senses. However, like our senses, each instrument has its own limitation. We will consider these limitations in more detail in Chapter 9; only one example will be given here.

In 1930, when anti-Oriental feeling was believed to be quite high in the United States, a social scientist wrote to 128 restaurants, hotels, auto camps, and tourist homes. He asked if they "would accept members of the Chinese race in their establishment." Of these, 118 said "no," 10 said "undecided; depends upon circumstances," and only 1 said "yes." To be sure, it was a rather resounding affirmation of the belief that Orientals were not welcomed. Yet six months previously, when the scientist and his Chinese friends had in fact traveled in that area, stopping at the very same establishments, they had been refused food and lodging only once. In addition, the subjective evaluation of the researcher was that they had been treated as cordially in the vast majority of cases as they would have been if they had all been white.

In this case, asking proprietors to commit themselves publicly about a socially sensitive topic that could affect their businesses was not the best way to determine how they would behave in the actual situation. Better instruments exist that clearly enhance rather than fog a researcher's ability to observe.

Try as we might, we cannot see the total world accurately; all we can hope for is to see part of it. Scientists, aided by instruments, can do a better job, but not a perfect one. There are just too many things to look at, and neither our senses nor the researcher's instruments are capable of seeing all. The fact that something must be left unseen is a major implication for readers of research.

Because scientists can observe only a little of what is potentially observable at any one time, we must realize that a lifetime of study allows not only for the collection of extensive observations, but also for the omission of infinite other observations. Scientists cannot avoid this restriction, but they can plan carefully what to observe and try to break out of the shackles that limit their perceptions. As evaluators of research, we must ask whether or not the author has attended to these problems and how different the findings would be if they were focused on different aspects of the event.

YOU INTERPRET EVERYTHING YOU SEE

A man, blind from birth and quite well adjusted to it, is operated on to have his sight restored. That is, all of the physiological mechanisms—the lens, the retina, the nerves leading from the eye to the brain, and so on—are repaired. The man can "see" for the first time in his life. What does he see? Not what most of us see, but just a blur. He does not suddenly see "objects" at all. One such man soon learned to find his way along the corridors of the hospital and to tell time from a clock. But he was also just as sure that his feet would touch the ground if he hung by his hands from his window ledge, when, in fact, the ground below was at least 50 feet away.

Learning to See

People learn to see. Seeing is not simply a collection of light waves that make sense in and of themselves. The adult with newly gained sight must learn to "see." Things he or she is familiar with by touch can be learned easily—hospital corridors and a clock, for instance. But things the adult has not touched are harder—how far away a distant object is, for example. The light waves entering our eyes only make sense if we know how to interpret them.

How each of us interprets what we see depends upon our total background—including our culture, education, language, and experiences—and the context in which we do the seeing.

What happens if each eye is simultaneously shown a different picture for a brief period of time? Will people see both pictures superimposed, both pictures separately, or will one of the pictures be dominant? When these questions are studied in a psychologist's laboratory, the most common result is that only one of the two pictures is "seen." Furthermore, the individual's background seems to have a lot to do with which picture is dominant. Police trainees more often see the picture of a person with a gun rather than the picture of a farmer walking behind a plow. People from all walks of life see the farmer about as often as the person with the gun. Mexicans more often see a bullfight scene when it is paired with a baseball game. Americans, on the other hand, are more likely to see the baseball game.

The Context

The context also helps determine which events are selected to be seen and how they will be interpreted. To learn more about what is meant by sanity and insanity, a researcher and seven other normal people asked to be admitted to psychiatric hospitals under false names and falsely reported that they had experienced certain symptoms of abnormality. Immediately upon entering the hospital all of the pseudopatients ceased all of the abnormal behaviors. These normal-acting people were discharged seven to fifty-two days later, all but one with the diagnosis of schizophrenia "in remission." Of interest here is the fact that these pseudopatients reported that the context within which they behaved (a mental hospital) strongly influenced what the staff saw them doing.

All pseudopatients took extensive notes publicly. Under ordinary circumstances, such behavior would have raised questions in the minds of the people around them, as, in fact, it did among the other patients. Indeed, before the study the researcher was so certain that the notes would elicit suspicion that elaborate precautions were taken to remove them from the ward each day. But the precautions proved needless. The closest any staff member came to questioning these notes occurred when one pseudopatient asked his physician what kind of medication he was receiving and began to write down the response. "You needn't write it," he was told gently. "If you have trouble remembering, just ask me again." One kindly nurse found a pseudopatient pacing the long hospital corridors. "Nervous?" she asked. "No, bored," he said. A psychiatrist pointed to a group of patients who were sitting outside the cafeteria entrance half an hour before lunchtime. To a group of young residents, he indicated that such behavior was characteristic of the oral-acquisitive nature of the syndrome. It seemed not to have occurred to him that there were very few things to anticipate in a psychiatric hospital besides eating.

So the problem of observation is confounded. Not only are researchers unable to see it all, but what they do see and how they interpret it are not completely under their conscious control. Their background and training play a role as does the context in which the observation occurs.

The "Halo Effect"

The well-known "halo effect" is a good example of interpretations not under one's conscious control. The effect means that an observer who has positive feelings about another tends to see all aspects of the person positively, and vice versa. Videotape interviews with a college professor depicted him as warm and likable in one sequence and cold and rigid in another. Students who viewed the warm, likable tape tended to evaluate all other characteristics of the professor as positive. Those viewing the cold, rigid professor perceived his other characteristics as negative, even though his appearance and mannerisms did not differ between the two videotapes. Though it is impossible to prevent these problems of observation, a competent researcher can to some extent control them and minimize their effect. One problem remains to be discussed, and is more difficult to handle.

YOU PRODUCE SOME OF WHAT YOU SEE

The World Changes

Time, as Einstein pointed out, is a fundamental part of the world. Nothing is static—people age, cars rust, and oranges rot. The world does not consist of "things" but rather "events." Our observations, however, often fail to take this into account. We are like a camera taking a snapshot of the world, and when we view it later we often have occasion to laugh at how much has changed.

Another scientist, Heisenberg, explains that at the most basic level, the study of elementary particles, it is theoretically impossible to know all you would like to know about them. If you try to observe and measure accurately a particle's speed, its location will be impossible to determine. Correspondingly, if you try to observe its location accurately, you cannot know its speed for certain. This paradox occurs because the very process of "looking" affects what is being "looked" at. As one tries to "see" an atomic particle, the light bouncing off it into our eyes (or, more correctly, the energy absorbed and emitted by our instruments) affects the electron enough to change its position, distorting our observation.

Heisenberg's uncertainty principle applies to all objects in the world, though the practical consequences of it when observing large objects such as people are practically nil. One parallel does apply to large objects—the effect of the observer on the observed. It is not difficult to imagine possible distortions that might occur because of the presence of an observer, such as a teacher participating in a student conversation about the course, or a manager watching subordinates, or a politician talking in the presence of a reporter.

There is also the related problem of expectations. People have a tendency to see what they expect to see. Or as David Berlo put it, "Seek and ye shall find, whether it is there or not."

Have you ever seen things that were not there because of your expectations? You hear a noise that sounds a lot like a dog rummaging in your garbage pail. It's dark outside. As you approach, the dog freezes. You can make out the silhouette of its head and body. You shout but the dog doesn't move. When you get closer, your mind seems to reassess the situation. Suddenly you can see that the "dog" was actually a trash bag that fell to the ground; a coffee can and some old newspaper had formed the "head" you saw.

Expectations

Expectations affect research also. In an extensive series of studies, Robert Rosenthal has demonstrated that experimenters often unintentionally influence their experiments so that the results coincide with the experimenters' expectations. In one of these studies, elementary-school teachers were led to believe that some of their pupils were "late bloomers" and would soon show marked improvement. In this study the teachers were purposefully deceived: the test used to identify the late bloomers was a sham, with late bloomers chosen randomly from the class list. Later testing indicated, however, that the teachers' expectations had had an effect. The designated late bloomers "bloomed" more than their classmates.

While these findings might be obvious or expected, they are a source of great concern to researchers who now must take more stringent measures to keep their expectations from biasing the findings. In evaluating research you must try to determine if the researcher's expectations were communicated to those being studied. And if so, are the results likely to be due to the researcher's expectations rather than the reason suggested by the researcher?

Charles Darwin, a scientist known for a wide variety of outstanding works, including the theory of evolution, is said to have been so concerned about this problem that he meticulously recorded all evidence that seemed to run counter to his beliefs. He wanted to be sure that he did not forget or ignore such evidence later.

Survey researchers are often troubled by a similar problem. They want to determine if a certain issue is important, but they know that people will think it must be important if they are being interviewed about it. Don't ask and you don't know. Ask and you change what you were asking about.

All scientists try to make carefully controlled observations to decrease the chances of affecting what they see. But the observer always contributes to what is observed. Sometimes the influence is slight or has been accounted for in some way by the researcher. Other times, the researcher's contribution seriously distorts what is there. Clearly, it is essential that readers of research be able to distinguish between these two situations.

WHAT CAN BE MADE OF ALL THIS?

We seem to be in a paradoxical state. On the one hand we know that observation is imperfect. Neither we nor a researcher can see it like it is. Yet we also know that, for the most part, we adequately observe the world: we do not cross streets in front of moving cars, or put our hand unknowingly into a fire. Our problem is that we do not know if we or another researcher would agree that a particular observation was made correctly. On the average, we seem to cope with our distorted view of the world, but for any given instance there is no guarantee that it was observed without distortion.

As a consumer of research, therefore, you must examine what the researcher observed. You have to try to determine whether you would have interpreted the researcher's basic observations differently. In the initial selection of what to observe, what was observed, and at each inferential step thereafter, a possibility exists that you will disagree with the researcher about what was observed and even what was not observed.

Develop Sensitivity to Error

But the extensive potential for errors in the observation process should not make you despair. Competent researchers are keenly aware of the problems of observation. Much of their training is concerned with how to avoid, minimize, or compensate for potential errors in observation. One simple tactic is the use of several independent observers, or perhaps the use of measuring instruments that do not impinge upon the people being studied; or perhaps something more complicated is needed. Many of the ways researchers treat potential problems of observation are mentioned later in this book. The point is that researchers can often cope with these problems. Your job as a reader of research is to be sensitive to potential errors in order to see if the researcher adequately dealt with them. If you can be reasonably convinced that a possible distortion has been controlled, you will have a more solid basis for believing that the original observations can be used to support the research results.

The process of observation is only one source of potential error in the research process. Because those observations have to be communicated to others, a second source of error can develop when observations are changed into a message, usually a written one. Chapter 4 deals with how writing adds other problems.

QUESTIONS TO ASK

1 **What is left out?**
   Since the world cannot be completely described, an observer intentionally or inadvertently selects a very small part of the world to observe. What is omitted may not be useful to that individual, but it may be extremely important to you.
2 **Are all interpretations acceptable to you?**
   Even direct observation includes interpretation. You must decide whether you, or another researcher, might interpret differently at this very basic level. Then findings are reported on the basis of the observations. They also involve interpretations. Finally, authors frequently interpret the findings in order to draw conclusions. You need to pay careful attention to the interpretations introduced in each step.
3 **What effect did measuring instruments or other "aids to observation" have on the observations made?**
   Questionnaires, trained observers, tests, and other devices are all aids to observation. Each has its own limitations that must be considered.
4 **Who did the observation?**
   Knowing something about the observer's background, training, expectations, attitudes, and so on may give you some insight into possible sources of distortion.
5 **In what context was the observation made?**
   Knowing something about when and where an observation was made may also help. What wasn't observed may have affected what was.
6 **Did the observer prevent possible distortions from occurring?**
   If the observer did not attempt to control for distortion it does not guarantee that the observations were in error; they may be, but we have no way of knowing. If the observer did attempt to control distortion, it does not prove that there was none, but it does lend weight to our confidence in the observation. Not only do observations occur directly, but in many cases "aids" to observation are used such as questionnaires, instruments, tests, and so on. Each has its own limitations and vulnerabilities in terms of possible distortions.

PRACTICE EVALUATIONS

Reminder: Answering the above questions yourself is good practice. Chapter 18 provides guidelines for you to follow in doing that. Chapter 19 provides two articles along with our evaluations of them. Chapter 20 provides two additional articles for you to practice on.

FOR FURTHER THOUGHT

1 It may be useful to compare the observation process with picture taking. Some of the factors that influence the picture one gets are listed below. Is there an analogue for these in the observation process?
  (a) Type of camera—still or motion
  (b) Type of film—color or black and white
  (c) Speed of film
  (d) Age of film
  (e) Competence of person using camera
  (f) Shutter speed
  (g) Size of aperture
  (h) Leaving the lens cover on
  (i) Focus
  (j) Depth of field
  (k) Use of filters
  (l) Size of lens—close-up or wide-angle
  (m) Quality of camera
  (n) How the object is arranged and centered
  (o) Size of negative
2 Philosophers and scientists have commented extensively about the observation process. Interpret the following quotations in terms of the material in this chapter.
  (a) "The world is not a fixed solid array of objects, for it cannot be fully separated from our perception of it. It shifts under our gaze, it interacts with us, and the knowledge that it yields has to be interpreted by us." (J. Bronowski)
  (b) "Man looks at his world through transparent patterns or templets which he creates and then attempts to fit over the realities of which the world is composed." (G. A. Kelly)
  (c) "The old saw that seeing is believing does not characterize the scientific mentality but its opposite. The task of inquiry is largely one of discovering what it is that needs to be done so that we can believe what we see." (A. Kaplan)
  (d) "An empiricist . . . thinks he believes only what he sees, but he is much better at believing than at seeing." (G. Santayana)
  (e) "Men occasionally stumble over the truth, but most of them pick themselves up and hurry on as if nothing happened." (W. Churchill)

FOR FURTHER READING

1 J. Marshall. "The Evidence: Do We See and Hear What Is, or Do Our Senses Lie?" *Psychology Today* 2 (February 1969), pp. 48–52.

A discussion of much of the material in this chapter, but presented in terms of courtroom trial. How accurate is a witness? Are better-educated witnesses better witnesses? What influences the testimony and accuracy of a witness? Do the legal rules of evidence have a solid basis in what is known about observation, inference, and influence?

2 J. B. Deregowski. "Pictorial Perception and Culture." *Scientific American* 227 (1972), pp. 82–88.

A report of experiments describing the effect of culture on perception.

3 M. D. Vernon. "Perception, Attention and Consciousness." In K. Sereno and C. Mortensen, *Foundation of Communication Theory.* New York: Harper & Row, 1970.

A more detailed treatment of research on perception and its implications for understanding how errors can occur in direct observation.

4 G. Gamow. *Mr. Tompkins in Paperback.* New York: Cambridge University Press, 1965, reprinted 1993.

This delightful introduction to the world of relativity and quantum mechanics takes the form of a series of dream worlds in which the effects of relativity and Heisenberg's uncertainty principle are large enough to be noticed by everyone.

5 J. Hanlon. "Uri Geller and Science." *New Scientist* (October 17, 1974), p. 176.

An interesting description of how a scientist as an observer apparently saw what he wanted to see in a public demonstration of Uri Geller's psychic abilities.

6 C. Wade and C. Tavris. *Psychology,* 4th ed. New York: HarperCollins, 1996.

See Chapter 6, "Sensation and Perception," for additional insight into what we know about how we take in information.

4

COMMUNICATION: WRITING ADDS OTHER PROBLEMS

It took four weeks to draft the questionnaire, one week to train the interviewers, three weeks to field the study, six weeks to analyze the data, and one week to write it up and submit it for publication. Fifteen weeks of research are distilled into one 20-page journal article.

Clearly, everything that was done can't fit into the article; something was probably left out. What's omitted is only one of the communication problems facing you as a reader of research. In the previous chapter we argued that the process of observation is a major source of error. In this chapter our concern is with the process of communicating those observations and its role in producing more errors. Researchers can no more tell it like it is than they can see it like it is. Here are some of the reasons.

WHAT'S LEFT OUT OF THE ARTICLE?

Deciding what to publish is a perplexing problem for serious researchers. If only the "best" results were published, the article might fail to communicate anomalies that a reader could make some sense out of and thereby use to get a better understanding of the problem under study. But journals prefer to publish shorter articles, and readers avoid longer books crammed with exceptions, details, and footnotes. In addition, if the anomalies are just sporadic errors, it is a waste of time to ask readers to wade through them. Good researchers take these factors into account when they decide what to say.

They know that anything left out might somehow turn out to be important. Thus they use their judgment to balance the conflicting demands of completeness and brevity. Poorer researchers don't even worry about the conflicting demands. In either case you may not get what you want. You need to be on the lookout for hints that important parts of the story aren't being told.

Conscious and Unconscious Decisions

A journal article should be thought of as an abstract, not as a diary or log. All parts have missing information. Sometimes the omission is unconscious, while other times it is more of a conscious decision. Assumptions that underlie the researcher's approach usually are in the unconscious category. Anomalies and results that run counter to the researcher's expectations often fall in the conscious category. In both cases, the consequences of the missing information may be serious. Assumptions and contradictory results are very important for a reader to know because they can put an entirely new light on the accuracy and applicability of the findings.

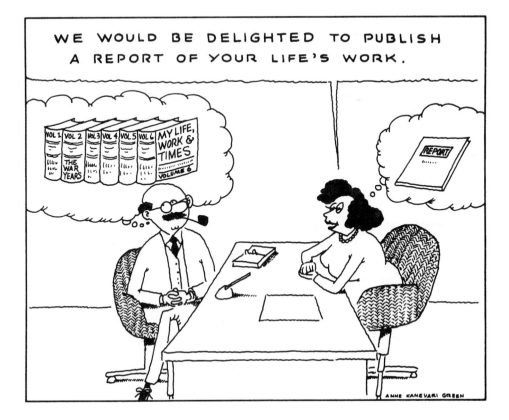

Evaluating What's Not There

Unfortunately, there isn't any particular strategy for detecting important omissions. Evaluating what is *not* included is difficult. It requires at least some knowledge of what fundamental elements ought to be there. If you've read enough journal articles in the social sciences, you have probably recognized some similarity in their organization. Reports of empirical research usually include the following components:

• The introduction contains a statement of the questions or problems under investigation and some justification for their importance.

• A summary or evaluation of related research is included to put the current study into a historical and scientific perspective.

• A description of the methods or procedures used is needed. In order to meet the norm of publicness, this section has to be detailed enough so that another researcher would be able to repeat it.

• The results section summarizes the data or observations. It also includes any computations or analyses of the data. This section should answer the researcher's specific questions.

• In the last section, the researcher goes beyond the specific questions asked and interprets the results in broader terms. The earlier literature may be reconceptualized as a result of this study, or the author may suggest implications of the results for current theory or existing practices.

To evaluate the *contents* of each of these sections of a journal article, you should read Section Four of this book first. Our concern here is with the *presence* of the information contained in these sections. All of it is necessary, though it is no crime if a different arrangement is used or if some of the sections are combined.

Academic journals generally require authors to include these sections. However, problems arise in some applied journals or in popularized accounts of social science research. Since these journals are published for an audience made up primarily of non-researchers, some of the more technical details are frequently left out. Occasionally, the entire literature review, most of the methodology section, and all of the analyses are omitted. But what you don't know does matter. Using these shortened accounts for more than just keeping informed—say, for actually implementing a policy change or some other application of the published results—requires a lot of faith in the editor and in the researcher.

Slightly Distorted Reconstructions

Not only is every article a shortened version of what occurred, it is also a distorted reconstruction. Journal articles have some underlying logic or structure that editors and readers prefer simply because the article is then easier to understand. But the actual practice of research is rarely, if ever, so logical. Usually many things are happening at once during the study, or in a sequence not implied by the structure of the article. For instance, after the results have been analyzed the researcher may find a better way to state the problem, or a colleague reviewing a rough draft of the manuscript may identify other relevant studies that were unknown to the author. Yet the published account reports the problem statement first, as if the researcher always thought of it that way. The literature review is given as a coherent whole. The method section usually includes only what they actually did—all changes necessitated by poor planning or unexpected events are omitted. When the major results don't come out as expected, the final section of the article may suggest that the minor results are all that matter. And sometimes the entire introduction is written last, giving the impression that the author was in total command of everything that happened and was able to predict all the results.

Accepting Author's Assumptions

Another type of information frequently left out of reports is information about assumptions. We pointed out in the last chapter that even direct observation involves interpretation of what the observer actually experiences. And the interpretation depends on past experiences that are influenced by the observer's culture, education, and language.

Findings are further interpretations based on observations. Given certain assumptions, researchers make statements that they believe have been supported by the observations (or the data) they gathered. Readers must be sure they can accept those assumptions. For instance, the data in a comparative study of two teaching methods might be the scores of the students in two classes on a final exam. The researcher might then state that the study showed that method A was better than method B. In so doing, the researcher is assuming among other things that final exam scores are indications of how good a teaching method is. A reader, on the other hand, might disagree and want to know, in addition, to what extent the methods encourage independent study techniques or self-confidence in the students. You should accept the researcher's findings only if you can accept the assumption that links the data to the findings.

Findings Are Based on Assumptions

Notice that there are innumerable ways of stating findings based on any set of data, and each may involve different assumptions as well as some of the same assumptions. The researcher in the example above, for instance, might have said that method A resulted in higher final exam scores than method B. In that statement no assumption is made about exam scores being the appropriate measure of the goodness of a teaching method. What is assumed both here and in the first statement is that the teaching method made the difference and not the teachers' abilities, or the IQ of the students, and so on. And, of course, you need not be limited to the way the researcher stated the findings. You can make your own assumptions and state the findings in the most meaningful way to you. What is important is to be aware of assumptions and evaluate them properly.

Conclusions Are Also Based on Assumptions

Conclusions are statements even further removed from the data by assumptions. When conclusions are discussed in a journal article (in the discussion, conclusion, or implications section), the author may mention the assumptions that were made. The assumptions may be values held by the researcher, beliefs about the findings from other studies, or anything that is related to the study. You as a reader must examine the assumptions stated, identify the unstated ones, and evaluate them as closely as the findings.

An author cannot report everything about a study, so you must look for cues to important omissions. In addition, observations, findings, and conclusions all involve assumptions that must be evaluated in order to assess the accuracy of statements that researchers make on the basis of their studies. Many of these omissions and reconstructions are necessary if we are to have readable journal articles. But some of them can seriously affect a reader's judgment. Good researchers will try to strike an acceptable balance between readability and a fair presentation of what happened.

HOW WAS MEANING CONVEYED?

What is left out of a report is only one of the problems. The language used also has an impact on the reader. The meaning a reader gets is determined by *how* a message is said as well as *what* is said.

Effect of Words on Meanings

The effect of words whose meanings are not so clear was demonstrated in a recent study. People were shown a short film of a car crashing into another car. After viewing the film, each person was asked how fast the car was going at the time of the crash. However, the wording was changed slightly for different groups of viewers. One group was asked, "How fast was car A going when it smashed into car B?" Another group was asked the same question except the word "collided" was substituted for "smashed." In other groups the words "bumped," "hit," or "contacted" were used. As might be expected, the average speed estimated by the viewers varied according to the word used. When "contacted" was the key word, the group estimated almost thirty-two miles per hour; when "smashed" was used, the group's estimate was nine miles per hour faster. The other words led to intermediate estimates of the car's speed. Nothing had changed in the film. The same event was seen by all the participants, yet the written description, presented as a question, seriously affected their interpretation.

This feature of words is sometimes referred to as the connotative meaning as opposed to the denotative meaning. Denotatively, it is clear that the collision between the two cars was referred to, but few of us would be aware that connotatively a slower or faster speed is implied by the author's choice of words. Most researchers try to avoid emotion-laden words. They try to pick words whose connotations are relatively neutral. However, all choices invoke some connotations in the mind of the reader.

Language as a Smokescreen

Language can also be used as a smokescreen to hide what is being said. Sometimes this is done in order to mislead the reader, as will be discussed later in the chapter. But other times smokescreening occurs because of the author's misconception of what technical and academic writing should be. Some authors seem to believe that obscure quotations (preferably in a classical language), complex equations, excessive foot-notes, or long strings of complicated words (that is, concatenations of polysyllabic ter-minology) are needed. It may be that this style is appropriate when aimed at a recep-tive and prepared audience. More often than not, however, these paraphernalia of pedantry—as David Hackett Fischer calls them—are likely to be distracting. They can either turn us off so that we don't read the article or intimidate us so that we come to believe that the author must be correct, because, after all, the writing is so "academic."

Smokescreens like this, in which the style or form of the message has more impact than its contents, affect everyone, not just the readers of research. Occasionally we come across documented cases in which researchers were fooled. In one such instance, an actor with fictitious credentials was introduced to a group of psychiatrists, psychol-ogists, social workers, and educators as Dr. Myron L. Fox of the Albert Einstein Uni-versity, an expert in applying mathematical game theory to physical education. The phony Dr. Fox gave a prepared lecture to this group, consisting of double-talk, contra-dictory statements, and fancy words. Afterward the members of the audience were asked their anonymous reactions. Most of the responses were positive, though one per-son thought the talk was too "intellectual." No one seemed to doubt what Dr. Fox said. It seems that how he said it, including the trappings in the introduction, spoke louder than the contents of his lecture.

Thus, how research is reported is likely to have one of two exactly opposite effects on you, the reader. As in the case of Dr. Fox, it may dull your evaluation abilities and induce you to accept information uncritically. Or it may so bore you or so offend you by its complexity that you refuse to take the time to consider the potentially valuable information hidden in the verbal jungle. Either way you lose.

Well-written, easy-to-understand journal articles are a joy to come by—perhaps be-cause we don't come by them often enough. Good, clear, concise writing is always de-sirable and some of the best researchers write very well. But even when research re-ports are not well written, they may still contain valuable information. Writing style can justifiably make or break a novel, but it should not stand in the way of evaluating accurate information. Readers of research need to compensate for a smokescreen when it is there, fight off boredom when writing becomes pedantic, and evaluate information on its merit, not on the author's writing ability.

WHY WAS THE ARTICLE WRITTEN?

So far we have looked at the written article itself as a potential source of error. The problems that were identified are created sometimes unconsciously, sometimes inad-vertently—but never malevolently. Now we want to consider the writer's motiva-tion, because writing has sometimes been used to intentionally conceal what really happened.

Creation of Phony Data

We doubt that much outright creation of phony data exists, but a number of notable cases have been exposed over the years. When dishonesty is discovered among scientists it has an especially repugnant air. It is comparable in some ways to cheating on an ethics exam or taking advantage of a helpless client under your care. Public expectations of how scientists should behave are so seriously violated that such dishonesty gets wide attention. Fortunately, outright fraud is infrequent.

A noted example of dishonesty was the case of Paul Kammerer, an Austrian zoologist. He was among many scientists in the early 1930s who were attracted to the theory that acquired characteristics can be inherited by succeeding generations. Kammerer reported that he found instances of the inheritance of characteristics that were originally caused by the environment. His colleagues became suspicious. After all, if Kammerer's findings were true, a lot of the theory of evolution would have to be rethought. So they independently examined the evidence and his procedures and eventually discovered that the supposed inherited characteristic (a dark patch of hair and skin) was actually caused by an injection of India ink by Kammerer or one of his associates.

Researchers as Safeguards

In findings of such importance, scientists keep a very close watch over one another. When important or unusual results are reported, other researchers in other laboratories repeat the study to scc if they can get the same results. If they cannot, the original findings are suspect—either something atypical happened in the original study or the scientist lied. This kind of cross-checking by other scientists is a valuable safeguard against fraud. There is little reason to be dishonest if the norms of your discipline suggest that you will be discovered quickly. However, the safeguard works only in those fields which support and encourage independent replications of the original study. If you are dealing with a less scrutinized area (and that includes much of the applied social sciences), you will have to be your own safeguard. Unfortunately, there are no certain methods for detecting fraud. We can only warn you of the danger.

Blatant cheating is a serious problem—but one, we believe, that occurs relatively infrequently and is often detected at a later time. A more common problem, and one that is harder to discover, involves the minor dishonesties and other questionable items that creep into reports to make them acceptable for publication.

Professors and other researchers need to publish. Today the phrase "publish or perish" is not without substance—if it ever was. We hope that untenured college professors do not create actual lies, but we suspect that standards are sometimes compromised a bit and some unsettling suspicions about accuracy are left unmentioned to ensure speedy publication.

The "Art" of Factifuging

To protect themselves and counter their critics, some authors may resort to a form of smokescreening. Writing in the British journal *The Lancet,* Dr. Nathan S. Kline humorously introduced the world to the art of "factifuging." Its purpose was to help the "oppressed authors defend their intuitively correct positions against contradictory data, irrefutable logic, and opposite conclusions." With tongue in cheek, he describes about 25 techniques. Each helps the author project a picture different from the facts, and each is ethically questionable.

For instance, under the heading "distracting," the use of *individualizing* was suggested. When overwhelming and incontrovertible statistical evidence is placed in their path, authors can distract the audience from this evidence by relating in detail an example of how an individual case or experience confirmed their position. A properly executed individualizing parry can easily leave the audience with the impression that something was wrong with the statistics. This form of factifuging occurs quite often, especially at conferences where criticism, questions, and rebuttals of the researcher's work are the norm. As readers of (or listeners to) this type of interchange, you need to remember that one or a few individual case studies do not prove very much and certainly do not disprove a statistical finding.

Though the factifuging techniques are funny as Dr. Kline presents them, they still show up occasionally in journal articles, convention presentations, and proposals submitted for funding. From the viewpoint of the reader they represent a distortion in communication or writing and may indicate that some weakness is being obscured.

But, you might say, journals check on things like that—dishonesties, smokescreening, and poor reasoning are discovered and removed. And indeed some journals do. The better ones send each article to one or more referees who are researchers in the same specific area. Each referee examines the manuscript in great detail, raises questions for the author to answer, makes suggestions for improving the report, and in many cases recommends that the article not be published because of one inadequacy or another. In fact, in many academic journals rejection rates of 60 to 80 percent are common. That's the ideal, and the best journals in all scientific fields probably operate in that way.

What Do You Know about the Journal?

Unfortunately, not all journals measure up to this ideal. Some do not use referees. They may accept all articles submitted, or screening may be done by the editor, who cannot be equally knowledgeable in all areas of the discipline. Some editors, in fact, need articles to publish. Rather than being careful to publish the best of what is available, they are forced to take whatever is submitted in order to fill the pages. Given the increasing appreciation for the value of empirical research, such articles, as opposed to opinion pieces or case studies, are in greater demand in many fields. Some journals seem to be willing to publish anything with numbers in it, because it may enhance the prestige of the journal.

Thus there is plenty of inducement to be a little dishonest in publishing. As a reader you need to learn something about the journals and authors in your field. What is the journal's reputation? Who is the editor? Are articles refereed? What percentage of submitted manuscripts does the journal publish? What is the author's status in the field? These and other similar questions all deal with external criteria for evaluation; we can raise them, but we cannot help you judge the answers. You need the answers to these questions before you can realistically decide if the author's communication is helpful, or if it is presenting a misleading picture of the research.

Finally, if observation can cause some error and writing about these observations can add more error, then even before you read the article there is reason to be cautious. In addition to these two sources of error, you as a reader are another source. The next chapter deals with those additional sources of error arising from the way you interpret what you read.

QUESTIONS TO ASK

1 **Is there anything missing that might be important?**
   It is difficult to evaluate what isn't there. Search for possible missing assumptions, hints that bad results were not included, and the presence of all necessary parts of a journal article. You will need to make use of your knowledge of the subject matter, the author, and the journal.
2 **Are the researcher's assumptions acceptable to you?**
   Assumptions usually are required for data analysis and to link the observations to the findings and conclusions. At least some assumptions will not be stated. You must be sure that both stated and unstated assumptions are acceptable.
3 **What is the effect of the language used in the article?**
   Did the author maintain neutrality in the choice of words, or are emotionally laden terms employed? Do the language and style reveal or conceal what occurred?
4 **Are purposeful distortions a possibility?**
   Who is the author and what are the editorial practices of this journal? It is difficult to see through a clever author who engages in some questionable publication decisions. Your knowledge of the field and the people in it are probably your best guides.

PRACTICE EVALUATIONS

Reminder: Answering the above questions yourself is good practice. Chapter 18 provides guidelines for you to follow in doing that. Chapter 19 provides two articles along with our evaluations of them. Chapter 20 provides two additional articles for you to practice on.

FOR FURTHER THOUGHT

1 Find a recently completed term paper or report, preferably one of your own. Review it in terms of the types of communication problems discussed in this chapter.
   (a) Identify the choices made in terms of what you included or left out. What distortions or false impressions might a reader get from these choices?
   (b) Examine the choice of language, particularly the neutrality of terms and their connotative meanings. Were all words chosen carefully to communicate what you meant? Was that meaning justified?
   (c) Can you find any weaknesses or counterarguments to the rationale that links the data to the final conclusions? Were those weaknesses mentioned in the paper?
2 Become familiar with the major journals in your field.
   Which are the more prestigious? This is not always easy to determine, but you can get some idea from the publisher (national or international professional organizations usually

ensure that their journals are respected), the lag time between acceptance for publication and actual appearance, and the status of the authors.

3 Interpret each of the following quotations in terms of the material in this chapter.

   (a) "Scientific reports almost never describe all the blind alleys, all the hunches that didn't work out, all the false starts and experimental errors. The tables are always nice and tidy, just as if nature itself handed out the data in tabular form. But nature doesn't give up its data easily; scientists have to seize it, and while they're grabbing they select and leave a lot behind." (D. Krech)

   (b) "Between what one observes and one concludes there is a long and tortuous chain of reasoning, inference and evaluation." (A. Rapoport)

   (c) "There have always been more historians who were more concerned that truth should be on their side than that they should be on the side of truth." (D. H. Fischer)

   (d) "Although the result is, I trust, tolerably ordered, this book arose in a haphazard way. Its genesis and execution were probably typical of most general treatises. We rarely separate the logical and psychological aspects of research and we tend to impute the order of a finished product to the process of its creation. After all, the abandoned outlines and unused note cards are in the wastebasket and the false starts are permanently erased from memory. It is for this reason that P. B. Medawar once termed the scientific paper a 'fraud'; for it reflects so falsely the process of its generation and fosters the myth of rational procedure according to initial outlines rigidly (and brilliantly) conceived." (S. J. Gould)

   (e) "Bad prose doesn't happen by accident: it's a conscious attempt to deceive." (G. Orwell)

   (f) "It is no use looking to scientific 'papers,' for they do not merely conceal but actively misrepresent the reasoning which goes into the work they describe." (Sir Peter Medawar)

FOR FURTHER READING

1 S. I. Hayakawa. *Language in Thought and Action,* 5th ed. New York: Harcourt, 1990. See especially Chapters 3 and 5.

An old, but not outdated, introduction to language and how it can affect human judgment and behavior. This is not a stuffy text, but an enjoyable learning experience.

2 N. S. Kline. "Factifuging." *The Lancet* (June 30, 1962), pp. 1396–99.

The full text of what we hinted at in the chapter.

3 D. H. Fischer. *Historians' Fallacies.* New York: Harper & Row, 1970, pp. 263–306.

These pages include two chapters that describe the fallacies of argument. Included are the fallacies of language and the fallacies of distraction.

4 S. E. Luria. "What Makes a Scientist Cheat." *Prism* (May 1975), pp. 16–18ff.

Some of the more spectacular examples of lying in science are reviewed and the author explores the possible motivations for why they might have taken place.

5 N. J. Pallone and J. J. Hennessy (Eds.). *Fraud and Fallible Judgment.* New Brunswick, NJ: Transaction Publishers, 1995.

A collection of 13 essays on fraud and deception in the social and behavioral sciences.

5

INTERPRETATION:
. . . AND THEN YOU READ IT

WHO, ME?

You're part of the problem also. One source of potential error that you have to guard against is yourself. In the previous two chapters we've argued that errors occur in the process of observation and in communication. Because readers of research need to observe the printed page and receive the message being communicated, many of the problems discussed earlier also apply to you.

YOU PROBABLY DON'T READ IT ALL

The first problem arises from the fact that most readers don't read it all. Even when the article is relevant to your needs, you probably do a lot of skipping and skimming. Most of the time you're generally aware of omitting some parts of an article. This may be due to the length of the article, to the writer's style, or to boredom or impatience. No matter the cause, the effect is the same—you can't learn anything from what you don't read and misinterpretations are more likely when you don't read carefully.

YOU ALSO HAVE TO INTERPRET IT

But even if you read the article completely, you cannot avoid the second problem, that of interpretation. Interpretation is a more insidious problem because you're less likely to be consciously aware of it. Each of us brings with us our own education, experience, prejudices, meanings, and purposes in reading. The content of the article must pass through each of these filters before a reader can get any understanding of what the researcher reports. It will not be exactly the same understanding the researcher tried to communicate in writing the report. In addition to the article's content, there is also the effect of its style, language, or format. The medium may not be the entire message, but it is certainly part of it. And lastly, there is the problem of remembering it all and remembering it accurately. Clearly the same filters that influenced your original interpretation of the article, along with any later experiences, have an effect on what you remember.

Obviously, much of what we want to say in this chapter has been said before; it just needs to be rephrased in terms of the reader rather than the researcher. Since you can do that on your own, we will limit our discussion in this chapter to those topics that specifically deal with interpretation as a source of error. It is a very short chapter, but we've included it in order to emphasize something you may not have considered before—*your* contribution to the problem of evaluating information.

THE AURA OF THE PRINTED WORD

The printed word has an enormous power to impress. Many people implicitly assume that the printed word is truthful. Naturally, no one believes all printed material. Tabloid newspapers are considered by some to be less than truthful. All people have their favorite culprits such as political propaganda (of either the left-wing or right-wing varieties) or some advertisements or astrologer's reports. However, scientific journals are frequently seen in a more hallowed light. Unfortunately, getting something into print does not necessarily mean that it is truthful.

An article with statistics has an incredibly positive effect on many people. We ask our students to tell how they reacted to statistics in articles they read. Many said that they always skipped them. Some indicated that they thought the article more authoritative if statistics were presented, even though they found them incomprehensible. In fact, of course, the presence of statistics neither adds nor detracts from the truthfulness of a report. Only if you can evaluate the statistics should they have any effect on you one way or the other.

Be sure that the aura of information put down in black and white (and especially that in statistical black and white) doesn't stunt your evaluation capabilities.

SOURCE CREDIBILITY

Your beliefs about the author and the journal affect how you interpret the content of the article. Studies investigating a communicator's credibility tend to support the notion that the identical message will be judged more favorably when it is given by a communicator with higher status and better credentials. Questionable statements may be readily and sometimes unknowingly reinterpreted so that they seem to be more accurate when you respect and are impressed by the author.

Your judgment of the journal has a similar effect. A journal with small type and lots of references at the end of each article is often considered scholarly. A magazine

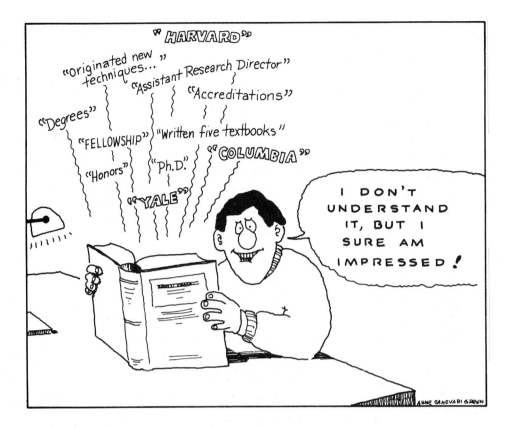

printed on attractive paper with well-arranged and tastefully selected illustrations generally is viewed as accepting and publishing only well-thought-out articles. Following the same kind of thinking, the articles published in an association's journal will be considered the best work in that particular field, simply because the association printed the journal. Obviously these inferences are not always correct.

We should make use of these external factors as we read an article, but we ought to be very aware of when and how we do so. That, of course, is easier to say than to do. The essence of our discussion of source credibility could easily be stated in a single sentence. But it is more difficult to stop yourself when you read an article and ask if you are being unduly influenced by the author or the journal.

YOUR APPROACH TO THINKING

Take a look at yourself as a thinker. Psychologists have shown that different people take different general approaches in evaluating information. One of the ways in which we differ relates to how we organize and structure our beliefs and attitudes, and this affects how we view the new information we read about. For example, Milton

Rokeach has found that some people, whom he calls closed-minded or dogmatic, are characterized by

1 a rigid manner of thinking and sharply defined differences between what they believe and what they don't believe
2 unqualified rejection of unacceptable beliefs, no matter how little or how much the beliefs differ from their own
3 lumping of conflicting views without differentiating among them
4 a view of the world as threatening and hostile
5 a regarding for authority figures as absolute and evaluation of other people according to whether they accept or reject the authority figure

Naturally, few people are completely dogmatic. People vary in their degree of dogmatism and in their ability to be open-minded. A revealing trait of dogmatic individuals is that they are not able to perceive differences between the attributes of a source and the attributes of a message. In other words, they are not able to evaluate information independent of the source. This kind of attitude varies all the way from the child's insistence that "My daddy's right, I don't care what he said" to an adult who has difficulty seeing contradictions in an article simply because the author is respected.

Dogmatism affects one's thinking in a rather general way. In judging research reports, readers (especially those with some, but not much, research training) occasionally have some specific, but mistaken, beliefs about what constitutes "good" research practice. These beliefs may be used to screen out quickly and rather automatically those studies which don't measure up to par. Some of the more common of these erroneous beliefs are that

- quantitative methods are always necessary
- random samples are always necessary
- a researcher cannot learn anything of value from a small sample
- if statistical procedures support a particular research finding, then that finding must be correct and it must be important
- what should happen in the long run, or on the average, will happen in the short run or in this single study

Later in the book we will touch on some of these matters. Our point here is to caution you to be aware of your existing criteria for evaluating research so that you are not too quick to denigrate a study because of some single apparent weakness—it may not be a weakness at all.

A related problem has to do with your motivation to read. Often your motivation isn't what you say it is. You may declare and perhaps believe that you are reading in order to become better informed, but you may be reading primarily to gain ammunition to refute someone else. Are you searching for the best assessment of the situation, the one that is based on a careful examination of all sides, or do you need to buttress an argument with some supporting evidence? Do you seek to persuade someone else or inform yourself? Again, your approach to an article affects what you get out of it.

Well, that's it. You were warned. This is a very short chapter. But its length can serve as an example of one of the things we've been discussing. You would be committing one of the errors we're trying to warn you about if you dismissed the content, simply because of the size of the chapter. It may be less than easy to accept your own responsibility as readers of research. Communication is a two-way street; both the sender and the receiver contribute to its overall effectiveness. To rephrase an adage from the 1960s: remember, you're not only part of the problem, you're part of the solution.

QUESTIONS TO ASK

All the questions given at the end of Chapters 3 and 4 apply here also. You need to reinterpret them so they apply to you as a reader rather than to a researcher or author. In addition to these, here are two other questions to ask that are suggested by the new material in this chapter.

1 **How much influence should the credibility of the author and the journal have on your judgment of the article?**
  This should be asked for each article evaluated.
2 **What is your "mental set" when you read an article?**
  Closed-mindedness limits your ability to accept new information and leads you to rely too heavily on your judgment of the author or the journal. In addition, what preconceived notions do you have about the characteristics required of "good" research? Are they correct notions? And, finally, why are you reading the article? If it is to bolster an existing belief or to tear down an opposing point of view, it may be difficult (or irrelevant) to assess the article honestly.

PRACTICE EVALUATIONS

Reminder: Answering the above questions yourself is good practice. Chapter 18 provides guidelines for you to follow in doing that. Chapter 19 provides two articles along with our evaluations of them. Chapter 20 provides two additional articles for you to practice on.

FOR FURTHER THOUGHT

1 What influence would each of the following traits have on a reader's reaction to and assessment of an article?
  (a) Intelligence
  (b) Paranoia
  (c) Tiredness
  (d) Conservativeness
  (e) Commitment to trying something new
2 Do you agree or disagree with the assertion that "no statistic is unambiguous?" Why?
3 Interpret the following quotations in terms of the material in this chapter.
  (a) "Printed data, like rumors, have the unfortunate property of gaining the appearance of reliability and respectability as they are successively quoted and go from hand to hand." (J. Simon)

(**b**) "I have met the enemy and he is us." (Pogo Possum)

(**c**) "Into every act of knowing there enters a passionate contribution of the person knowing what is being known and this coefficient is no mere imperfection, but a vital component of his knowledge." (M. Polanyi)

FOR FURTHER READING

1 H. Kahane. *Logic and Contemporary Rhetoric: The Use of Reason in Everyday Life,* 7th ed. Belmont, CA: Wadsworth, 1995.

One of the better introductions to fallacies of thinking. What makes it particularly applicable to our needs is that it spends several chapters (5–9) evaluating the logic and language of lengthy written presentations.

2 S. I. Hayakawa. *Language in Thought and Action,* 5th ed. Harcourt Brace, 1990.

Most of Book Two is applicable here.

3 C. W. Offir. "Floundering in Fallacy: Seven Quick Ways to Kid Yourself." *Psychology Today* 8 (April 1975), pp. 66–68.

A good introduction to a few of the more common fallacies that may appear in research studies. These are methodological fallacies and are different from the fallacies of language discussed in the previous two books.

4 S. Sutherland. *Irrationality: Why We Don't Think Straight.* New Brunswick, NJ. Rutgers University Press, 1992.

An up-to-date, nontechnical survey of what cognitive and social psychologists know about our everyday thoughts and behaviors. How and why we are "irrational," and what we can do to improve our chances for acting wisely in our personal and professional lives.

5 T. Gilovich. *How We Know What Isn't So.* New York: The Free Press, 1993.

Another look at "The Fallibility of Human Reason in Everyday Life" (the author's subtitle for the book).

6 R. S. Feldman. *Essentials of Understanding Psychology,* 3rd ed. New York: McGraw-Hill, 1997.

The discussion of language on pages 236–45 is helpful for understanding how we interpret the written words of others.

THE NATURE OF ERROR

What kinds are there?

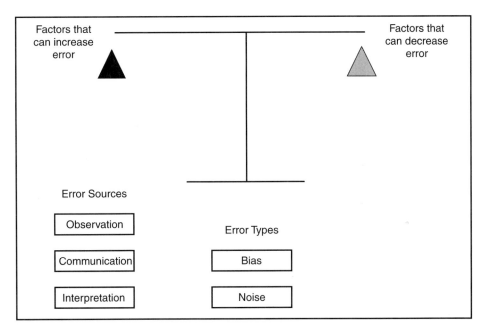

Factors that can increase error

Factors that can decrease error

Error Sources

Observation

Communication

Interpretation

Error Types

Bias

Noise

THE ERROR MODEL: IDENTIFYING, CONTROLLING, AND REMOVING ERROR

We classify all error into two fundamental types—bias and noise. Each may seriously distort the factual accuracy or the generality of the research findings. However, what researchers do to deal with them is quite different and what you need to look for when evaluating their effect is quite different. In this section we describe bias and noise and show how each can affect the accuracy and generality of research findings.

6

BIAS:
A SYSTEMATIC ERROR

IT'S HARD TO BELIEVE SIDWELL WOULD BE A GOOD MAYOR IN SPITE OF WHAT HE'S BEEN SAYING, DON'T YOU THINK?

NOT UNTIL YOU ASKED ME.

ANNE CANEVARI GREEN

You probably would agree that the question in this public opinion poll is biased. As stated, it makes it difficult for the respondent to declare his support for Sidwell. The question is biased not because it demonstrates a prejudice of the interviewer, but because these words may systematically distort the final results of the poll. The number of Sidwell supporters may be underestimated and any conclusions based on the results may be unjustified and in error.

All research has some error in it. Some is haphazard and essentially random. This type of error will be discussed in the next chapter. Other error is systematic—it is always in the same direction and is the result of some specific source. A bathroom scale that always registers five pounds light is a source of such error. It systematically distorts all weighings the same way, making them inaccurate or invalid—or to use a more general term, it makes them *biased.*

Identifying Sources of Bias

Since some type of bias is possible in all studies, it is your job as a critical reader to identify the major sources of bias and to judge whether the bias is serious enough to warrant reinterpretation of the results of the study. Not all sources of bias are significant in every study, however. For instance, the sex of the interviewer may influence the responses to questions about women's rights, but not to questions about support for teachers' salaries in the local schools. Similarly, some sources of bias will have a real influence but be so small that they don't matter. In fact, a number of minor biases may actually cancel one another out by working in opposite directions.

For some studies you examine, some biases will not be accounted for because they are either irrelevant or too small to matter. You will be left with sources of bias that may have significant effects on the findings of the study. Your major concern, then, is to determine whether the researcher had detected and corrected them. Or, equally effective but usually very difficult to do, you can correct for the biases yourself. If the amount of bias can be reasonably estimated, then the findings of the study can be adjusted so that they are factually accurate. However, in most studies it is almost impossible to know the extent of the bias. So unless the researcher has eliminated or controlled them, biases will probably seriously reduce the accuracy of the findings.

The most serious problem of all, of course, is the case where both you and the researcher have failed to detect some important biases. In such a case, the biases would invalidate the study's results, but no one would know that.

Knowing that you should look for biases is of little help if you do not know what to look for. The problem is that any variable can be a bias; which ones are and which ones aren't depends upon what is being studied as well as how the study is being conducted. A variable that is theoretically relevant in one study may have to be treated as an undesired bias in another. Your ability to identify this type of biasing variable and estimate its effects on the findings depends on your knowledge of prior research and your familiarity with the theoretical issues pertinent to the topic under investigation. Because this type of biasing variable comes under the heading of external criteria, we cannot be of much help here.

However, many potential biases are a result of how the study was conducted: these fall under the heading of internal criteria. The rest of this chapter describes three major potential sources of bias—the researcher conducting the study, the people being studied, and the research plan.

BIASES DUE TO THE RESEARCHER

As researchers interact with the people they study, a host of human frailties can introduce bias. Training in how to do research includes considerable emphasis on how biases can creep into studies and how researchers can minimize them. For example, researchers are taught to use laboratory notebooks or to take extensive field notes in order to prevent any biases which may be caused by a lapse of memory. Most researchers have a wide variety of tools and techniques to use, but the safeguards cannot be assumed to be built into every researcher.

The Researcher's Expectations

In all of social research, the expectations of the researcher may bias the results. We've already introduced this topic in Chapter 3, but now we shall take a closer look at it. The expected or desired outcome of the study may distort the judgment of the researcher. Ambiguous situations may be systematically treated as unambiguous—but always in the direction that the researcher expects. For example, a researcher working with gifted children may expect complex and mature insights in their written compositions. Written work that others might have judged as average could easily be classified as excellent by the researcher.

This source of bias also occurs when researchers communicate their expectations to the people being studied or interviewed. Good researchers will not do this purposefully, but through a series of unplanned cues, nonverbal gestures, and subtle reinforcements the researcher often communicates what outcome is expected and how the people should act. These clues have been called the "demand characteristics" of the study. They may lead to results that are biased in the direction of the researcher's expectations, but neither the researcher nor the respondent may know what has happened.

One way to minimize this possibility is to keep whomever is in contact with the people being studied uninformed about the purpose of the study. The people doing the research should hire assistants to conduct the study under their direction. These research assistants can then be kept in the dark as to the expected outcome of the investigation. Studies can also be designed so the respondents will not know the purpose of the study or whether they are being treated differently from any other participants in the study. Studies in which neither the research assistant nor the people being studied know enough to bias the outcome in this manner are called "double-blind" investigations.

A typical example of a double-blind study in medical research—where the technique is widely used—is the testing of a new drug. A number of doctors are used as research assistants. They prescribe and administer the drug to their patients. Each doctor is given the drug by the researcher in separate vials; each vial is identified by a number and contains enough of the drug for one patient. About half the vials contain the drug to be tested, the other half contain a safe placebo; the doctors cannot tell which vial contains which, so they are, in effect, blinded. Thus their judgments about the effectiveness of the medication cannot be influenced by their beliefs about the new drug. And the patients will not receive any greater or lesser encouragement from the doctors as to the speed or certainty of the drug. Since the patients are also blinded, their expectations cannot bias the outcome of the study; patients receiving the drug and patients receiving the placebo will have similar expectations.

Age and Sex

The age, sex, and race of researchers may also affect the respondents. Studies about the role of women in society often produce different results depending upon the gender of the person doing the interviewing. Similarly, public opinion questions dealing with integration, open housing, or busing of school children to achieve integration may produce systematically different results depending upon the race of the person conducting the interview. In situations like these, researchers could probably use a number of interviewers who differ in age, sex, race, and other apparent characteristics. The extent of any possible bias can be determined by comparing the results obtained from different interviewers who differ on the characteristic in question.

A similar phenomenon may occur in a noninterview situation. If the researcher is conducting a laboratory experiment, the characteristics of the research assistant interacting with the people may produce a distortion. For example, a highly authoritarian assistant might easily intimidate people who were being tested for the degree of assertiveness they expressed.

Inadequate Training

Other sources of distortion occur because of inadequate training of interviewers or research assistants. Poorly trained interviewers are more likely to communicate their expectations to the respondents. There may not be the high degree of standardization necessary in the interview process. Questions may not be asked in the same order for all respondents. Some questions may be skipped entirely because the answer was "obvious" to an interviewer or because an interviewer was too embarrassed to ask it. Sometimes interviewers may reword the question because they feel more comfortable with their wording or because they think the respondent will understand it better. All these practices must be avoided if the results of an interview are to be believed, and all these practices can be avoided through proper training.

Intentional Deception

Finally, there are biases due to intentional deception on the part of the researchers or their assistants. Examples of researchers lying when communicating their findings have already been discussed in Chapter 4. A different type of cheating shows up in surveys that hire interviewers. Interviewers who have no inherent interest in the topic being researched have been known to complete questionnaires themselves or to interview only their friends rather than trudging around town talking to strangers. Many interviewers consistently avoid entering rundown homes or buildings that appear to be "dangerous." As a result, the people who live in older, more dilapidated structures may be systematically eliminated from contributing to a study. The absence of their opinions or reactions may bias the generality of the outcome.

BIASES DUE TO THE BEHAVIOR OF SUBJECTS

Social research studies people, and the people themselves can bias the study in many of the same ways as the researcher can. People in a study are not unthinking empty machines. Some will be sensitive to the demand characteristics which suggest (rightly or wrongly) what the study is about and what will be expected of them. These people may try to "psych out" the investigation as an intellectual challenge or guess at what is really going on because they are afraid of being judged harshly by the researcher, because they want to do what is expected of them, or because they want to behave in a manner that is socially acceptable.[1]

The Hawthorne Effect

A related bias is the so-called Hawthorne effect. In the 1930s, researchers were studying the effects of lighting conditions, rest periods, and other factors on worker performance in the Hawthorne plant of the Western Electric Company. For one particular group of workers, the investigators were able to control the working conditions. As various conditions were "improved," the researchers found that the performance of the workers also improved. An uncautious researcher might be ready to conclude at this point that the change in working conditions led to the increases in performance. But in the Hawthorne study the researchers also made conditions "worse" and found that the workers' performance continued to improve.

It became clear that the improvement in working conditions did not improve performance. The results had to be related to the research project itself. The researchers, in fact, found that the workers were flattered by the attention they received, and the more attention they got, the harder they worked. Each time a study was conducted, regardless of the direction of the change in working conditions, performance improved. This kind of bias can easily occur in many of the typically uncontrolled studies conducted by managers who want to determine the consequences of a proposed change in the operation of the organization. Without proper research design, managers will have a difficult time separating the effect of the new change from the Hawthorne effect. Chapter 12 goes into this topic in more detail.

By now, undergraduate psychology students have probably been subjects in more reported research in the social sciences than any other individual group. Even though they have been shown to be more questioning and more jaundiced about the intentions of the experimenter, research continues to use students such as these in psychological experiments. However, even subjects other than psychology sophomores come to experiments with expectations. If their expectations are numerous and extremely varied, no bias will result. But if the expectations are systematic—a subject group always "expecting the worst," for example—a bias can occur because the majority of people outside the experimental situation don't feel that way. Usually, the researcher tells the subject some minimal information about the study (e.g., "we are interested in how people work in groups") and blinds the subjects from any more specific information that may give direction to their behavior (e.g., "we want to know how social position and self-assurance affect leadership in newly formed groups").

BIASES DUE TO THE RESEARCH PLAN

Some research plans are more susceptible to biased distortions than others. While it is impossible to eliminate all potential sources of bias, adequate concern for research design will eliminate the major ones. Many procedural biases are presented more fully in Sections Four and Five of this book, and still more are defined briefly in the glossary. Only a few examples will be given here.

Use of Pretests

Some research plans make use of pretests. Suppose a researcher wants to determine audience reactions toward a proposed change in the layout of the front page of a newspaper. The researcher reasons that the audience's initial reactions are important to obtain as a beginning baseline measure. That is, reactions to the new page layout need to be compared with reactions to the current layout. If the researcher determines the audience's reaction to the current page by means of a questionnaire or interview, there is a danger that a bias might result. People are not often consciously aware of newspaper layouts, and their attitudes and feelings toward such things are probably not well formulated. However, questions asked in an attempt to get a measure of the audience's reactions to the current layout will make people more aware of the issue. Respondents therefore may be changed by the pretest and will react differently toward the new page layout than if they were not pretested. The bias, then, is the constant tendency for people to be more sensitive to the page layout. The researcher is interested in how everyday people will react to the new layout when they pick up the paper, but everyday people will not be subjected to the pretest and will not react the same as those who were pretested. So, much of what is learned in this study can't be applied to the people that matter. The findings will be biased and the generality of the results will be diminished.

Pretest bias can often be avoided. Most of the time other research plans are available. Some will enable the researcher to answer the same question without making use of a pretest. In other cases, a pretest could be constructed so that a respondent would not react as much. If a pretest were necessary, a researcher would ideally use one that would not be recognized as a test. Tests that do not interfere with a person's normal behavior are called "unobtrusive." If people cannot learn from the pretest or do not even know that a pretest has been given, it is impossible for them to change because of the pretest.

A similar problem arises whenever a group of people is studied over a long period of time. Frequently called a "longitudinal study" or a "panel study," this technique involves making many observations or getting many reports on the subjects' behaviors or attitudes. Each of these observations may function as a pretest, changing the person studied. The problem for you as a critical reader of research is to determine if a particular panel study is making someone more aware of an issue and therefore is making the results less applicable to people who are unaware. If the measures used do not make people react too differently from their normal behavior, then they may learn to calmly accept their role in the study and behave in a normal way. Members of a panel usually need some time to adjust to their role. Researchers, therefore, will sometimes begin the study early and make some observations that can be ignored.

The Selection Process

Another entire class of biases are those due to selection: who or what shall be studied and where and when shall the study be done. For example, people who volunteer to participate in studies can add a bias simply because of their volunteer status. Evidence strongly indicates that volunteers tend to be better-educated, to have higher occupational status, to be higher in the need for approval, to score higher on intelligence tests, to be less authoritarian, and to be better-adjusted (except in medical research) than nonvolunteers. Other differences exist but cannot be claimed with as much confidence as the list just given. When these listed characteristics are related to the topic being studied, a volunteer group, by being unusual, can bias the results. People used simply because they're available may be equally troublesome. The key question is: How representative are they of the larger group of people to whom the researcher would like to apply the findings?

A similar problem exists whenever the researcher selects one (or a few) event(s) to study from a complex interrelated ongoing set of events. Researchers who use participant observation may have to be concerned about this, and so might researchers who review and analyze already completed case studies. When these approaches have been used, it is always useful to ask how and why the selected set of events were chosen and how the results might be changed if other events or other available case studies were examined.

BIAS AND ERROR

Bias exists to some degree in every study, but the presence of bias is not always a signal that the study must be totally discredited. Readers of research need to know how bias can creep into a study. Then you need to determine if bias has occurred and, if so, whether it is of major concern. This chapter has been just an introduction; most of the remaining chapters will identify other common biases and the clues you should search for to determine whether the researchers adequately prevented their occurrence.

Unfortunately, bias is only part of the larger concept called error. It is a systematic error that can usually be eliminated, or at least reduced, by proper research techniques and precautions. The other type of error has very different properties and thus must be treated differently when you evaluate its influence. This other error is called noise and is the topic of the next chapter.

QUESTIONS TO ASK

> **1 What are the potential sources of bias in the study?**
> In order for a distortion to be a bias it must be systematic—it influences the results in only one direction. Biases may be due to researchers, the behavior of subjects, and the research plan. Each of these categories should be considered in your search for biases. In addition, there are a multitude of substantive variables (i.e., nonmethodological) that can bias the research results.
>
> **2 What procedures did the researcher use to compensate for, or eliminate, potential biases?**
> Did the researchers deal with the expectations of their assistants and the respondents? Were the interviewers well trained? Were volunteers used? What about the use of pretests? Review the chapter for other specific questions of this type.
>
> **3 Which of the potential biases might actually affect the observations made or the results of the study?**
> When you've discovered some potential biases, you need to determine if they actually had an effect. Potential sources of bias might not have an effect because they are simply not relevant to the study, or because they are too small to matter, or because the researcher has eliminated them.
>
> **4 Are there any undetected biases?**
> There are always undetected biases. We've included this question to remind you to search for one the researcher missed. If both you and the researcher do not notice a sizable bias, the findings will not be factually accurate or generalizable. The study will be useless, but no one will know it. Researchers are aware of this problem, and they can sometimes eliminate biases that they are not aware of by converting the unknown biases to noise.

PRACTICE EVALUATIONS

Reminder: Answering the above questions yourself is good practice. Chapter 18 provides guidelines for you to follow in doing that. Chapter 19 provides two articles along with our evaluations of them. Chapter 20 provides two additional articles for you to practice on.

FOR FURTHER THOUGHT

1 Compare the common everyday use of the word "bias" with the more technical use employed in this chapter. How different are they? Using the information from this chapter as a guide, describe the consequences of someone being biased, in the everyday meaning of that word.

2 Suppose a researcher has some biases (in the everyday meaning) and these biases are directly related to the study to be conducted. What safeguards science from erroneous conclusions caused by these biases? (*Hint:* review Chapter 2.)

3 The reason medical researchers prefer to use double-blind studies is that some patients taking placebos say they have less pain or an improvement in symptoms in comparison with their situation before taking the dummy drug. Estimate the percentage of patients taking placebos who report positive results from this medical "treatment."[2]

4 Biases might arise because of problems with missing, unavailable, or preliminary data. For each of the following hypothetical research studies decide if there is a potential for biased conclusions.

(a) In a study of the changes in housing costs, what would be the effect if in 1947 the town hall had a fire and all housing records for that town were destroyed?

(b) In a study of the foreign policy decisions of former President Bush, what would be the effect if 25 percent of his papers were not made available to the public because they were identified as dealing with personal matters?

(c) In a statewide referendum on making English the official language of the state, what would be the effect if the voting booths closed at 6:00 P.M. in the northern half of the state, but remained open until 7:00 P.M. in the rest of the state?

5 For each of the research studies described above, see if you can invent one plausible situation in which the situation would *not* necessarily lead to a large, biased conclusion.

6 Do you sometimes correct for the biases of friends and associates when discussing politics, religion, or other topics? Describe how you do that as specifically as you can.

7 Interpret the following quotations in terms of the material in this chapter.

(a) "All looks yellow to the jaundiced eye." (A. Pope)

(b) "Finnegan's Finagling Factor: That quantity which, when multiplied times, divided by, added to, or subtracted from the answer you got . . . gives you the answer you should have gotten." (Anonymous)

(c) "The measure is man himself." (J. Charon)

FOR FURTHER READING

1 E. J. Webb; D. T. Campbell; R. D. Schwartz; and L. Sechrest. *Nonreactive Measures in Social Sciences,* 2nd ed. Boston: Houghton-Mifflin, 1981.

A much-acclaimed and rather enjoyable look at alternatives available to social researchers if they want to make their observations and measurements less reactive and sensitizing.

2 R. Rosenthal and R. L. Rosnow (Eds.). *Artifact in Behavioral Research.* Orlando, FL: Academic Press, 1969.

A bit more difficult reading, this is a collection of articles reviewing the evidence about the major causes of bias or artifact in a research study. Sometimes it is a wonder that anyone has ever learned anything from any study.

3 J. A. Ricketts. "Powers-of-Ten Information Biases." *MIS Quarterly* (March 1990), pp. 63–77.

A study that demonstrates how difficult it is for educated adults to recognize sizable biases in data. Only 15 percent of the people in the study discovered data that were purposefully distorted by making them 1,000 times larger than they should have been. When the researcher strongly warned the people about the possibility of large errors, the percentage of people recognizing the thousandfold error only increased to 23 percent.

7

NOISE: THE OTHER
TYPE OF ERROR

The purchase of a bathroom scale is usually a simple matter. For many people the major concerns would be price, color, style, and accuracy. Price, color, and style don't have much to do with research, but accuracy does. In order to explain what we mean by noise, we will examine the accuracy of bathroom scales. Lofty ideas have humble beginnings.

One way to check the accuracy is to weigh yourself on the scale and compare that weight to what you believe your true weight to be. And because scales sometimes stick a little or give different readings depending on where you stand on them, it would be wise to weigh yourself several times. Suppose that there are four different bathroom scales for sale and that you weigh yourself 10 times on each one. For the purposes of discussion assume your true weight to be 150 pounds. The table on page 65 shows the 10 weights obtained on each scale; each small dot indicates the result of one weighing. Also included is the average of the 10 weighings so you can get an idea of what weight each scale would show on the average.

It is readily apparent that scale A is preferable because the 10 weighings are all close to the weight assumed to be true. Hence there is no systematic distortion, or bias. Also, little variation exists among the weighings—any one weighing would not be far off of the true weight. So scale A is your first choice for purchase. But, alas, the sales-clerk tells you that it is too expensive.

What then is the next best choice? Scale B has the advantage of weighings that center around the true weight; there is no bias. Scales C and D are clearly biased. However, if all scales have an adjustment mechanism in the form of a little wheel that can

Scale	Results of 10 weighings	Average of the 10 weighings
| A | ```
        .
      ..:...
       ...
──────────────────────────
145       150        155
``` | 150 lb |
| B | ```
      . .  .. . ... ..
──────────────────────────
145       150        155
``` | 150 lb |
| C | ```
:::
..:
..
──────────────────────────
145       150        155
``` | 144 lb |
| D | ```
                  ...:.. .
──────────────────────────
145       150        155
``` | 155 lb |
| | (true weight) | |

initially set each scale to zero, you can possibly remove the biases from C and D. Given such an adjustment, scale C is definitely preferable because each weighing will be close to the true weight.

The scales point out the differences between the two general kinds of error: bias and noise. Biases are all those distortions which cause the scale's average weight to be wrong by affecting each weighing in the same way. Those distortions which cause variability from one weighing to the next, on the other hand, are called noise.[1] Scales B and D are noisier than the other scales; in fact, they are so noisy it's a wonder that anyone would buy either one.

Of the two kinds of error, bias is more serious because an unknown bias can cause the results of a study to be wrong. In addition, the bias will not only cause the same error whenever the study is repeated but can easily continue to go unnoticed. Noise will also cause the results of a study to be wrong, but not systematically. If the study were repeated several times, the noise would not affect the results the same way each time.

Keep the Noise Down

These concerns for the accuracy of bathroom scales are analogous to the concerns you should have for the ways studies are designed and carried out. In all research, error of one form or another is possible. In general, a situation like scale A is preferred: no biases and little noise. But situations like scale A do not occur naturally in social research. The researcher's job in designing a study is to eliminate or correct for biases and to keep the noise as low as possible; your job is to be sure this has been done. In the previous chapter we've looked at the effect of biases on research findings. In this chapter we complete our introduction to error by looking at the effect of noise on research findings and the implications of noise for you as a reader of research.

CHARACTERISTICS OF NOISE

Pervasive and Inevitable

Noise makes reality difficult to see correctly for researchers and readers just as electrical noise or static in a TV picture makes the picture hard to see. Competent researchers, like competent TV repairers, can reduce the noise to an acceptable level, but they can never eliminate all of it. Any attempt to obtain information that is factually accurate and generalizable will be affected by some noise at various points in the research process. If a description is being developed, noise introduces inaccuracies. If two situations are being compared, you may have difficulty distinguishing between real differences and differences that occur only because of the noise. Noise is both pervasive and inevitable.

Unsystematic Error

Noise is unsystematic error, sometimes in one direction and sometimes in the other direction, sometimes large and sometimes small. Thus noise has a very important characteristic: it is zero on the average. That is, given the opportunity, the errors in one direction (say, overestimating your weight) will balance out the errors in the other direction. As a result, noise is not biasing.

Among the four bathroom scales, scale C was the second choice, but only because the nature and extent of the bias was known and could be corrected. If the amount of bias were not known, most researchers would prefer an unbiased scale even if it had some variability in the weighings. You also should prefer a known variability to an unknown bias. Scale B is like that: the measured weights vary but center around the true weight.

Mix the Biases; Live with the Noise

Noise may be preferred to an unknown bias, but is there anything that can be done about it? Can noise be substituted for biases? Readers of research can't do anything about it, but in some situations researchers can. They randomly mix the unknown biases to eliminate any systematic effect. The biases may have been eliminated, but the process of mixing will have increased the noise. Details about the mixing process aren't necessary here, but we can remind you of an earlier example. Possible sources of bias mentioned in the previous chapter were the age, sex, and race of the interviewer. If all interviewers were alike in terms of these characteristics, a bias might result. To remove the threat of bias, researchers use interviewers who are not all alike. By mixing up the characteristics among the interviewers, they may prevent a potential bias, but the noise will probably be increased.

Because the mixing process removes the worst type of error, unknown biases, researchers will use it if they can. Researchers will, first of all, try to identify and remove all large biases that are known. As a second step, they will use the mixing process as a safeguard against any remaining but unknown biases. With this two-step approach researchers can significantly reduce error due to bias, but noise will still be present.

NOISE AND RESEARCH

We've identified three important characteristics of noise: it is inevitable, it is nonbiasing, and it can sometimes be substituted for biases. All these characteristics have the same implication—research results are going to be noisy. Researchers clearly need some way to deal with the noise and to determine how much is present in the results. Readers of research, just as clearly, need to be able to interpret noisy research findings.

View Noisy Results as Estimates

When the results of a study are noisy, you should not treat them as exact answers. Instead you should consider them as estimates. All research results can vary if the study is repeated, much like the variations among the weights given by any of the bathroom scales. As readers of research you need to know how much variation is possible because the usefulness of the findings is directly related to this variation. Scale B, for example, may show a person's weight as 151 pounds, but on the next weighing that scale could show any weight from about 148 pounds to about 153 pounds for the same person. Knowing the range of possible results (148 to 153) helps you interpret the result actually reported (151) by reminding you of how wrong that result can be.

Social science measures have the same problem. Suppose a researcher is interested in comparing the average income of two groups of people. For our purposes it doesn't matter what these groups are: they can be private university graduates versus public university graduates, or right-handed car sales agents versus left-handed ones, or any other distinct groups. We'll simply identify them as group A and group B. If there are thousands of people in each group throughout the country, the researcher cannot query each of them. Instead, the researcher carefully selects, say, 500 people from each group and finds out the income of each. The major result of the study shows that the average person in group B earns $400 more than the average member of group A.

This result, like all results, is noisy. If the study were repeated using different people from group A and from group B, the result would probably not be exactly the same. The range of the different possible results is important. A narrow range (say group B earns between $325 and $450 more) and a wide range (say group B earns between $100 and $800 more) will give you a different impression of how wrong the $400 original result might be. Both of these ranges, however, agree that group B earns more.

But what if some repetitions of the study found that group B earns more, and other repetitions found that group A earns more? In such a case, neither you nor the researcher can be sure which group earns more. This uncertainty is serious, and you would have to treat these results quite differently than you would if the range, regardless of how wide, always showed that one group earns more.

In these examples, we've arrived at the ranges by considering what would happen if the study were repeated many times. With the bathroom scales, several weighings were taken. In the comparison of incomes, we guessed what might happen if other people were queried. Social research is more complicated and more costly than weighing people on a bathroom scale. Social researchers cannot usually afford the effort or the expense of repeating a study. Without a great many replications, noise does not have the opportunity to cancel itself out. That is, in any single study noise will produce error. How can researchers tell if that has happened? How do they determine the range of the possible results? And what can you learn from the research report about these issues?

Learn to "See" through Noise

Of the several tools that help a researcher answer these questions, statistical inference is the most important. Don't let the name scare you—we aren't going to include any formulas or complex computations. A thorough understanding of statistics would help you, but you can do a lot of good evaluating by just knowing what statistical inference is about. And what it's about is very simple to state in terms of noise. Statistical inference is a mathematical way to help a researcher "see" through noise. Systematic results are isolated by discounting the effect of random variation. To use the television example once again, statistical inference can be thought of as a method to make the picture clearer in spite of the interference.

Statistical inference is based on probability. An estimate is made of what would happen if the study were actually repeated many times, telling the researcher how wrong the results can be. In the income example, the researcher found that on the average group B earned more per year. Using statistical inference, the researcher will be able to determine the range of results and the probability of the conclusion (B earns more) being wrong. If the probability is high, it means that the apparent systematic result (B earns more) may not be real, but could be due solely to noise. The researcher could find out the same thing by repeating the study many times, but statistical formulas and computations are cheaper.

Obviously the kind of information supplied by statistical inference is invaluable. You should, therefore, expect to see many examples of it in published research. To be a critical consumer of that research, you need to know more about statistical inference than what is given here, a general introduction to the concept of noise. Chapters 13 and 14 continue this introduction by presenting a more thorough, but still nontechnical, look at the most common applications of statistical inference in social research.

SOURCES OF NOISE

Random variability has many possible causes. In fact, any of the causes of bias discussed in the previous chapter can also produce noise, if the effect is not constant. For example, consider a poorly written item on a questionnaire. If most people react similarly to it, its effect is to bias the results. But if the item is ambiguous and respondents react to it differently, it will contribute to noise, not bias.

Differences among People

One source of noise in social science is relatively uncontrollable. It is the noise due to differences among the people being studied. Any test performance, for instance, is influenced by the amount of sleep a participant had the night before, prior food consumption, health, personal problems, education, personality traits, and much more. These factors influence people differently: for some people and for some research projects the influence is so small it can be safely ignored, but for other projects or other people it adds some variability to the results. And we would expect this variability to be unsystematic, contributing to the noise.

Fuzzy Criteria

Other sources of noise are more controllable, and their presence may indicate some degree of weakness in the study. When experts are used to judge the behavior of people or to judge something produced by people, it is important that the standards be specific and applied consistently. If the criteria are initially fuzzy, or if the criteria change over time, or if different judges apply the same criteria differently, noise is likely to occur. Research assistants can affect the results in the same way by treating the people or objects being studied differently. If the same procedures are not followed for everyone, if the directions are slightly changed, if different equipment is used, if the environment is changed—if any of these occur, noise is likely to result. The best research practices cannot prevent all the noise. Some will remain, but it hopefully will be so slight that the results will not be hidden.

The "Mixing" Process

Finally, we will remind you of the noise that is purposefully added to a study by the researcher. In order to remove any remaining unknown biases, the researcher uses a random "mixing" process that produces noise. In well-conducted studies this process may very well be the largest source of noise, but the researcher is willing to live with it in order to remove the biases. When the mixing process is done properly, statistical inference will help the researcher determine if the research findings are due to the effects of this mixing or whether they are due to something substantive, something the researcher is actually studying.

QUESTIONS TO ASK

---

1 What are the potential sources of noise in the study?
Noise is produced by inherent differences among the people or objects studied, by inconsistencies in the research process, and by purposeful "mixing" by the researcher.

2 What procedures did the researcher use to minimize the noise?
Look for standardized instructions and procedures, trained interviewers and research assistants, pretested instruments, and consistent use of criteria. These and other procedures will be discussed in the remaining chapters of this book.

3 What range of results is possible?
The presence of noise means the results may vary. The researcher should report the extent of this variation so you will be able to determine if the results are useful for your needs.

4 Was statistical inference used?
Statistical inference can provide important information about the possible range of results and the probability of results occurring solely because of noise. Chapters 13 and 14 explain more about the use of statistical inference in social research.

PRACTICE EVALUATIONS

Reminder: Answering the above questions yourself is good practice. Chapter 18 provides guidelines for you to follow in doing that. Chapter 19 provides two articles along with our evaluations of them. Chapter 20 provides two additional articles for you to practice on.

FOR FURTHER THOUGHT

1 Given the inevitability and pervasiveness of noise, what could a scientist mean by the word "truth"?

2 The term "noise" was given a technical meaning in this chapter. The everyday meaning is more varied. For each of the following situations is the "noise" completely unsystematic or are some systematic sources included?

(**a**) A "strange noise" in your car

(**b**) The "buzz" of conversation in a lecture hall before class

(**c**) The "static" on a radio

(**d**) A baby "crying"

3 Are the causes of noise fundamentally different from the causes of biases, or is noise the result of many uncontrolled and perhaps unknown biases? What are the implications of your answer on the process of research? On the evaluation of research?

FOR FURTHER READING

1 L. Gonick, and W. Smith. *The Cartoon Guide to Statistics.* New York: Harper, 1993.

Though this book does not explicitly deal with the idea of "noise" it does provide a reasonably-good introduction to statistics—presented through cartoons.

FACTUALLY
ACCURATE INFORMATION

Can you believe it?

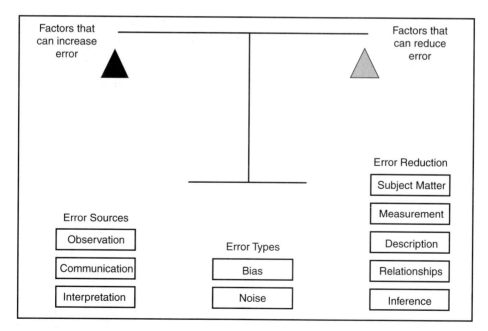

THE ERROR MODEL: IDENTIFYING, CONTROLLING, AND REMOVING ERROR

ERROR MODEL

- Error is pervasive. It keeps the "truth" from being easily discovered.
- The researcher's responsibility is to identify all potential sources of error that could have an important impact on the results. Biases must be prevented or removed so that the results will be both factually accurate and generalizable. Noise must be reduced so that the results can be recognized.
- The reader's responsibility is to determine if the researcher dealt with these errors appropriately and to search for any sources of error the researcher might have missed.

In Chapter 1 we mentioned an "error model" of research. This model can now be re-stated a little more precisely.

We would not have written this book if we didn't believe that good researchers can remove biases and reduce noise so that we as readers can have some confidence in the factual accuracy and generalizability of the results. When you analyze the methods a researcher employed, you are deciding if the researcher identified all the potentially important errors and dealt with them appropriately.

The chapters in this section present six major concerns you should have about what the researcher actually did or did not do. Remember, no one research study can control or eliminate all possible sources of error. What you need to do is to assess the strengths and weaknesses of a research report so that you can decide what degree of trust is appropriate.

Each chapter in this section represents a theme that is applicable to all forms of in-quiry. Our emphasis is on social science research, but the questions raised apply to in-formation obtained by any means. A concern for each is essential if you are to answer the fundamental question you should ask of information: can you believe it?

8

SUBJECT MATTER: WHAT IS BEING STUDIED?

A methodological riddle: When it comes to reading the report of an empirical study, what is the difference between a layman, a researcher, and a methodologist?

Answer: The layman reads the text and skips the tables; the researcher reads the tables and skips the text; and the methodologist does not care very much about either the tables or the text, as long as they agree with each other.

T. Hirschi and H. Selvin

Undoubtedly, people differ in what they choose to read in a journal article. Skimming or reading only certain parts of an article may be useful if time is short or if you want to get a general overview of what an author has to say. But imitating any one of the three characters in the above riddle is a dangerous practice—particularly when it comes to reading in the social sciences and related professional areas.

Most readers are inclined to look for errors and distortions in the sections of journal articles on procedures, results, and conclusions. That's where numbers frequently appear, and it's generally easy to equate error with numbers. But error can occur in any part of an article. The best qualities of the layperson, the researcher, and the methodologist combined are needed to determine the strengths and weaknesses of an article. You must look at the entire article. Limiting yourself to certain parts means that you may overlook errors that can seriously affect the author's findings and conclusions and in turn the usefulness of the article to you.

This chapter is concerned with the first part of a typical journal article—with what a researcher uses to describe, define, or delimit the subject matter of the study. We will consider the problem statement, the definitions, and the literature review. The three topics are presented in the order in which you will sometimes encounter them in journal articles. Not all articles progress in this way, but there is a certain logical neatness in knowing first the author's purpose, then what is meant by the terms used, and finally the relationship of the study to other related investigations.

Our trichotomy is somewhat artificial, however, because good definitions and problem statements must often be based on extensive knowledge of previous research. And previous research includes both definitions and problem statements. Thus, although we discuss each topic separately, they are in fact quite interrelated.

Our concern throughout most of this book is with internal criteria for the evaluation of information. This chapter is the closest we come to dealing with external considerations. Your knowledge of the subject matter, your beliefs about what makes sense, and your familiarity with other research on a topic are especially important in evaluating problems, definitions, and literature reviews. Use your own expertise, but add it to some of the more general concerns discussed below.

PROBLEM STATEMENT

The problem statement consists of those sentences in an article which identify the research objectives. Sometimes these sentences are called the "statement of the problem" or the "research question" or the "research hypothesis" or something similar. Whatever form it takes, we will refer to it as the "problem statement."

On first thought it may seem that the problem statement is important mainly as an adjunct to the title; it helps you decide *if* the article should be read. Our concern here, however, begins after you decide to read the article. What effects can the problem statement have on the research findings?

Try to solve the following problem.

> A tennis tournament needs to be arranged for 98 players. Two people play a match, the loser is eliminated from the tournament, and the winner is paired to play again with another player. This process of removing losers and pairing up winners is to continue until one person remains.
>
> What is the fewest number of matches needed to find the single final winner of the tournament?

Unless you look at it in a certain way, this problem is not trivial. A common approach to solving the problem is to make a list of the various matches (i.e., A versus B, C versus D, and so on) and then count them. This is a tedious process; unless one is careful a mistake can easily be made. And, when finished, how can you be sure that it is the minimum number of matches?

A simpler and more direct approach to the solution becomes possible when the problem is stated differently: given 98 participants in a tennis tournament that eliminates one player in each match, how many matches are needed until only one player is left? Well, if each match eliminates one player from tournament, 97 people must be eliminated in order to end up with a single winner. Thus, there must be exactly 97 matches in the tournament.

Books on problem solving and creativity often seem to take some perverse delight in presenting problems like this, which are agonizingly difficult to solve until restated in a slightly different manner. Their point, of course, is that how one views or states a problem has some bearing on the kinds of solutions that are likely to be found. Books about propaganda, logic, and persuasion present a similar message: the language in an argument can lead to invalid conclusions. The same is true in research. The way in which the researcher thinks and talks about the subject matter of the study may affect the findings.

Is It Relevant?

To begin with, we should point out that the author's problem statement is sometimes irrelevant. That is, the usefulness of a journal article to a reader may not be related to the author's purpose. The problem statement helps you evaluate a research report, but it does not prescribe a use for the findings. Someone who needs to construct a questionnaire may search the literature for examples of questionnaires used in similar situations, but he or she would not care much about the findings. Or a reader who needs a particular factual item of information may discover it as a minor finding of a study. At the extreme, if a bibliographic citation is needed, a reader may scan the article's footnotes without reading anything else.

Limits and Restrictions

When a problem statement is relevant, the major requirement for a reader is that it be nonbiasing. A good problem statement will guide a researcher's investigations but should not put unnecessary limitations or restrictions on the answer. The language used in the problem statement can be one source of bias. Either-or questions are prevalent in everyday language, and they occasionally spill over into the research reports. "What is the best way to teach beginning reading: by phonics or by word-sight?" This search for the best approach excludes anything other than phonics or word-sight. It also excludes from consideration various combinations of these approaches. This example is obviously exaggerated, of course, but either-or questions as problem statements do exist and simply may not be as blatantly presented.

The language of the problem can also create a world that is not supported by what is known. A communications study of the "nonverbal cues used by Kennedy to win the first debate with Nixon" implies that Kennedy won the first debate and that nonverbal cues helped. Depending upon how one measures winning, the first implication may be acceptable; the second definitely needs to be studied, and not taken as already proved.

The Author's Orientation

Another potential source of bias is the author's theoretical or philosophical orientation, which is often implied in the problem statement but not acknowledged. Sometimes readers can determine the author's viewpoint by examining the title of the article or just by noting the journal it is published in. For example, a problem statement concerned with the recommended treatment of claustrophobia might not by itself indicate any unstated assumptions on the part of the writer. But that same problem statement would have different implications if it appeared in the *Journal of Psychiatry* rather than the *Journal of Applied Behavioral Therapy.*

The "Importance Fallacy"

There is another, more subtle, kind of bias caused by the problem statement. For lack of a better label we will call it the importance fallacy. This fallacy occurs whenever readers assume that the problem statements they read are the important problems in the field. Many times what gets studied is that which has been funded by federal and local agencies. Such agencies usually fund only research of interest to them. This is not to denigrate the value of funded research. A great many social science advances, in both theoretical and applied areas, are due to funded research programs. Our concern here is with what these funding agencies choose to support.

James Coleman recently argued, for instance, that social science research is most often not politically neutral when it is carried out in order to provide factual information to policymakers. He argues that its bias is not in the methods used or the dishonesty of researchers, but rather in the aspects of problems that are or are not researched.

The 1954 Supreme Court decision cited social science research in its decision to declare segregated school systems illegal. That research was provided by the NAACP and naturally enough dealt with the effects of segregated schooling on black children. Additional research was funded as a result of the Civil Rights Act of 1964 for the expressed purpose of assessing the extent to which individuals were being deprived of educational opportunities because of race or other attributes. Again, the aspects of the problem that were researched were limited to those of interest to oppressed minorities and federal agencies trying to protect their rights.

The authors and most readers of this book probably feel that the moves toward desegregation were needed. Thus, research that helped carry forward this social movement is laudatory. One must still face the issue that research was clearly providing facts for one side of an argument.

A comparable situation exists in many areas of social research and professional practice. There is a lack of consensus about what should be done as well as a lack of research on all sides of the issue. And in most debates, research findings will have a decided edge over speculation. You must decide how to weigh what is known (because it was funded and researched) against what is still unknown because it wasn't funded.

Compare the Findings with the Problem

As a final concern, you need to compare the problem statement with the findings and conclusions. For a variety of reasons, authors may not answer the questions asked, and as a reader you must be sure you know the difference. The only way to determine what question was really answered is to read the entire article with some care. No matter what researchers *say,* it is what they *do* that matters. If, as is common in social science, the author raises an important, but broadly stated, problem and for any number of practical reasons limits the investigation to some smaller part of the problem, then you need to be very careful to see the answers as relevant to only part of the problem.

Thus, there is no guarantee of a match between the problem stated and the problem answered. Because of this you may want to consider changing your reading habits. Readers of research, like everyone else, are overloaded with information and responsibilities, so there is an understandable tendency to read the abstract *instead* of the article. Reading the abstract or the problem statement and the conclusions is a good way to determine in general what the article is about. But if the article is about something relevant to your needs, there is no substitute for reading the complete article.

DEFINITION

Everyone appreciates, in a general way, the value of good definitions. But definitions can sometimes be used in ways that do not help the reader as much as first impressions suggest. Consider the following dialogue:

> *Beginning student:* Why is John always so mean to everyone? He seems to get some personal satisfaction in being nasty and cruel.
> *Advanced student:* That's easy, it's because he's sadistic.
> *Beginning student:* Oh, I see.

Or does he? What exactly has the beginning student learned from the conversation? We contend that he has learned much less than he believes. A sadist, at least as the term is commonly used, is someone who seems to enjoy being cruel to others. So all the advanced student contributed to the conversation was a label—the arbitrary term used to name this type of behavior. And unfortunately, the beginning student may believe he has gained something far more important, an *explanation* as to why John behaves as he does.

We can rewrite this conversation differently, substituting the term "sadistic" for its definition. Then the emptiness of the interchange becomes clearer:

> *Beginning student:* Why is John sadistic?
> *Advanced student:* Because he is sadistic.
> *Beginning student:* ???

Presumably, definitions are only the beginning of explanation, not explanation itself. Sadistic is a useful term for frequently referring to individuals who seem to enjoy being cruel to others. Unfortunately, once the term has been defined, its application, as in the conversation above, is easily accepted as an explanation.

We realize that this example isn't earthshaking. However, educators have argued that many psychological concepts are being widely misused in just this way, and as examples pointed specifically to "intelligence," "motivation," and "creativity." Intelligence can be defined as learning rapidly or behaving effectively. However, someone's rapid learning can hardly be explained by referring to that person's intelligence. At best we would be saying that the reason the person is learning rapidly is because she or he previously learned rapidly—and thus was labeled intelligent. In a similar vein, motivation is defined as persistent efforts to succeed and can't be used to explain persistent efforts to succeed. Creativity is defined as the production of original work and is similarly limited.

Critics of these examples may well argue that intelligence, motivation, or creativity are in fact defined differently and thus can provide an explanation. For instance, if intelligence could be defined as a certain brain chemistry that could be determined independently of rapid learning, then an explanation of rapid learning would be conceivable. In any event, the critic points out only that there may be ways to define the concepts so that they can be used as explanations and not just as descriptions.

Circular Definitions

Several related versions of this kind of definitional error may also occur. Circular definitions are those which define a term by using the term itself. Now you won't often see something as blatant as, "safe nursing is when the nursing staff acts in accordance with acceptable and current standards of safety." Usually the circularity will be better-concealed (often from the researcher as well as from the reader).

For instance, a research project might set out to determine how well patient care in a hospital measures up to current standards. A conclusion might be that safe nursing is practiced in that hospital. In one sense there can be no quarrel with the findings. As defined, safe nursing is practiced. To be clear, however, the practices are what has been *defined* as safe by current standards. Someone, or some committee, came up with that definition and all the researcher has done is show that the hospital can be described that way.

A more meaningful, and less circular, definition of safe nursing would be one that defines safety in terms of absence of bed falls, accurate dosages, equipment failures being detected, and the like. If a study showed that the latter were accomplished, the researcher could say in a much more meaningful way that safe nursing was being practiced. And the researcher could also check to see if adherence to current standards seemed to contribute to safety.

Frequently, careful thought and reading are needed to uncover circular definitions. A researcher interested in predicting consumer satisfaction should not be very surprised if the term could be measured by a questionnaire that in essence asks consumers if they are satisfied. However, this sort of circularity can only be discovered when the items on the questionnaire are studied.

Specific Definitions

Definitions must also be specific. In Chapter 2 we presented several norms of science. These norms have direct applicability to the problem of definition. The concern for publicness, for example, requires that an author report the definition chosen. If the definition isn't reported, then there's a question about which of a variety of related definitions was used. In a literal sense, you can't know what the author is talking about.

The norm of replication requires that the definitions be specific enough so that another researcher could use them to carry out the entire study a second time. This requirement fills the journals with long, single-spaced details of the research procedure or method. But what's important here is not repeating a research investigation but understanding it. Specific, well-detailed definitions are important to readers because they help determine how the research relates to their needs.

Unless a definition is specific and detailed it may inadvertently be stretched beyond its applicability. For example, if a writer defines *participatory management* somewhat loosely as "management in which subordinates participate in planning," then it will be difficult for readers to know if their particular situations are covered by the definition. Does participatory management include those situations in which a supervisor

1 receives regular status reports from subordinates?
2 uses a suggestion box to get input from subordinates?
3 socializes and maintains informal contact with a few subordinates in order to discuss business problems?
4 meets regularly with each subordinate?
5 forms an advisory planning committee consisting of subordinates chosen by their colleagues?

Or does it mean something else? Since the author did not supply an adequate definition, readers will often supply their own meaning for the term and may attempt to apply findings to their situation that the author never meant to be applicable.

Vague Definitions

Another problem for readers is that authors who write vague, nonspecific definitions can more easily defend their positions against all forms of conflicting arguments and evidence. If someone disagrees, vague authors can easily sidestep the criticism by saying they meant something slightly different from their critic. Or if some supportive evidence on a related topic is uncovered, vague authors can stretch their definitions to include that situation. Given free rein to defend their positions, vague authors will find confirmation everywhere and contradiction nowhere.

Given numerous vague definitions, each of which has been stretched here and there so it seems to be supported by evidence, there is no sensible way for users of research to choose among these definitions. Practitioners can justify whatever they want by choosing definitions and evidence appropriately. Students have more and more definitions and theories to study without a corresponding increase in learning. And the field as a whole suffers because it is in such confusion that progress is slow. Moreover, in this kind of situation, anti-intellectual and antiresearch biases are often produced; readers may end up believing that they cannot trust the literature in their field and need to decide for themselves how to solve the problems that confront them.

In contrast, specific definitions are less stretchable and can therefore be evaluated more directly. Useful definitions will remain, and others will be weeded out of the field. Advocating a specific definition that doesn't turn out to be useful is far better than advocating a vague definition and being unable to evaluate it. Francis Bacon puts it more directly: "Truth arises more easily from error than from confusion."

Definitions, in fact, are a key link in your attempt to understand the subject matter. Definitions can lead to error when they are erroneously offered as explanation, when they are circular, or even when they're too vague. With all these pitfalls, it's important for you to know if the researcher avoided these errors.

Definitional Goals

Competent researchers attempt to create definitions that ensure publicness, replicability, and, if possible, fruitfulness. These definitional goals are part of an attempt to create definitions that reduce error. Because publicness and replicability are easier to achieve, they will be considered first.

When researchers talk about reality, you will want to know specifically what they mean. Thus you must look for clear, unambiguous definitions of terms. A researcher studying "eating" should specify whether the consumption of liquids (such as milk shakes) is included and whether taking vitamin pills falls under the definition. In normal usage of the term "eating," lack of specificity is not very important, but if a physical education researcher is studying the effects of various diet programs you need to know precisely what is meant.

Fortunately, research does not usually involve just talking. To generate factually accurate information, researchers must check what they say against reality, and this means they must do something. What they do is another way in which they define what they are talking about. A researcher who studies eating by simply asking subjects how many meals a day they eat is using a very different definition than if she or he follows them around recording everything that they put in their mouths. The researcher may have had the same conceptual definition in mind in both cases but then chose different methods to actually observe eating.

Operational Definitions

How researchers define things by what they do is called an "operational definition." When this type of definition can be given it helps both researchers and readers. The "operations" in an operational definition are procedures or steps one must go through in the real world in order to observe the concept being defined. Thus, they are words that are used to link what the researcher is talking about (concepts) to reality.

The recipe for a cake is an operational definition. It makes public what someone means by "white cake." It makes it possible for anyone with basic cooking skills to replicate the author's white cake.

White Cake

Preheat oven to 375 degrees.
Sift together 3½ cups of flour, ½ teaspoon salt, and 4 teaspoons baking soda.
Cream together 1 cup of butter and 2 cups of sugar.

Add 1 teaspoon of vanilla to 1 cup of milk.
Slowly mix together in stages the flour mixture, the milk, and the creamed sugar.
Whip the whites of 7 eggs until stiff and fold them into the batter.
Bake in lightly greased pans for about 25 minutes.

The cake recipe above seems complete. Anyone with basic cooking skills could follow it and probably end up with something similar to what the author of the recipe had in mind. But would the cake be identical in terms of taste, weight, height, moistness, and so on? Probably not, because even though the recipe is quite specific, many aspects of it are still missing. What size eggs are called for? What quality of butter? How accurately do we have to measure each of the ingredients? How do we correct the recipe for a difference in altitudes? Each of these probably affects the outcome of the cake. Presumably, they do not affect the outcome a great deal or else the recipe would have included them. In addition, other cookbooks have slightly different recipes. If followed, those recipes would also produce a cake much like the first one. There is no "correct" recipe for a white cake. Similarly, there is no one correct operational definition for a concept.

Notice that even though the operational definition makes it all quite clear and specific, it is somewhat sterile. After all, we mean much more by the words "white cake" than the recipe can convey. We may mean a birthday cake, a cake with frosting, or something baked by mother. And in some situations a dictionary-like definition would be more helpful than the recipe. Or for a three-year-old, a "yummy dessert" would be satisfactory.

These points are true for all kinds of operational definitions. First of all, they are never completely specified, nor can they be. Second, there will probably be several possible operational definitions for a given concept—the choice among them is left to the researcher to justify. Third, operational definitions are by themselves sterile: they need to be supplemented with conceptual definitions in order to better communicate the breadth and richness of the concept. So while operational definitions go a long way toward improving a reader's understanding of a research report, they are neither perfect nor sufficient by themselves. But when they can be given, they are very useful, especially to readers of research.

Finally, keep in mind that some concepts cannot be operationally defined. As a reader of research, however, you should search for operational definitions and make a careful examination of them because they make your job much easier.

Fruitfulness

An acceptable operational definition helps readers and researchers by linking words with reality and by being public, specific, and replicable. But this is not enough. The major criterion for the evaluation of any definition is its fruitfulness, and this is the most difficult to assess. First, to be fruitful, the conceptual definition must build on current theories and prior research. And secondly, the operational definition should coincide with the conceptual definition in a useful way.

Fruitful definitions usually fit into the research traditions of a field. They build on what exists. There is occasionally justification for writers to construct new definitions, but they ought to be reasonably sure that the existing ones are not suitable. One of the characteristics of the less developed sciences and professions is the overabundance of nearly synonymous concepts and concepts with similar operational definitions. Researchers should not introduce new terminology into a field unless they are convinced that the existing set of concepts is inadequate. With new terms or definitions, you have a more difficult time fitting the study into the perspective of other work in this area. As readers you ought to be sensitive to this and demand that authors justify their additions. Otherwise you will be confronted with an even larger array of confusing terms and definitions that can only hinder use of the literature.

Another requirement for a fruitful definition is that it be useful, though what is useful to a researcher is not always so to a reader. Readers require definitions that are understandable and applicable within the context of their needs. Compare two studies of user satisfaction with a local public library. In both studies, accessibility was considered to be a key aspect of satisfaction. In one study, accessibility was defined in terms of location—how close is your home to the library? In the other study, accessibility was defined in terms of service hours—of the hours the library is open each week, how many are available to you? Both definitions of accessibility are acceptable. Both are also useful to the researcher who can determine the relationship between (1) location of a patron's home and satisfaction, and (2) the availability of service hours and satisfaction. To the library manager, the second definition is clearly more useful. To increase satisfaction, the library manager can perhaps change the service hours of the library, but the manager cannot as easily change the distance between the library and the patron's home.

Ideally, both operational definitions of accessibility could be used in the same study. That would increase not only the usefulness of the study but also the likelihood that the study actually dealt with the concept of accessibility. To pursue this idea for a moment, consider the term "accessibility" as a researcher might think of it conceptually. In the library situation, accessibility includes anything that affects the ease of use of the services and materials in the library. This conceptual definition is the researcher's target—it is what the researcher wants to find out about. Any single operational definition is an attempt at hitting the target. Yet most of the time a perfect bull's-eye is impossible. Sometimes operational definitions include things that aren't conceptually involved, and sometimes they fail to include things that conceptually should be included. Both operational definitions of accessibility above include only part of what was meant. An example of an additional question might be the adequacy of library hours. Users might suggest fewer hours because they felt the library needed to save money, even though the shorter hours would make it harder for them to use the library. Thus, the operational definition would include attitudes toward both allocation of funds and accessibility.

Since operational definitions seldom include exactly what is of interest, several operational definitions that, taken together, encompass the conceptual definition completely are usually needed. This goal should be of particular concern to the researcher and to the reader or user of research. Having more than one operational definition increases the chances that at least one will be useful.

Notice that what is advocated here is one conceptual definition and several related operational definitions. The opposite is not desirable and probably goes a long way toward hindering progress in any field. If there are several different concepts with very similar operational definitions, then the field is cluttered with concepts which are indistinguishable but which generate a lot of discussion. The current confusion about IQ illustrates this. A standardized intelligence test is the single operational definition, but does it measure prior knowledge, ability to solve present problems, ability to solve future problems, academic potential, ability to take tests, and so on? If we could get the experts to agree, it would be better to have separate operational definitions for each of these concepts. Then we would know what we were talking about and would be more certain that we were measuring the concept of interest. Or, in a word, the definition would be more "fruitful."

A Brief Summary

Before going on with the remainder of this chapter it would be wise to quickly review what was said about definitions. Because they are arbitrary and verbal, they are very easy to create. But *good* definitions are much more difficult; they need to be specific, generalizable, and public. They should not be used as explanations or proof. When possible, they should be both operational and conceptual. And readers of research should evaluate the fruitfulness of a definition primarily in terms of its usefulness for their purposes.

REVIEW OF RELATED RESEARCH

Between the problem statement and the description of the procedures, you will usually find a summary or evaluation of previously completed work that in the author's opinion is relevant to the present study. You don't need great experience in reading the social science journals to discover the lack of uniformity among reviews of related research. This lack of uniformity is probably due to different understandings on the part of authors as to the role and purpose of the literature review.

Reviews Differ

Some literature reviews focus solely on conclusions of earlier work, while others are equally concerned with procedures. Some reviews just summarize, others evaluate. In some reports the review forms the largest part of the article, while in others the review may be entirely absent or reduced to a few sentences that give a box score of supporting and nonsupporting studies. For example, a hypothetical, but common type of box-score sentence might look like: "Three studies (Smith, 1957; Jones, 1962; Dingman, 1964) found similar results, but only one study (Martinson, 1966) did not."

Within this context it is understandable that journal readers do not know what they can learn from the literature review. Naturally, what can be learned depends to a great degree upon the kind of literature review given. It is our belief that the most useful kind of review is evaluative in approach. Its purpose is to provide a unified point of view—to integrate the present study and put it into perspective in terms of its research history and theoretical context. This type of review serves the reader of research very well. But even if the review is not set up this way, it can still provide some clues that will help the reader make an overall assessment of the accuracy and generality of the entire journal article and its findings.

In the beginning of the book, we stated that the most compelling argument for believing the outcome of an empirical investigation is its agreement with numerous other well-conducted studies; it is an argument based on replications rather than on reasoning or methods. Readers should search for this kind of information in the literature review and should assume that a knowledgeable author would not fail to include it if it were known.

Replications Are Seldom Identical

However, a simple box score of the outcomes of a number of studies is not enough. One reason that a box score is not sufficient is that replications are seldom identical to the original study or to each other. For most topics of interest, an attempt to duplicate an earlier study exactly would fail. For one thing, the time would have changed—the replication would take place after the original and would often be based on whatever knowledge and insights the second researcher could get from the original. For some investigations the simple passage of time may make a significant difference. This is particularly true for those studies affected by current events, new technologies, or the effect of time on humans or machines. Public opinion studies are often affected by current events; asking the same questions several weeks, or even several days, later may no longer be appropriate because the populace is better informed. Similarly, a new study of the early intellectual development of children would not be likely to obtain the same results as one conducted 20 or even 10 years ago. The effect of television on children is striking.

If we can discount the effect of time, we simply turn our attention to the methods used in the original study and in the new one. Usually, replications in social research occur in different laboratories run by different researchers who use different people as subjects or respondents. So at least in this sense, the new study is not a perfect copy of the older one. Furthermore, it is common to see slightly different operational definitions used in the two studies.

A second weakness of box scores or any simple listing of the earlier findings is that all studies are not equal. They differ in quality and therefore in the believability of their findings. Box scores or itemized conclusions by themselves do not include any judgment about the correctness of the findings. It may be that the author carefully evaluated all the earlier studies and included only those of high quality. That is possible, but we think rather unlikely. Besides, when reading journal articles you may want to trust the author's honesty, but the author's competence should be demonstrated. Unless you have some indication of how the author chose and evaluated articles, you should be uneasy.

Criteria for Inclusion

Some selection by authors is necessary, but the proper standard is relevance—not quality. We would hope that after scanning the earlier studies and choosing the relevant ones for inclusion, authors would judge their merits publicly in the literature review, giving as much information as is practical so readers can make an independent assessment. Readers can then check to see that an author evaluated all parts of the cited studies, including the methods used.

The selection process deserves further consideration. One useful tack for a reader is to list or think about the kinds of studies the author chose to include in the review of related research. One obvious consideration is recency. Older studies should be included if they are important or in some way seminal. But a literature review that does not contain any recent work should be suspect. There are several possibilities. It could be that no recent work has been done on that topic, though if that were true the author ought to say so and the reader ought to ask why that is so. Or, there are more recent studies, but they were excluded either purposely or because the author was unaware of them. Again, both of these possibilities should raise some questions in your mind as you read the article.

A more subtle consideration has to do with the articles omitted from the literature review. In some topic areas it would be impossible to include everything done earlier. Some journals will not allocate enough pages for inclusion of all these studies even if the author wanted to be comprehensive. What you are looking for is some indication of a biased literature review—one that might distort the researcher's approach to the problem or the interpretations of the findings.

Assuming that you have done some reading in this area before, try to identify one or more pertinent articles that disagree with the beliefs or hypotheses of the author. Were they included in the literature review? If not, why are they missing, and what effect does their omission have on what the author learned from reviewing the literature? Sometimes authors act like high school sophomores writing their first term paper. They seek only those articles which support their viewpoint. While this approach may be appropriate for opinion pieces or editorials, it should not be the model in science. So, on the one hand, agreement between the literature review and the findings should increase the credibility of the study. On the other hand, unanimity among the articles cited in the literature review should raise some questions.

Prior Predictions

Of final interest in the review of related research is not how the research was constructed, but how it was used. Frequently, a carefully examined review of the literature culminates in a refinement of the problem statement and a prediction or hypothesis of what the author expects to discover in the findings. These expectations are based on a critical analysis of the literature coupled with the researcher's reasoned beliefs about what is true.

You need to distinguish between those studies which contain such predictions (either explicitly or implied) and those which do not. All studies have some kind of results. Sometimes the results are due to poor procedures, or luck, or even causal factors that the researcher never considered. For a researcher who has invested time, energy, and resources in an investigation there is a great motivation to find out something substantive from the study. It is surprisingly easy for a motivated researcher with some tools of analysis to find "meaningful" patterns, even if only chance occurrences produced the data. Clearly you need to protect yourself from accepting atypical results as the major findings. While there is no guaranteed way to do this, we can give more credence to those findings which agree with the researcher's predictions.[1] If prior research and current theory are strong enough to lead to a prediction, then findings in agreement with the prediction may very well be due to more than chance or poor procedures.

This is not to say that studies without prior predictions (prior to collection of the data) have no value to us as readers. They do have a value. But they suggest rather than support. They indicate possibilities rather than probabilities. They are useful to explore and consider rather than explain and conclude. In general, they are a weaker form of evidence than are studies whose findings agree with earlier hypotheses. Therefore, in your analysis of the literature review, you need to determine how well the cited studies and the author's analysis of them led to a prediction. Sometimes a careful examination of the discussion section will help you determine if the prediction is justified or if it seems to have been created out of thin air or perhaps after the results were in.

SUMMARY

We began this chapter with a methodological riddle that focused on the last part of a journal article: the methods, the data collected, the findings, and the author's interpretation of those findings. For readers of research and especially for practicing professionals, the findings and interpretations are probably the most important parts of a journal article. They are often so important that uncritical readers skip most of the article and limit themselves to the abstract or the conclusions. As we will demonstrate in the remaining chapters of the book, the factual accuracy and the generality of the findings depend to a large extent on the methodological procedures employed by the researcher to collect the data.

An equally important but more indirect effect on the research findings is the framework for the investigation. The first part of a journal article provides this framework; it introduces the subject matter under study by providing a problem statement, by defining terms used, and by putting the study and its findings into perspective. The framework of a research investigation is like the foundation of a house. It structures and orients much, if not everything, that comes afterward—particularly the methods and conclusions sections. In the methods section, the operational definitions, the measuring and analysis procedures, the selection of subjects or respondents, and even the choice of variables to include in the study are all affected by what the author learned or stated in the first part of the article. In the conclusions section, the author will frequently interpret the results in the context of the current state of knowledge as reflected in the review of related research.

All in all, the framework, or first part of an article, is important to readers of research because it helps them understand and interpret the second part. There are few, if any, rules for constructing the framework of a study; researchers have a lot of latitude. Correspondingly, there are no set rules for evaluating the framework of a study; readers need to be careful and to question continually.

QUESTIONS TO ASK

Problem Statement
1 **Is the problem stated so that it can be solved?**
   A problem may be simple or difficult depending on the way it is stated.
2 **Is the problem statement open-ended and nonbiasing?**
   Some ways of stating a problem can restrict the scope of a study and eliminate useful alternatives from consideration.
3 **How important is this problem to your more general concerns?**
   Researchers are free to choose any problems they wish. They may not choose to do research on the aspect of a topic most important to you. Remember that what has been researched is not necessarily what is important.

Continued

4 **Does the research answer the questions asked?**
If not, what questions does it answer?

Definitions
5 **Are definitions being misused as explanations?**
Definitions tell us how to label things, but labeling is not explaining.
6 **Are circular definitions used?**
It will not always be obvious that a word is just being defined by itself. Sometimes questionnaires or other procedures must be examined in detail to discover whether the concept is linked to anything besides itself.
7 **Are definitions sufficiently specific?**
Definitions are arbitrary; you don't know what is meant unless the author takes some pains to tell you. If definitions are not sufficiently specific, your meanings and the author's meanings may well be different.
8 **Are operational definitions used and are they adequate?**
Operational definitions help ensure that you know what the researcher is talking about in terms of the real world. However, they are seldom wholly adequate for the concepts they define. They may include something that should not be included. You must decide to what extent they are on target. Having more than one operational definition for each concept helps ensure that the conceptual target is hit.
9 **Are the definitions fruitful?**
Definitions should build on the research traditions in a field, and they must be useful to you.

Review of Related Literature
10 **Is there a review of related research?**
The absence of a review does not by itself suggest that the information presented is inadequate. However, a good critical review is useful to the reader and shows the author has thoroughly considered the topic.
11 **What is included in the literature review?**
The selection of articles should be based on relevance. Articles should be recent and should not exclude disagreeing or contradictory findings. Ideally, the review should be evaluative, but it should also include enough descriptive information for you to completely understand the research cited.
12 **Did the author thoroughly consider what might be found and the corresponding implications prior to gathering the data?**
"Interesting" findings can be gleaned from almost any research study after the data have been collected. "Conclusive" findings are much more likely, however, to come from a prior commitment about what will be learned from specified findings.
13 **Do the findings make sense in terms of the literature cited?**
This question doesn't quite fit here because it is concerned with findings, which are discussed in the second half of an article. But if the current findings agree with those of earlier studies and your own experiences, you are making an argument based on replications and you will probably want to trust them more than if they are clearly at variance with the earlier work. The major exception to this is when the researcher predicted a contradictory result before the data were collected.

PRACTICE EVALUATIONS

Reminder: Answering the above questions yourself is good practice. Chapter 18 provides guidelines for you to follow in doing that. Chapter 19 provides two articles along with our evaluations of them. Chapter 20 provides two additional articles for you to practice on.

FOR FURTHER THOUGHT

1 Comment on each of the following statements:
   (a) It snows in Syracuse because Syracuse is in the snow belt.
   (b) Lewie is the best handicapper that ever lived. He picked the last 100 winners in a row.
   (c) Every study in our extensive review supported the contention that premarital sex is related to high income.
   (d) An operational definition guarantees that the writer is at least speaking "sensibly," but it does not guarantee that the writer is saying anything important. ("Sensibly" means, literally, "having sensory input.")
   (e) A decision was made in this article not to state explicitly the purpose in order to reduce the investigator's bias.
2 Find a journal article that includes a critical review of the literature. *Psychological Bulletin* or any issues of the *Annual Review* are good places to begin your search. Compare the reviews in these articles with the reviews found in the articles you normally read.
3 Comment on the following operational definition of a foot from a 16th-century German regulation:

"Stand at the door of a church on Sunday, bid 16 men to stop, tall ones and short ones as they happen to pass out as the service is finished, then make them put their left feet one behind the other and the length obtained shall be a right and lawful rod, and the 16th shall be a right and lawful foot." (*National Geographic,* August 1977, p. 288)

4 Interpret the following quotations in terms of the material in this chapter.
   (a) "The true meaning of a term is to be found by observing what a man does with it, not what he says about it." (P. W. Bridgman)
   (b) "Truths based on definitions require a justification of the definition." (C. W. Churchman)
   (c) "For good answers, good questions can always be found, but some good questions have no answers." (Anonymous)
   (d) "If the proposed problem is big enough to be significant it cannot be done; if the problem is delimited enough to be feasible, it is not worth doing." (Anonymous)
   (e) "If I have been able to see farther it was because I stood on the shoulders of giants." (Newton)

FOR FURTHER READING

1 R. F. Mager. *Goal Analysis,* 2nd ed. Palo Alto, CA: Lear Siegler/Fearon Publishers, 1990.

An easy-to-read, even humorous, treatment of analyzing goals to produce researchable objectives. Used extensively in the field of education to translate concepts into operational definitions. Mager's fable of the "fuzzies" drives home the point.

2 C. Sellitz et al. "The Logic of Analysis" (Chapter 2) and "Selection and Formulation of a Research Problem" (Chapter 3). In *Research Methods in Social Relations,* 3rd ed. New York: Holt, 1976.

These chapters from an introductory research methods book provide some ideas underlying the testing of hypotheses, the development of a research problem, and the construction of a literature review.

3 J. S. Coleman. "Intellectuals and Public Policy." In *The Public and Public Policy: Reflections on Bi-Centennial America.* Syracuse, NY: Maxwell School of Citizenship and Public Affairs (The Maxwell Summer Lecture Series), Syracuse University, 1976.

We cited Coleman's argument that social science research is often not politically neutral. In this paper he covers that topic and related issues concerning the contribution of research to policymaking.

4 R. L. Ebel. "And Still the Dryads Linger." *American Psychologist* 29 (1974), pp. 485–92.

We cited Ebel's discussion of concepts that he feels have been inappropriately used as explanations when they are, in fact, only labels. His concerns continue to be reflected in many areas of social science.

5 D. B. Pillemer and R. J. Light. "Synthesizing Outcomes: How to Use Research Evidence from Many Studies." *Harvard Educational Review* 50 (1980), pp. 176–95.

Combining the results of different studies of the same research question is an important, but perplexing, pursuit. This article identifies some alternative ways of carrying out such a synthesis. The authors believe that the reader needs to pay careful attention to the specific details of the methods employed in each study.

6 C. J. Drew; M. L. Hardman; and A. W. Hart. *Designing and Conducting Research: Inquiry in Education and Social Science,* 2nd ed. Boston: Allyn and Bacon, 1996.

Chapter 4, "The Research Process," includes a discussion of how researchers decide what to study.

9

MEASUREMENT:
HOW DOES IT SIZE UP?

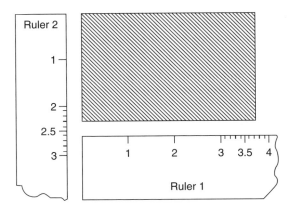

The shaded portion of the figure above is a rectangle whose area we want to determine. Below the rectangle is ruler 1, which is evenly aligned with the left edge of the rectangle. Ruler 2 is evenly aligned with the top of the rectangle. Both rulers measure inches and each is divided into tenths of an inch.

Using ruler 1, how long would you say the rectangle is? Look at the figure carefully to get an accurate measure of its length. After you have determined the length of the rectangle use ruler 2 to determine its width. Then multiply the two numbers to calculate the area of the rectangle.

TAKE SOME TIME TO MEASURE THE AREA

Before going any further in this chapter you should try to determine the area of the rectangle. There is no prize for the correct answer, but the exercise does have some value.

Many people would report the length to be 3.7 inches and the width to be 2.3 inches. Multiplying these numbers together, they would report the area to be 8.51 square inches. If they reported this answer they would be misleading anyone who read it. And probably many of you who arrived at different answers would also be either misleading or mistaken.

The answer 8.51 isn't misleading because of the arithmetic. If you assume the length to be approximately 3.7 inches and the width approximately 2.3 inches, then 3.7 × 2.3 equals 8.51. It is misleading because the concept of "approximately" was not incorporated in the answer. This same type of error is rather common in many of the social sciences, and if undetected, it has serious implications for the users of the research findings.

A Closer Look

Take another, closer look at the bottom right corner of the rectangle. If that corner were magnified along with ruler 1, it might look like the figure below. With this degree of magnification it is clear that the length of the rectangle is not quite 3.7 inches but a little less. Yet because you did not originally have this picture, your eyes had a difficult time seeing the length as less than 3.7 inches. Since the length is obviously close to, if not exactly, 3.7 inches, you used that figure to determine the area.

How much less would the length have to be before we would estimate the length to be 3.6 inches? Take another look at the preceding figure and decide what length less than 3.7 inches but more than 3.6 inches you would use as a cutoff point. The obvious choice for this cutoff point is halfway between 3.6 and 3.7 inches. That is, 3.65 is really the lowest point at which the edge of the rectangle could fall and still

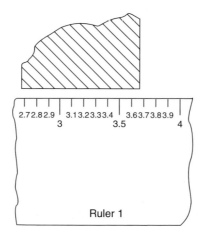

Ruler 1

have the length reported as 3.7 inches. Similarly, 3.75 is the highest point the edge of the rectangle could be for the length to be reported as 3.7 inches. Thus, what is meant by 3.7 in this particular measuring situation is anything between 3.65 and 3.75 inches.

Now if we had had this degree of magnification available to us originally, of course—or if our rulers measured finer than tenths of an inch—we could report a more precise measurement. But no matter how great the magnification or how fine the measurement of the ruler, there still will be a range of values in which the true length belongs. Suppose, for example, we could measure to the thousandths of an inch. With this degree of fineness the length might be reported as 3.683 inches. But what is meant by 3.683 is really anything between 3.6825 and 3.6835 inches. Thus, no matter how good our measuring instrument, every measurement produces an *estimate* within which the true length lies. This is, of course, the same conclusion we reached in Chapter 7 when we introduced the concept of noise.

A Range of Possible Values

Getting back to the problem of computing the area of the rectangle, we now know that the length could really be anything between 3.65 and 3.75 inches. Similarly, the width could be anything between 2.25 and 2.35 inches. So the smallest the area of the rectangle could be is $2.25 \times 3.65 = 8.2125$ square inches. And the largest the area could be is $2.35 \times 3.75 = 8.8125$ square inches. And the true area of the rectangle could be anything between 8.2125 and 8.8125 square inches. This range of values around the midpoint can be conveniently written as $8.5125 \pm .3$. Now, the answer is not misleading; the range of possible values is given.

Notice that determining the range required much more than just multiplying the two estimates of length times each other. In general, determining the appropriate range of values is not simple. Frequently it is much harder than this, but whenever measurements are reported, it is essential that you have some idea of what range of values surrounds an estimate. We cannot overemphasize the importance of this seemingly obvious principle. Unfortunately, the principle is violated daily, and its misuse has probably affected each of us at least once.

For example, consider students who take standardized tests as part of college admission procedures. Their scores, like all measurements, are estimates of their true ability. The scores can be interpreted reasonably only if the range is considered. Yet many admissions officers consider only the scores of the applicants. For the aptitude tests of the Graduate Record Exams (GRE), the scores usually range from about 200 to 800. Suppose two applicants are being considered—one with the score of 680 and the other with a score of 655. Is the first clearly more capable?

Differences and "Real" Differences

By now you should refuse to answer until you learn something about the range of scores that might be a true representation of each student's abilities. If the range were plus or minus 5, the higher score would indeed indicate greater ability. But, if the range were plus or minus 50, 75, or 100, the difference between the two looks less convincing. In fact, the organization that constructs and scores the GRE suggests that two scores need to be at least 50 points apart before you can be reasonably sure that the student with the higher score is really more capable. The closer the scores are to each other, the smaller your chance is of knowing which student is really on top. In the case above, a 25-point difference should not be given much weight in choosing between the students. Other factors such as grades or letters of recommendation should be considered relatively more important.

NOISE AND BIAS IN MEASUREMENT

So far our concern has been with the measuring instrument. How precisely can it measure? It is important to consider carefully the instruments used in published reports—particularly the home-grown sort of questionnaire devised rather quickly by someone not well versed in research.

Measurement as a Process

But a concern for the instruments themselves is not enough. Measurement is a process that includes everything the researcher does to arrive at the numerical estimates. Measurement includes the instrument, but it also includes the manner in which the instrument was used, the skill of the person using the instrument, and, in social research, the various attributes or characteristics of the people being studied. All these factors can affect the actual numerical measure the researcher obtained. Sometimes the effect is systematic, biasing the final measure; while other times the effect is random, which widens the range around the estimate.

As an exercise we occasionally ask students to measure as best they can the perimeter of their classroom. They are asked to bring with them to class good instruments for measuring length, such as rulers, chains of known length, tape measures, and so forth. The class is divided into groups of about five people and each group measures the room's perimeter. Results of the different groups are then compared.

Everyone expects the results to differ, but rarely do they expect such a magnitude of difference. A common result for the maximum difference among the groups is at least 40 or 50 percent. This exercise was conducted once with groups of college teachers and their maximum difference was 100 percent; the largest estimate of the perimeter was twice as big as the smallest. Now, neither the students nor the teachers were engineers or surveyors, but they were college graduates, and measuring length seems pretty easy and straightforward—not quite in the same category as measuring the boiling point of some unknown gas or something equally "technical." If well-educated people have such difficulty measuring length, imagine what happens when some well-intentioned, but untrained people try to measure something more complicated.

What about measuring the room's perimeter? What are the potential causes of the differences among the groups' results? And are these causes systematic or random?

The Measuring Instrument

What usually comes to mind first is the measuring instrument itself. While no one would purposely use a rubber tape measure, a cloth one—which stretches somewhat—is often used. Every instrument to some degree changes over time. To the extent that these changes are not systematic, they contribute to the noise in the measurement, but a ruler that loses part of the first inch with repeated use would be biased, not noisy.

Certainly the instrument is important. But it is unlikely that the instrument alone produced the large difference among the groups. The other contributors to the difference should be considered as important aspects of the measurement process.

Other Measurement Factors

First, there is the operational definition. What is meant by "perimeter"? That is an easy question in a geometry class, but operationally there is some confusion. Some student groups measure all four walls. But if they measure along the bottom of the walls where they meet the floor, what should be done with molding, or the door jambs, or the air vent, and so on? Some groups measure one floor tile and count the tiles in each direction, but there are difficulties with the cracks between the tiles, uneven tiles, and rooms that have opposite walls of unequal lengths. No matter what operational definition is agreed upon, some unforeseen problem will arise. Furthermore, the groups rarely begin their task by agreeing on a definition. Rather, some students end up measuring one wall by their unique definition, while other students are measuring other walls using different definitions. Operational definitions that are not sufficiently detailed or are not used consistently throughout the measurement process will contribute to random variability. In contrast, operational definitions that are inadequate, but are used consistently and carefully, will be biasing.

Second, the person doing the measuring contributes to error. One's mood, one's visual acuity, one's patience, and other temporary psychological and physiological states contribute to measurement noise. Students who consider such exercises silly may not be as careful as others who take the exercise seriously. Similarly, students who did not get enough sleep the night before or who are not feeling their best may not measure the room as carefully as they might if they were more rested or healthier. Random error occurs in the arithmetic as students try to convert all their measures into inches so they can be added together. Personality and intellectual characteristics of the students (such as persistence, or quantitative ability) along with their prior experience in similar tasks would affect the measurement in a more systematic manner.

The context also plays a role. If the lighting in the room was inadequate, the lengths obtained would be noisy regardless of one's visual acuity. The presence of the instructor in the room may have affected different students differently. And the time of day—some people are morning people, some are evening people—time of year, weather, and a number of other contextual factors could add random disturbances to a group's estimate of the room's perimeter.

The procedure employed can also distort the measurement. After the groups measure the room's perimeter, we ask which group has the most accurate answer. Once, one group claimed to be the most accurate because its instrument measured to the nearest ¹⁄₆₄ inch. Admittedly, such an instrument can, in principle, measure more finely than the everyday sort of ruler, which can distinguish at best around ¹⁄₁₆ inch. But the instrument doesn't do the measuring; people do. When asked how they used their very accurate ruler, members of this group innocently explained that they placed the ruler on the floor, then put their thumb down to mark the end of the ruler, and then moved the ruler over to begin at the other side of the thumb. This procedure wiped out any advantage the group might have had by using the more accurate instrument. The width of the thumb must have raised the uncertainty from ¹⁄₆₄ inch to ¾ inch or more and produced an underestimate of the perimeter of the room.

Acceptable Error: How Much?

With a little thought, other possible sources of bias and noise can be identified in the measurement of the room's perimeter. We expect, of course, that with practice the groups would become better at measuring the room's perimeter. But no amount of practice or training would remove all sources of error. Some of it is inevitable. What matters is how much error is present, and whether that amount is tolerable. For example, how much error would be acceptable if you wanted to know whether a room were large enough to hold 50 people? In this case a rather large error component wouldn't matter—plus or minus a few feet shouldn't make much of a difference. But if expensive carpeting were being installed, an error of one or two feet would not do and the measures (as well as the procedures for their use) would have to be refined so that the error was reduced to plus or minus a few inches.

RELIABILITY

The noise, or random error, in measurement is usually considered under the topic of reliability. The more random variability, the less reliable the measurement, and vice versa. Reliability in this technical sense is similar to our everyday use of the word. People are reliable if they are trustworthy or dependable. Similarly, a measurement is reliable to the extent it is trustworthy or dependable. A dependable measure is one that gives the same or very similar results each time it is used. Reliable measurements are repeatable or stable measures.

Degrees of Reliability

Researchers have an obligation to include in their writing the reliability of their measures. Sometimes the form taken is a range of possible error such as 50 feet 2 inches, plus or minus 3 inches ($50'2'' \pm 3''$) or possibly 49 feet 11 inches to 50 feet 5 inches. A smaller range reflects a greater reliability. Sometimes a reliability coefficient—a number between zero and one—is given. The lower the coefficient, the less reliable the measurement procedure; the higher the number, the more reliable. Notice that

THE NOSE - CONE
WILL HAVE TO BE
7' 3.2437689"
IN DIAMETER.

ANNE CANEVARI GREEN

reliability is a matter of degree. Measurement procedures are not simply "reliable" or "not reliable." There is an infinite gradation of degrees of reliability and what might be acceptable to researchers may not be acceptable to you as a potential user of that research. So you should try to determine for yourself if the measures are reliable enough. If they are not, then any findings, results, or conclusions based on them are not justified by the evidence.

Cautions in Reporting

There are some common cautions to consider when interpreting reported reliabilities. First of all, the plus or minus form used to describe reliability is usually a measure of the instrument itself. A good tape measure, for instance, may be capable of measuring to the nearest sixteenth of an inch, and so based on this fact alone, the reliability of the instrument is no better than $\pm\frac{1}{32}$ inch. But as we pointed out earlier, a whole host of factors are potential sources of a lack of reliability. The instrument is only one source and may not be the most important one. Plus or minus measures of reliability may be, at best, optimistic estimates of the reliability of the obtained measures.

A second consideration arises more often when people themselves are used as measuring instruments. Suppose judges have to identify the best painting in a collection, or

Contestant	Ratings of 10 judges			Average of 10 ratings
Miss A		.:... ...		150
	145	150	155	
Miss B		. . ..		151
	145	150	155	

choose the next Miss America, or decide on the proper diagnosis of a mental patient. In all these cases the judges are serving as measuring instruments and the measure of reliability depends upon their consistency—that is, upon whether they are all measuring the same thing. When they can agree, their judgment is reliable—at least in the sense of being consistent.

Some situations require a decision by judges whether they agree or not. In gymnastics competition, for example, each judge independently rates the performance of a gymnast, and the final measure of the performer's ability is the average of these ratings. Athletic competition requires a decision—the average score. Your concern with reliability, however, leads you to note how much the judges' individual scores differ. An average score can be computed no matter how much the judges differ, but you may want to consider the process unreliable if there are large differences among the judges.

When researchers attempt to measure, they will usually report the degree of interjudge agreement. The problem exists when all you know is the judges' decision—not how it was obtained. The Miss America contest is a case in point. It's hard to believe that the final decision is based on consensus among the judges. If that were true, there should have been some years when they could not agree among themselves and no one was chosen. Since a new Miss America is picked each year, we have to assume that some sort of averaging among the judges is done.

If the judges did not agree, the chosen Miss America may not be the "best" (of whatever they are measuring), but she may be the "best on the average." Two different notions of "best" can be seen in the table above, which is similar to the representation of the bathroom scales presented in Chapter 7. Each mark represents a judge's rating of a contestant.

Now compare Miss A with Miss B. The ratings on contestant A are in agreement, meaning that if one of the judges were replaced there is a good chance that the average rating for Miss A would not change much. The ratings of Miss B are less uniform and therefore less reliable. Clearly, the choice between the two contestants can be resolved only when some agreement is reached on the meaning of "best."

Classification and Reliability

Classifying people or objects into categories is another kind of measurement. The reliability of categorizing depends primarily on the operational definitions of the categories. If the definitions are vague or not sufficiently detailed, the classification will be less reliable—objects may not be put into the same category if the task were repeated. This is precisely the problem facing psychologists and psychiatrists as they try to diagnose some of their patients. The definitions that distinguish among the various kinds of schizophrenia or between neurotic and "normal" behavior are not always clear-cut. There is often a lack of agreement in diagnosis, even among doctors who have similar orientations.

A Restatement

Before we leave the subject of reliability, a restatement is necessary as to what it is about. Reliability is a desired attribute of the process of measurement, describing how accurate or believable the measures are. Reliability depends only upon the amount of random error or noise in the measurement process. Good researchers can improve the reliability of a measure to acceptable levels because they are aware of the potential sources of noise and they know how to eliminate or reduce some of it. As a reader of research be very wary of missing reliability estimates—particularly if you cannot tell if the investigator adequately dealt with the random sources of measurement error.

VALIDITY

Reliability is needed, but it is not enough. Measures that are perfectly reliable may be absolutely useless unless they also have some degree of validity. Validity is a complex subject that is primarily concerned with *what* is being measured. In general, a measurement is valid to the extent it measures what one wants it to measure and not something else. This criterion seems to be such an obvious requirement that you may question if the problem of validity ever really occurs—or whether it's another of those esoteric academic subjects.

Let us assure you that the problem of validity is real. Obviously, no one would measure a person's weight with a tape measure, but you need to be sure that a researcher isn't making a similar error with less obvious things. The Scholastic Aptitude Test (SAT) and the Graduate Record Examination (GRE), which are used to make college admissions and scholarship decisions, are supposed to measure certain abilities . . . or is it that they are supposed to measure a person's knowledge . . . or are they just supposed to predict college performance? The debate over which, or whether they do any of the above, is a debate about what the tests are valid for. Until this debate is resolved, it is premature to expect administrators and faculty members to use the tests in any consistent manner.

Prediction as Validity

Pragmatically, the question of validity often comes down to the question of how well a measurement can predict some other characteristic of the individual. What is actually being measured is of little importance if the predictions hold true. If, for instance, the number of hairs on a student's head was an excellent indicator of how well that student would do in college, admissions officers would probably ask for that information in the application form.

If the measurement predicts, the result is valid for making that prediction. One of the arguments against SAT and GRE tests is that though they predict rather well, they do not predict well enough. Students who have low scores sometimes do well in college, and students who have high scores sometimes flunk out. Admissions officers seem to be placing less emphasis on these scores than they did a few years ago. Instead, the SAT and GRE scores are being used as only one of several indicators of how well an applicant is likely to do.

Predictive validity is only one type of validity, but for practitioners and for those who want to apply research findings in real situations, it is probably the most important kind. As you read the literature, you need to search for evidence of predictive validity. Did the author test the ideas on a group of people, and did they work out? Did the predictions agree with the actual outcome?

Construct Validity

Sometimes there is a need to go beyond predictive validity. If you are really trying to understand a concept, you want to know if it is being measured correctly—to make sure that concept is being measured and not something else. This concern is frequently referred to, somewhat obscurely, as a concern for "construct" validity.

A test for reading comprehension, for instance, involves students reading passages and then answering questions about the content of those passages. Obviously, students will be able to answer the questions better for topics they already know a lot about than for those they were not familiar with before taking the reading test. Regardless of how well the students were able to read a particular passage, they may obtain a high score on reading comprehension because of their prior knowledge about the subject matter. If the test were constructed so that prior knowledge could bias a person's score in this way, it would lack some degree of construct validity. Prior knowledge as well as reading comprehension would be measured instead of just reading comprehension.

"Library use" is sometimes measured by counting the number of people who come into the library. But the library is also used by people who read books checked out by friends and members of their family. A researcher who tries to find out how many people are using the library by counting individuals as they come in the door may underestimate the correct number because such a count would miss people who used the books but did not check them out themselves. Such a count may also overestimate the correct number if, for instance, the only public bathroom in the area were in the library.

Researchers usually indicate the degree of construct validity by explaining how well their measures agree with other measures of the same concept. In measuring library use by counting the people as they come in the door, the researcher could compare this count with other measures of library use such as circulation records, membership rolls, wear and tear on the card catalog, and so forth. The extent to which a simple head count agrees with these other measures is an indication of the construct validity of the "head count" as a measure of library use.

Validity, like reliability, is a matter of degree. And, like reliability, it is affected by noise or the random components in measurement; the more the noise, the poorer the reliability and the validity. Validity, however, is also affected by systematic error—by biasing aspects in the measurement process.

Combined Measures

A frequent threat to validity is the combining of a number of measures into one. There is seldom any naturally correct way to combine the elements, and information is lost about the component concepts that have been lumped together.

People who run state fairs wish to reward farmers who raise good cows. To do this, they must measure the goodness of a cow. They know that "goodness" is the combination of many separate things. A dairy cow must have strong legs, good udder support, a strong back, and markings characteristic of her breed, among other things. But which cow is better—one with especially strong legs and a slightly weak back or one with an exceptionally strong back but with slightly inappropriate markings? The judge must not only rate each cow on each attribute, but must decide how to combine the ratings across all attributes in order to determine which cow is best overall. This rather haphazard approach to combining the different components is fine for state fairs and perhaps for similar events like speech contests or ice skating competitions. In other cases you must ask if the various components of the measure are weighted appropriately.

Grades make a good example. Suppose a final course grade is determined by combining the scores for an exam and a paper. Say that the exam scores ranged from 50 to 92 and that the papers were graded either 4, 3, 2, 1, or 0. In such a case the paper would have very little effect on the final grade if the two scores were simply added. Someone getting an 86 on the exam and a 4 on the paper would get the same final grades as someone who got a 90 on the exam and a 0 on the paper. It seems unlikely that four points on the exam should be equivalent to four points on the paper. So in order for the final course grade to validly reflect the two component scores, the scores must be combined in some way that weights them as the instructor would want. This involves some statistical notions beyond the scope of this book, but it can be done.

Sometimes such combining is not acceptable to a researcher or to the person who wishes to use the results of that research in real situations. If an instrument measures both apples and oranges when you want to measure only apples, you are in trouble. Since you do not know how much of the final measurement depends on the apples and how much depends on the oranges, you cannot use the measuring instrument intelligently in any situation in which important decisions will be made.

Evaluation of employees is a case in point. A single instrument that judged each employee all the way from poor up to excellent would probably not be very useful to anyone if no information were available about what different attributes produced that rating. Was the employee easy to get along with, hardworking but not very competent—or vice versa? For this reason, most employee evaluation forms are multidimensional. That is, the person doing the rating will be asked to make separate judgments on work performance, communications skills, ability to work under direction, relevant personality considerations, and so on. Usually there will not be any attempt

Number of points	Contributor
72	What was learned in class and by studying.
12	Reasoned guessing based on Frank's two years of studying Latin.
2	Frank's sitting next to a particular friend.
–4	A fight with his girlfriend before the exam.
–7	Ambiguity in the directions to part of the test.
3	Repetition of some items in the exam, though the wording was slightly changed.
–1	A scoring error by the teacher.
77 Total	

to combine these separate ratings into one single description of the employee; employee performance is not a single dimension and its measurement has to reflect that fact.

Another example comes from the research that tries to describe a person's personality. At cocktail parties a common preoccupation is to sum up someone's personality in a simple way: "Jennifer is introverted," or she is "repressed," or "her superego is insufficiently developed," or any of a variety of other ways to catalog a person. But these simple classifications of personality are not very useful because they are too simple. With more complex models of personality, human behavior can be predicted better than with a cocktail party diagnosis.

RELIABILITY AND VALIDITY

Both reliability and validity are central to measurement of any kind. And measurement is the key to scientific understanding. To paraphrase Lord Kelvin, if you can't measure it, you don't know what you are talking about. No profession will advance if its theories and practices are based on concepts that are unmeasurable or can only be measured so imprecisely that little faith can be placed in the outcome. For without good measurement there is no way to test one hypothesis versus another, and there is no way of determining if a new practice actually works as well as or better than the existing practice.

To help put these two important concepts into perspective, here is an example of a paper-and-pencil examination. Suppose Frank, a high school senior, scored 77 on his French final examination. That score is composed of several components, only one of which is a measure of what Frank learned in class and through studying at home. Suppose the breakdown of his score looked as shown in the table above. Frank scored a 77 when he should have gotten a 72. That is, the test was designed to measure what was learned, but as with all measuring instruments, error was present. That part of the error due to Frank's knowledge of Latin is probably systematic. Anyone who knew some Latin would have had an advantage in the examination over those who did not have any Latin training. All other contributors to Frank's total score are most likely random.

The random contributors are sources of unreliability; another day, or a slightly different test, and Frank's total score might change dramatically. But even if these contributors were eliminated, the biasing effect of Latin tends to weaken the validity of the test. As constructed, it measures French and Latin knowledge, not just French.

Good measurement is relatively free from both noise and bias. It is reliable and valid. Reliable measurement can be obtained without being valid, but valid measures aren't useful without also being reliable. Thus, validity is the more important of the two. Unfortunately for the consumer of research, researchers can more easily increase the reliability of a measure than the validity of that measure. Increasing reliability takes hard work, but it can be done by double-checking all measurements, observations, and calculations; standardizing and controlling all procedures; and minimizing ambiguity or operational definitions and directions. Usually these safeguards will be enough to raise the reliability to an acceptable level.

But validity of measurement is a different thing altogether. To measure something validly implies that the "essence" of it, or its "true nature," is known and can be recognized. Otherwise you can never be sure that what is supposed to be measured is in fact being measured at all.

QUESTIONS TO ASK

1 **Is the researcher trying to measure more precisely than the instrument allows?**
A ruler calibrated in sixteenths of an inch cannot be used to measure to ¼₄ inch. The instrument just doesn't have that degree of precision. Very precise measurement is a goal in all scientific fields, but you can't let researchers imply they have achieved a finer degree of measurement than their instruments allow.

2 **Is some measure of reliability given?**
With such a measure your job is easier—you get not only an estimate of the reliability, but also a clue about the researcher's concern for careful measurement. If no measure is given, you may want to estimate the amount of noise present.

3 **Is the reliability sufficient for your purposes?**
As consumers you need to make this decision. Researchers often have the freedom to wait for the slow accumulation of replicated studies. Professionals often must make decisions with insufficient information. And what is good enough for the researcher may not be good enough for you.

4 **What type of reliability measure was given?**
There are two different aspects to this question. First, is it a measure of stability or repeatability, or is it a measure of consistency or agreement? Having one when you need the other is not of much use. Secondly, is the reliability of the instrument alone or of the entire measurement process? If the former, then the reported reliability is a restricted one because the entire process is what's important, not just the instrument.

5 **What is really being measured?**
Could the instrument be measuring something other than what the author indicates? If so, search for some evidence of the construct validity of the measure.

6 **Does the measure predict well enough for your purposes?**
An intelligence test might predict college grades but not job performance. You need to ask, "validity for what?" to see if the measure is useful for you.

7 **How many dimensions are being measured at once?**
Often there are several components or dimensions that need to be measured—like employee performance. Did the researcher acknowledge all the important dimensions or were some omitted? A good rule of thumb is to prefer a separate measure for each of the dimensions, but if the researcher combined them into one measure, check to see if they were weighted appropriately.

PRACTICE EVALUATIONS

Reminder: Answering the above questions yourself is good practice. Chapter 18 provides guidelines for you to follow in doing that. Chapter 19 provides two articles along with our evaluations of them. Chapter 20 provides two additional articles for you to practice on.

FOR FURTHER THOUGHT

1 Choose a measurement (or judgment) you frequently make in your professional practice or everyday life.
   (a) Identify the random error components in it.
   (b) Estimate how reliable this measurement or judgment is.
   (c) Consider the implications on the job (or to you personally) if this measurement were much more reliable.
   (d) Consider the implications on the job (or to you personally) if this measurement were much less reliable.
2 Repeat Exercise 1, but consider biasing error components in the measurement instead of random components, and orient your discussion in terms of validity instead of reliability.
3 Interpret the following old joke in light of our discussion of measurement.
   Question: How old is that mountain?
   Answer: It is 4,000,000,010 years old.
   Question: How do you know that?
   Answer: Well, ten years ago I read that it was 4,000,000,000 years old.
4 Take another look at the table on page 100. Are there any conditions under which you believe the best choice for Miss America should be Miss A, the contestant with the lower average score? Why?
5 Write for information on how to interpret your favorite standardized test. It should include what range of scores correspond to any obtained score. It may also state how different two scores must be in order for you to be confident that the students who got the scores really do differ in ability.
6 Interpret the following quotations in terms of the material in this chapter.
   (a) "There are always more mathematical theories than one whose results depart from a given set of data by less than the errors of observation." (G. A. Bliss)
   (b) "The value of an observation not only depends on its own level of accuracy but also upon the particular way it has been combined with other observations (many of them nonnumerical), the nature and number of computational steps involved, etc. In this manner the topic soon stops being primitive; on the contrary, very deep-lying problems are encountered, some of which have only recently been recognized." (O. C. Morgenstern)
   (c) "To say that a measure of observation is reliable does not necessarily indicate that a significant variable is being measured, or one that we wish to measure, or one that is uncontaminated by irrelevant influences." (H. Peak)
   (d) "You can't get blood from a turnip." (Anonymous)

FOR FURTHER READING

1 W. S. Torgerson. *Theory and Methods of Scaling.* New York: Wiley, 1985, Chapter 1.

Measurement is a technical topic, and few reading sources introduce the topic for nonresearchers. Except for the first chapter, this book is difficult reading. In that chapter the author discusses some of the same information we've presented and puts it into a broader framework of social science measurement in general.

2 E. Babbie. *The Practice of Social Research,* 7th ed. Belmont, CA: Wadsworth, 1995.

Babbie's chapter, "Conceptualization and Measurement" (pp. 109–30), ought to be read in conjunction with Chapters 8 and 9 of *Evaluating Information.* It offers a useful review of the same ideas, but incorporates them into a single, integrated chapter.

10

DESCRIPTION:
ARE THE RESULTS
SUMMARIZED FAIRLY?

An American and a Russian were the only competitors in a footrace. The American won. The U.S. newspapers reported that the American beat the Russian. The Russian newspapers reported that the Russian came in second, while the American was next to last.

This ancient anecdote points out the difference between accuracy and fairness. Both press reports are true. But are they fair? Well, it depends on one's perspective. When seen in terms of the annals of political propaganda, these stories may be commendable because they are at least accurate. In research reports, however, you should expect a fair summary of what occurred and what was found, and that involves more than accuracy.

Researchers collect only a small portion of possible observations. But even this amount is usually too much to cope with. Neither the researcher nor the reader wants to wade through, analyze, and remember great masses of data. The data need to be summarized so that the effect of idiosyncratic observations is minimized and general patterns can be discerned and reported. In Chapters 3 and 4 our concern was with the original observation of data and the possible consequences of not being able to see or tell everything. In this chapter we will also be concerned with the effect of possible errors of omission but our focus is on summaries of data rather than on the data themselves. Since something must be left out, one characteristic of a fair summary is that important information is not omitted.

However, what's important in one research study may be trivial in another. The objectives of the study and the researcher's point of view help determine which information is important. As a result, the summaries of information cannot be considered completely impartial or objective. A fair summary, therefore, is relative; it depends upon purpose and person. You need to be sure not only that the researcher provided a fair description given the purposes of the study, but also that the description is fair for your purposes.

SOME GUIDELINES

There are three questions to ask that will help you decide whether a description is fair. The questions remind you to evaluate summaries in terms of their two possible distorting characteristics: leaving something out and choosing items to suit the researcher's purpose.

How Summaries Are Determined

First of all, you need to know exactly how the summary was arrived at. Be sure you know what observations, measurements, or raw data the researcher started with and how they were used to calculate the summaries given in the article. The procedures section of the journal article ought to describe the researcher's method in enough detail so you can answer this question. For instance, an anthropologist might collect observations in the form of detailed daily notes or instead might try to recall all experiences at the end of several weeks. Naturally, you would be more confident with summaries that were based on the more reliable daily notes. But even with daily observations, there still are many ways in which the researcher could produce a summary, and it is important that you understand what was done.

The Alternatives That Exist

The second question is to ask yourself what alternative summaries could have been used. Sometimes only one type of summary makes sense, but most of the time real alternatives exist. Naturally, you are limited here to the alternatives you can think of; in short journal articles you cannot expect the author to weigh all the various options. But even if you can think of only one alternative, compare it with what the researcher used. What kind of picture do you get from each? Which of them presents the fairest description from your perspective?

What Might Be Left Out

The third question is simply an explicit reminder to consider what was left out. Since the purpose of a summary is to present the data in economical form, research reports do not usually include the original measurements or the raw data. However, the researcher should have carefully examined what was left out and provided the reader with some information about it—in essence, a summary of what was left out.

In the remainder of this chapter we will apply these questions to two very common summaries—verbal descriptions and descriptive statistics. Even though our examples involve only one type of verbal description (field notes resulting from naturalistic observation) and two manipulations of numbers (resulting from measurement), the three questions can usually be applied to all types of summaries, including pictures, graphs, and diagrams.

VERBAL DESCRIPTIONS

The most basic form of data gathering is simply the recording of observations—verbal descriptions of what was seen. This approach is well-suited for many research problems, and some social scientists, especially sociologists and anthropologists, use it extensively. The data are notes, audiotapes, videotapes, films, or other records; the findings are the researcher's summary of what was learned from the extensive observation.

For instance, from a classic anthropology text:

> The Zuni are a ceremonious people, a people who value sobriety and inoffensiveness above all other virtues. Their interest is centered upon their rich and complex ceremonial life. Their cults of the masked gods, of healing, of the sun, of the sacred fetishes, of war, of the dead, are formal and established bodies of ritual with priestly officials and calendric observances. No field of activity competes with ritual for foremost place in their attention. Probably most grown men among the western Pueblos give to it the greater part of their waking life. It requires the memorizing of an amount of word-perfect ritual that our less trained minds find staggering, and the performance of neatly dovetailed ceremonies that are charted by the calendar and complexly interlock all the different cults and the governing body in endless formal procedure.

This is a summary. If you wanted to evaluate the sample text you would need to know how the summary was arrived at, what alternative summaries might be given, and what was left out.

For the most part, the crucial bridge from observations to the summaries that are reported is invisible—it happens inside the researcher's head. And, there are few explicit rules or norms for summarization. The most pronounced concern of researchers is the accuracy of the data itself. Careful researchers try very hard to avoid inaccurate descriptions by controlling for biases which arise from the process of observation and the process of recording those observations. We have in mind here those biases due to the behavior of people (see Chapter 6) such as the Hawthorne effect, and the effects of evaluation apprehension, expectancy, and social desirability. In addition, there are those difficulties caused by the richness, scope, and duration of the phenomenon being observed.

When you examine a verbal description to see if it is an adequate summary, you need to check carefully for the presence of controls. Did the researcher attempt to prevent these biases or minimize their effects? For example, if either unobtrusive measures or deception is possible, the biases due to people can often be controlled; if the phenomenon of interest can be recorded over a long period of time in some automatic or mechanical way, it is possible to decrease the biases of selection (are the observed events representative?) and memory (did the researcher remember all essential details?). These particular methods of control are not always possible in every investigation; they wouldn't be possible in the study of the Zuni. But methods[1] do exist, and researchers who provide lengthy descriptions of their observations are also obligated to explain in detail how they controlled for these biases.

AVERAGES

Averages are probably the most common type of summary found in social research. By means of an average a researcher can characterize an entire collection of measurements (such as the heights of 30 children or the time it took to complete 14 tasks) with one number.

Before considering the question of fairness, we will review some basic information about averages. First of all, the word "average" is ambiguous. At least five different kinds of averages exist, and the word average can be legitimately applied to each (though researchers are usually careful to identify the specific kind of average being used). Two of these averages appear most frequently, and we will confine our discussion to them. One is the arithmetic mean. It tends to be the average that most nonresearchers think of. The mean is computed by adding up all the scores and then dividing by the number of scores. The other average is the median. It is the middle score, the one that is bigger than half the scores and smaller than the other half.

The mean may or may not be the same as the median. The result depends upon the numbers involved. Obviously, if they are equal, one is just as fair a summary as the other. The problem arises when they are not equal. For a simple example look at five scores.

$$1 \quad 3 \quad 4 \quad 7 \quad 10$$

The mean of these scores is 5 and the median is 4. When fairness is the issue, one important consideration is how each of these averages is affected by a change in the scores. To compute a mean, all the scores must be added, so the mean depends upon each and every score. If one score is changed, the mean will also change. Thus a large change in only one score can change the mean dramatically.

The median, on the other hand, has a quite different reaction to changes. Since the median is always in the middle, it is not affected much by changes in a single score. In fact, it is not affected at all if the score that changes gets bigger or smaller. For instance, change the 10 in the above set of scores to a 70. The mean should be sizably affected, and it is. The new mean is 17. But the median remains the same. The 4 is still the middle score.

Certainly a different impression would be given if an average of 4 were reported rather than an average of 17. Imagine how people with an ax to grind could choose the average that best supports their position. Take another look at the five numbers, but this time consider them hourly wages. The union could lament about an average wage of $4 per hour while management thinks an average of $17 per hour is too high. In this case neither average is necessarily fair because each hides important information. Probably the best a researcher could do with these data is to report both averages. A reader would then know that half of the scores (or wages) were below four, but one or more very large scores (or wages) must exist because the mean is so much larger than the median.

We've already responded to the first two questions for judging fairness—at least indirectly. The third question asks what has been left out. In terms of an average, the answer includes all the other scores. It is not necessary for the researcher to include all the raw data. One of the reasons for having summaries is to avoid this. What is needed is a summary measure of how different the scores are.

The closer the scores are to one another, the better the average represents all the scores. But if the scores differ markedly, the average is not a good substitute for all the individual scores. One type of summary is a simple statement by the researcher indicating how close or how far apart the scores are. Usually, however, a quantitative summary is used. Two commonly used summary measures are the standard deviation and the variance. You need to be able to recognize their names and interpret them for what they are—a summary of how the scores differ from one another. The larger the standard deviation (or the variance), the more the scores spread apart; if the standard deviation is very small (near zero), then you should expect most of the scores to be close or even to equal one another. In order to answer the third question for judging fairness, you need a summary measure of disparity like the standard deviation. Researchers, in order to report averages fairly, should always include such a summary measure.

Before ending our discussion of averages, take another look at the three questions. When answering them, don't forget the importance of knowing the operational definition and ascertaining the validity of the measurements.

For example, one indicator of the quality of public school education is the average number of students in the classroom. The lower the average, the better. Suppose you find the following summary statement in the principal's annual report to the PTA: "The average number of students has decreased over the last five years. It is now about 20 pupils per teacher."

To understand this summary, knowing that 20 pupils per teacher is the arithmetic mean, and the range of scores goes from a low of 8 pupils in one class to a high of 31 in another isn't enough. You also need to get behind these figures, interpret what they mean, and explore their implications. Whom did the principal include in the count of teachers? Just regular, full-time classroom teachers? Or were subject specialists (art, music, physical education), librarians, and guidance counselors included as well? Obviously the answer matters because the more teachers included, the lower the student-teacher ratio will be and the better the school will appear.

You are told that the range goes from 8 to 31 students per class, but the class of 8 has only pupils with special educational problems. Should that class be included in the average? A class of only 8 children does lower the mean. Eliminating that class changes the range to a low of 18 and a high of 31 students per class. Are these numbers close enough so that the average fairly represents each class? The answer is probably no when you are considering the quality of elementary school education. Well, then, is there any interesting pattern among the scores? For example, is first grade, which usually would benefit most from a low pupil-teacher average, at the low end (near 18) or at the high end of this range?

We could go on for a while posing questions about the principal's seemingly clear and straightforward statement. But the point has been made—to judge the fairness of a summary you need to be aware of a lot more than the average itself.

PERCENTAGES

Percentages are simple but often-misused summaries. A percentage is a summary that makes a comparison between two numbers. One number is the base, and the other number is what is to be compared with that base. If we say that 5 is 50 percent of 10, then 10 is the base; but when we say that 10 is 200 percent of 5, then 5 is the base. The base number is the key to percentages. By keeping the base firmly in mind, you will discover many of the typical distortions that keep a percentage from being a fair summary.

One common distortion occurs whenever the base number is small. When you see a report that says 50 percent of the people interviewed had a certain opinion, the figure sounds impressive. But remember that 50 percent is not only 2,000 out of 4,000, it can also be one person out of two. When the base is large, the percentage is reasonably reliable. But when the base is small, the percentage is probably quite unstable: a fairer description would make use of the actual numbers themselves (one out of the two people interviewed).

A second distortion shows up when percentages are treated like ordinary numbers. Percentages can be added or averaged but only if all the bases are equal; otherwise it's like adding apples and oranges. If worker productivity improved 10 percent in one plant and 20 percent in a second plant, saying that the average improvement was 15 percent may not be correct. The percentage depends on the bases, the existing level of productivity in the two plants. If plant No. 1 was originally producing 10 widgets per hour and is now producing 110 widgets, the increase is 10 percent. Plant No. 2 is much larger in size. It originally produced 400 widgets per hour and with a 20 percent increase it now makes 480. The original base production for the two plants was 500 (100 + 400) widgets per hour, now it is 590 (110 + 480). That is an 18 percent improvement, not 15 percent.

Finally, don't forget to consider the operational definition of the base figure. Many times researchers can choose among alternative bases. A question that's always worthwhile is to ask why they chose the one they did. Does it give a fair picture, or would another base give a different portrayal? A social work agency, for example, may want to compare the amount of service now being given with that of earlier years. But what earlier year ought to be the base? If the first year is used, you would expect a large percentage increase because of the typical startup problems of most new agencies. If last year is used as the base, was last year also part of an increasing service trend, or an unusually poor year? The point is that if the base year is not representative of the other years, the percentage may not fairly portray the agency's service record.

So far we've been concerned with the first of our three questions, "How was the summary computed?" When analyzing percentages, focus on the base number in your consideration of this question. The second question, regarding alternatives, can be seen in two ways. Keep the percentage as the summary but choose a fairer base figure. Or find a fairer alternative to the percentage itself. Most often, that alternative will be use of the actual scores themselves—probably the fairest way to treat the small-base problem. If the researcher says 50 percent, try to translate that percentage into the actual numbers involved.

Percentiles

Before considering the third question, let's take a look at a type of percentage called the "percentile," or "percentile rank." Percentiles are often used in the areas of psychological and educational testing to compare a single individual's score with all the other scores. Each person tested will have an actual score on the test (the raw score) and a percentile score, which is computed from the raw score. A person's percentile score tells the percentage of all the people who scored lower on the test.

For instance, a raw score of 280 by itself doesn't tell you very much. If the researcher also tells you that the maximum possible score was 300, you know a bit more, but not as much as you may think. A score of 280 could be the highest score anyone received on the test, the lowest, or somewhere in the middle; you can't tell. One way to tell is with a percentile. If the raw score of 280 turns out to be in the 99th percentile, then that person scored higher than the vast majority of test takers. But if the raw score was in the 35th percentile, that person scored higher than only 35 percent of the others.

Percentiles are meaningful in relation to some particular group. Sometimes the group chosen by the researcher will not be the fairest for your purposes. Standardized college entrance examinations (such as the SAT or the GRE) are frequently reported as percentiles of three different groups—all people who took the test, all males who took the test, and all females who took the test. Since males tend to have higher raw scores on the quantitative portion of the test, any particular male's raw score will translate into a lower percentile when compared with other males than when compared to all the people who took the test. That is, a raw score of 650 may be in the 70th percentile when compared to males but in the 75th percentile when compared to everyone. So interpreting a percentile requires that you know the comparison group. And when there are alternative groups, you must decide which is the fairest.

Examining how a percentile is calculated will also show that the maximum percentile rank may be quite low if there are only a few scores (or test takers) involved. If there are only four scores, the top score has three-fourths of all the scores below it, yielding a percentile rank of 75.[2] That may not be very impressive, but it is the highest possible. As the number of scores increases, the highest percentile also increases. When there are few test takers, there is an artificial limit on the maximum percentile, which in turn may give an unfair summary of a person's performance. A fairer summary would include a statement to the effect that the individual scored the highest of all four people who took the test.

With regard to the third question, determining what is left out when a percentile is given, let's look at some raw scores and their corresponding percentiles.

Raw score	Percentile
50	80th
12	60th
7	40th
6	20th
5	0th

A raw score of 12 converts to the 60th percentile. If that raw score were any score greater than 7 but less than 50, it still would convert to the 60th percentile. What should be apparent then is that percentiles leave out the degree to which (how much) one score is higher than another. Percentiles only tell you *if* one score is higher than another. In cases like this, you might get a better picture of the situation by studying the entire set of raw scores along with their percentiles.

We've just touched on two of the more common types of summaries found in social research. And for our purposes that is enough to raise the question of fairness and suggest a strategy for making that decision. For your purposes, a little more understanding of summaries and possible distortions would be valuable. Rather than try to duplicate some first-rate presentations of these topics, we will simply end here and recommend that you look through one or more of the books listed at the end of the chapter. They are all pleasant enough to be bedtime reading.

QUESTIONS TO ASK

1 Is this a summary?
All descriptions are summaries to some extent. You need to be able to recognize a summary when you see one.

2 Is the summary fair?
Fairness in terms of summaries is a relative notion. All summaries must leave something out and reflect someone's viewpoint. So in this regard, all summaries are unfair. But in a more pragmatic vein, you need to decide if a fair picture is given for your purpose. To help evaluate a summary, ask (a) how was it computed or determined, (b) what alternatives are there, and (c) what was left out.

3 Was an average reported?
What kind of average (mean or median or something else)? What picture would you get if some other type of average were used? Does the average represent all the scores fairly, or is there a wide range among the scores?

4 Was a percentage reported?
What is the base, how big is it, and how was it chosen? Compare the picture you get from the percentage (or percentile) with one you would get from the raw scores.

PRACTICE EVALUATIONS

Reminder: Answering the above questions yourself is good practice. Chapter 18 provides guidelines for you to follow in doing that. Chapter 19 provides two articles along with our evaluations of them. Chapter 20 provides two additional articles for you to practice on.

FOR FURTHER THOUGHT

1 When witnesses are sworn in, they promise to tell not only the truth, but also the "whole truth." What could be meant by the "whole truth"?

2 We have given mostly numerical examples of descriptions that may, or may not, be fair. Think about descriptions that are not numerical in your field. How well does our approach work in evaluating these descriptions for fairness?

3 A map is a type of summary of the territory it represents. But the map is not the same as the territory. Does that mean the map is not accurate? Does that mean it is not a fair summary?

4 Is there any value to summaries that "lie" to the reader? What is your reaction to the following quotation?

"Not only is it easy to lie with maps, it's essential. To portray meaningful relationships for a complex, three-dimensional world on a flat sheet of paper or a video screen, a map must distort reality. As a scale model, the map must use symbols that almost always are proportionally much bigger or thicker than the features they represent. To avoid hiding critical information in a fog of detail, the map must offer a selective, incomplete view of reality. There's no escape from the cartographic paradox: to present a useful and truthful picture, an accurate map must tell white lies." [Mark Monmonier, *How to Lie with Maps*. The University of Chicago Press, 1991, p. 1.]

5 Do you agree with the following quote by the English philosopher, Alfred North White-head? "There are no whole truths; all truths are half-truths. It is trying to treat them as whole truths that plays the devil."

6 Analyze the following descriptions using the three questions suggested in the chapter.

(a) "Sam, you're really going to like this girl—she's got a great personality, an inner beauty, she's a great listener . . . and her father, Sam, her father is . . ."

(b) "I tell you friend, this car is a little beauty. It's got real class. Look at the shine on that hood. I've even marked it down for a fast sale to the right person."

(c) "As part of my application for this job, I want to emphasize selected highlights from my rich past experience."

(d) "The average salary in this agency has shown a steady increase that comes to about $2,000 over the past two years." "But only the top executives' salaries have changed. You fink!"

(e) "I'm a physics major and my grade-point average is 4.0." "You have 16 pass/fail courses and only one graded course—basket weaving. That's a weird school you go to."

FOR FURTHER READING

1 H. Schwartz and J. Jacobs. *Qualitative Sociology: A Method to the Madness.* New York: The Free Press, 1979.

A qualitative methods textbook which combines what one needs to know in order to actually conduct such a research investigation with a critical examination of each method's strengths and weaknesses.

2 M. Monmonier. *How to Lie with Maps.* The University of Chicago Press, 1991.

Equally delightful, equally readable. An informative and enjoyable introduction to what maps can do *to* us as well as what they do *for* us.

3 S. K. Campbell. *Flaws and Fallacies in Statistical Thinking.* Englewood Cliffs, NJ: Prentice Hall, 1974.

4 D. Huff. *How to Lie with Statistics.* New York: Norton, 1993.

5 R. Reichard. *The Figure Finaglers.* New York: McGraw-Hill, 1974.

6 R. P. Runyon. *Winning with Statistics.* Reading, MA: Addison-Wesley, 1977.

7 H. Zeisel. *Say It with Figures,* 6th ed. New York: Harper & Row, 1985.

These are enjoyable, nontechnical introductions to distorted summaries and how to recognize them. The chapters are short, the examples are amusing, and the cartoons are funny. All the books review some of the material we've talked about in terms of averages and percentages. They also discuss graphs and other kinds of summaries you may be subjected to.

8 M. H. Maier. *The Data Game: Controversies in Social Science Statistics,* 2nd ed. Armonk, NY: M. E. Sharpe, Inc., 1995.

Are reports based on governmental databases unambiguous? Maier's delightful book looks at various social issues (e.g., unemployment, crime) and demonstrates how descriptions based on alternative, but official, databases lead to different conclusions.

11

RELATIONSHIPS:
MORE INFORMATIVE,
BUT MORE DIFFICULT
TO UNDERSTAND

Although he put in a full night studying for the social studies test, his grade was only 56. Later, he had the following discussion with the teacher:

Student: I'm very upset with my grade. I worked very hard for this exam and all I got was a 56.

Teacher: That is very upsetting. How about if we go over what you did to see if I can help you for the next exam?

Student: What really annoys me is that I stayed up almost all night; I must have studied about six hours. I can't work any harder than that. Perhaps social studies is just too difficult for me.

Teacher: Well, I don't think it's too hard for you. I know you're interested in what we're talking about.

Student: Yes, I am interested, and I put in so many hours preparing for the exam.

Teacher: I believe you. I don't think a lack of motivation or interest it the problem. My hunch is that the problem lies in your studying.

Student: But I can't work any harder than I did.

Teacher: I agree—and you shouldn't have to. The problem is learning to study smarter rather than harder.

Student: What do you mean?

Teacher: Well, for one thing, we know that it isn't good to cram the night before. It's much better to spread your studying over a couple of days. That way you aren't as tired or as pressured, and you have a chance to think about what you're reading so it makes sense to you.

Student: There was a lot to learn that night.

Teacher: I think you can do a lot by improving your study skills. Remember, "smarter" not "harder."

Student: You mean like studying a few hours for several nights instead of cramming just the night before?

Teacher: Right. You keep up your interest and hard work, but make that one change, and I'm pretty sure your grade will go up on the next exam—perhaps quite a lot.

Notice that the student didn't question his grade. He simply didn't answer many questions correctly and, as a result, got a low score. In terms of the previous chapter, we would say that a 56 was part of a "fair description" of the student's performance. But as a description it took into account only the grade. As you can tell from the conversation, just focusing on the grade or the number of hours studied wasn't enough to help the student understand *why* he got a low grade or *what* he can do about it. To help with these questions, other aspects of the situation such as motivation, interest, and the distribution of study time also needed to be considered.

What was true for the student is true for consumers of research as well. A fair description of each single aspect (or variable) of what's being studied is necessary, but it will usually not be enough. Instead, readers of research (and researchers as well) are interested in a variable, such as exam scores, because they want to understand it better or because they want to be able to make predictions about it. To gain understanding or to improve our ability to predict requires that we learn how the one variable we're interested in relates to other variables.

Notice that the teacher has an idea of what some of the important variables are which are related to test performance: interest, motivation, and study habits. In addition, the teacher believes the student can make good use of one of these relationships. She predicts he will do better in the course if he distributes his studying instead of just cramming the night before. The teacher is able to make this prediction because the two variables (study habits and test performance) are related.[1]

THE IMPORTANCE OF RELATIONSHIPS

The discovery of relationships between variables is probably one of the most important things researchers try to do. If one variable turns out to be related to another variable, the researcher has learned something which may help lead to a better understanding of the first in terms of the second. Once a relationship has been spotted, researchers try to describe it in a way that increases our understanding of the variables or our ability to predict one from knowledge of the other.

The point of this chapter is not to explore the more technical details about how to figure out relationships mathematically but to emphasize the importance of checking to see whether the researcher has even thought about relationships. Describing variables one by one is often important to do, and it's important to make those descriptions fair, as discussed in the previous chapter. But to stop there without considering relationships between the variables will not provide much insight into what is being studied. So it's very important that you check to see if researchers have gone beyond

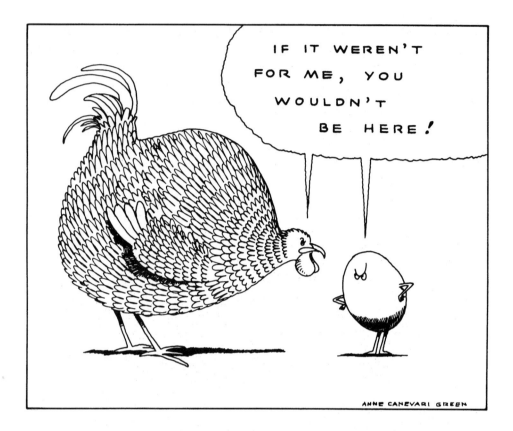

looking at variables one at a time, that they have searched for and interpreted how two or more variables relate to one another. You should expect researchers to try to find out if there is a relationship, and if so, how it can be best described.[2]

But even this is not enough. Many researchers do analyze relationships, but sometimes not properly. When this happens, the result will not be a "fair description" of the relationship. Several different factors can affect the interpretation and use of relationships. If the researcher doesn't know about these factors or can't recognize them when they occur, the conclusions reported are very likely to be questionable and, on occasion, blatantly wrong. These factors can affect all relationships, regardless of how they were found or of the style used to report them. It does not matter whether the relationships were discovered by an analysis of statistics or through a study of historical writings or whether they were based on the author's considerable experience. If any of these factors affect a relationship in something you're reading, you will need to be very cautious in the conclusions you draw from that study.

Third Variables

The first of these factors addresses the role of "third variables." A relationship exists between two variables, but other variables (each of which is, somewhat awkwardly, considered a "third" variable) may affect the interpretation of that relationship. For example, if you analyzed over the last 30 years the amount of children's allowances and the price of whiskey, you would probably find that these two variables are positively related: the amount given in weekly allowances increased and so did the price of liquor. But that relationship, regardless of its strength, is meaningless because both of the variables are affected by a number of third variables, such as the increase in all prices due to inflation. That is, the relationship as presented suggests some direct link between the two variables (whiskey prices and children's allowances), but such an interpretation would be incorrect because it is likely that general economic factors such as inflation affected both variables.

Similarly, you can also question the relationship which exists between the ages of elementary school children and their reading ability or between the amount of education people have and their incomes. It isn't that these relationships don't exist; instead it is a question of how third variables affect our understanding of the relationship. Thus, we would expect the amount of reading instruction to be a third variable, affecting the relationship between the age of elementary school children and their reading ability. Similarly, occupation probably plays a role in the relationship between education and income.

A Hypothetical Case   Sometimes our understanding is completely changed through the consideration of a third variable. Consider the following hypothetical example.

> The local Community Center has been charged with sex discrimination in its athletic program for 8- to 10-year-olds. The center runs a spring softball and a winter basketball league. All the teams are coed. There are always more youngsters interested in joining than there are teams to put them on. So a small group of coaches and parents makes the final decision based on their estimates of the children's abilities. Parents of those children who are not selected are, of course, disappointed. This year, however, a few of them noticed that more boys were playing than girls and claimed that the leagues discriminated on the basis of sex. To support their claim, they pointed out that over the past two years, 120 boys and 120 girls signed up to play in one of the leagues, and of these, 79 boys and 64 girls were selected. In percentage terms, 66 percent of the boys who applied, but only 53 percent of the girls, were chosen for the sports teams. From these figures, the disgruntled parents concluded that sex discrimination exists: it favors boys in the amount of 13 percent.

Is that correct? On the face of it, the evidence seems compelling; there are more boys playing in the leagues even though an equal number of boys and girls applied. Moreover, a 13 percent difference is not trivial. So, do the facts support the conclusion?

Well, as you might have guessed, the answer is not as simple as it appears. There is a relationship between the two variables, sex and rate of acceptance, and these two variables are obviously the most important ones when thinking about the possibility of sex discrimination. But other variables may also play a role here. Athletic ability of the children is one. Another might be the amount of previous experience the children had playing each sport. You can probably think of others. If we had information about these variables, we could see whether they might have played a role here.

Include Third Variables in the Analysis   Unfortunately, looking at any of these variables one at a time is not likely to reveal very much. What must be done is to somehow incorporate the third variable into the analysis of the relationship between sex and rate of acceptance in the sports program. Let's do that with a specific third variable, the sport (basketball or softball) each child wanted to play, and see how it might affect our interpretation of the data. To do that we simply need to find out the percent of boys and girls accepted in each of the sports. We know that 13 percent more boys than girls were accepted in the athletic program, but is that 13 percent difference true for both softball and basketball? The following table gives the information about how many boys and girls applied to and were accepted by each sport.

	Boys			Girls		
	Number applied	Number accepted	Percent	Number applied	Number accepted	Percent
Softball	92	69	75	40	32	80
Basketball	28	10	36	80	32	40
Total	120	79	66	120	64	53

Note 13 percent difference

The bottom row of this table provides the same data that were presented by the parents in their charge of sex discrimination: overall, 66 percent of the boys, but only 53 percent of the girls, were accepted. Now look at the situation for each sport. In softball, 75 percent of the boys who applied were accepted and 80 percent of the girls were accepted. In this sport at least, there isn't any sex bias favoring the boys; there is a slight, but probably not meaningful, difference in favor of the girls. In basketball we see a similar pattern: there is a slight difference in acceptance rates favoring the girls (40 percent versus 36 percent).

So what appeared to be an overall sex bias in favor of boys disappears when the third variable (sport desired) is taken into account. What happened here is that lots of boys, but few girls, applied for positions in softball, and a high percentage of *both* sexes were accepted to play in that sport; the result was that more boys were selected. Basketball, in contrast, is much harder to get into (perhaps because there are fewer players on a basketball team), but that is where most of the girls applied. Both sexes had relatively low rates of acceptance for basketball. Taken together, the different sport preferences of each sex coupled with the different rates of acceptance for each sport led to the overall result that more boys were playing in the athletic program.

The Added Value of Relationships   The point of this example is that relationships by themselves usually communicate more than variables analyzed one at a time; they provide the context needed for a better understanding. But it may not be enough to think about relationships presented just in terms of two variables. We need to consider possible third variables, because they can change our interpretation of the relationship, often dramatically. Good researchers will include key third variables in their analyses, but that does not mean they've thought of all of them. More importantly, there will also be many relationships reported in the literature you read in which the author did not build in an explicit consideration of third variables. Though you can't redo their analysis with third variables, you can think about them and try to guess if there would be a different relationship if they were included.

Crossing Levels

In the 1930 census the United States was divided into nine geographic regions. From that census it is easy to obtain data for many variables in each of the nine regions. Of these, let's look at just two: the percent of the population in the region which is illiterate and the percent which is black. The relationship between these two variables was computed from the census data and summarized in a single statistic of .95.[3] This is a very strong positive relationship, since the statistic is close to its maximum value of 1.00. This means that if the percentage of illiteracy is high in the region, there is a corresponding high percentage of blacks living in that region.

We don't doubt this figure, but we must remember it for what it is: a relationship between the two variables in the nine regions. In this example, researchers would say that the analysis was at the region "level." But, the same relationship could also be studied at several other levels. Some of these levels (such as nation) would be "higher" than the level of region, while some (such as city) would be at a lower level than region.

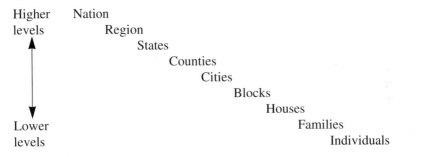

For the same two variables, there is no guarantee that the relationship computed at one level will equal the relationship at another level. In fact, it is highly unlikely that the same relationship from two different levels will be equal. Using census data from the preceding example, the relationship between race and illiteracy was also computed at the level of the state and at the level of the individual. What was .95 for the region dropped to .77 for the states. At the level of the individual, the relationship between the same two variables dropped dramatically to .20. That is, the relationship between an individual being illiterate and being black at that level was only .20. The difference among these results (.95, .77, and .20) is so striking that it is easy to understand that vastly different kinds of conclusions are called for, depending upon the level used.

Crossing Levels Can Be Risky   What we've seen in this example is true in general. Looking at relations at one level, but making conclusions at another level, will usually lead to mistakes—often sizable ones.[4] Given what happens when levels of analysis are crossed, you might wonder why anyone would use data from the wrong level. Crossing of levels occurs because it is often easier to obtain existing information about relationships at a (too) high level than it is to collect new information about the relationship at a lower level where the researcher wants to make the conclusions. Organizations and governmental agencies regularly collect data from which relationships can be uncovered. But this information is usually at a high level of analysis. For instance, an organization often cares more about the performance of each of its divisions than it does about each of its work teams. Similarly, governmental archives have more data about cities than they do about individuals. So data at a high level can be found, often easily, and it is tempting to use these data to provide clues about the relationship at another level, where the data are harder to come by. But such "clues" are usually so far off base that it would be wiser to ignore them altogether.

As a reader of research, you need to watch out for crossing levels when relationships are being discussed. If you discover that levels have been crossed, the safest bet is to not believe the researcher's conclusion about that relationship.

Freedom to Vary

The relationship between two variables also depends upon how much "freedom" each of the variables has. For example, look at the variable height for adults. If a group of adults were selected haphazardly off the street, their heights would spread out between five and seven feet. We could say that height, in this case, would have about two feet of freedom. In contrast, suppose we were studying the heights of professional basketball players. For this group, the heights might range from six to seven feet, only one foot of freedom. To take another example, consider intelligence. For most of the people in the general population, intelligence scores could be as low as 76 and as high as 124; there would be 48 units of freedom. Compare this to the amount of freedom in the IQs of doctors. Because it is unlikely that people with very low IQs would have been admitted to medical school, the amount of freedom in the IQs of physicians will be much less than 48.

How does this idea of freedom affect relationships? A relationship exists when the values of one variable tend to change in some systematic way when the values of the second variable change. Height and weight are related, and therefore we would expect tall people in general to weigh more and short people to weigh less. Thus, there is a general pattern of height changing as weight changes. Relationships require a systematic pattern between the variables, and that pattern (if it exists) can occur only if both variables have some freedom to vary.

The Other Extreme—No Freedom   To understand this, consider the most extreme opposite situation. Suppose one of the variables has no freedom at all, such as people who weigh exactly 110.235 pounds.[5] The heights of these people would still vary somewhat, but notice that there could not be any systematic pattern of relationship between the two variables: as the heights change, the weights remain the same. Therefore, for this group of people, there cannot be any relationship between height and weight.

That's the extreme case; it rarely occurs in real research projects. What does occur is something between the two extremes of complete freedom and no freedom. When this happens, the relationship turns out to be somewhere between what it would be at the extremes. Suppose the relationship between height and weight among a general group of adults turned out to be moderately strong when calculated statistically. Let's assume the statistic would have a value of .65, out of a maximum of 1.00. This figure represents the size of the relationship when both variables are completely free to vary. If one or both of the variables could not vary at all, the statistic would equal zero. Somewhere between zero and .65 is the value the statistic would equal if there was some (but not complete) constraint on the freedom of one or both of the variables. Thus, if a researcher who was studying the relationship between height and weight based the results on a sample of basketball players, the statistic would have to be lower than .65, perhaps quite a bit lower.

Now, there is nothing wrong with the answer the researcher gets for basketball players. The problem emerges when the researcher isn't aware that one (or both) of the variables is not completely free to vary. In such a situation, the researcher will report the relationship and the reader will naturally assume it applies to a more general population, rather than to the "constrained" group which was actually studied. Thus, the readers will be given incorrect information about the relationship. But perhaps more importantly, it is also possible that readers will be told nothing at all because the results may be so low that the researcher will mistakenly conclude that no relationship exists and as a result will not publish the study.

Causality and Relationships

Among all the factors about relationships, probably none has been discussed more often than the topic of cause and effect. In the social sciences, this discussion is particularly important because most of the relationships studied are done in the hope that a causal connection can be discovered.

Most people are probably well aware that all relationships are not causal relationships; just because one variable is related to another does not mean that it caused the other. Well-known it may be, but surprisingly you can still find examples which suggest otherwise. While no one would argue that the amount of allowance given children causes specific whiskey prices, we can find examples which at first do suggest a causal connection between the variables, but on closer inspection, the causal link is seen as weak or nonexisting. Consider the following examples:

Example 1

The two variables are: the degree to which the husband distances himself from his spouse, and the amount of complaining his wife does.

In this first example, the husband believes that he keeps away from his wife because she complains all the time, that is, the cause is her complaining, the result is his distancing. While that may be true, we can learn something if we could turn the causal relationship around. Could it happen the other way, that the wife complains *because* her husband is not available? This view of the causal connection between the two variables also seems plausible; in fact, we would predict that the wife believes that this is the accurate version of what is happening in their relationship.

What this example demonstrates is that some relationships can be thought of in either direction; variable A could cause variable B, or it could be the other way around. Obviously, when a relationship can be seen this way, it makes it very difficult to argue for any causal connection between the two variables, because in order for one variable to cause another, the first must precede the second.

Let's look at another relationship that can be considered in either direction: It is well known that many cancer patients are depressed. From this relationship, some people have claimed that depression can lead to cancer. But isn't it also possible to turn this around and say that if a person has cancer, that person will become depressed? Because you can turn the relationship around, we can't be sure which variable came first and which came second. To determine a causal connection between these two variables will require more information than just the fact that depression and cancer may be related.

Example 2

The two variables are: one's height at age two and one's height at age 20.

In this second example, the relationship can't be turned around because there is only one way to order the variables: height at age two comes before height at age 20. So *if* the author wanted to say that these two variables are causally related, the earlier heights would have to be the cause of the later heights. But, knowing the direction of the relationship, as in this example, still isn't enough to argue convincingly that the relationship is causal. In this case, we are able to dismiss the causal connection between the two variables because we can probably think of other possible causes of one's height at age 20, such as heredity, health, or diet. Probably one or more of these third variables is the cause of both infant and adult heights.

Three Guidelines for Determining Causal Relationships   For a researcher to claim that one variable caused another, the researcher must first of all demonstrate that a relationship exists between the two variables. Given the existence of a relationship, the researcher must then deal with the lessons learned from the above examples. The researcher must be able to convince you that the two variables can be ordered in only one way. And, the researcher must ensure that other possible causes (third variables) do not exist in the setting being investigated. As a critical reader, you need to ask yourself the following questions:

• Can you find a weakness in the researcher's claim that a relationship exists?
• Can you turn the relationship around or argue that the variable that is supposed to be the cause did not occur before the other variable?

• Can you identify plausible third variables which might be the cause or part of the cause?

Answering yes to any one of these questions means that the researcher has not been able to make a strong case that a causal relationship exists between the two variables.

Causality is a very complex issue involving research methods, philosophy, and argument. It would be difficult to deal with it adequately in a lengthy essay, let alone in one section of a chapter about relationships. We began this discussion of causality in the context of relationships, because they are the key to understanding a lot of research that is reported. But as the preceding paragraphs note, there is more to causality than relationships. These other considerations are discussed more completely in the next chapter.

QUESTIONS TO ASK

1 Was the analysis or the conclusion based on a single variable?
Rarely will this type of simple analysis be sufficient. Usually, to understand what's occurring, you will need to think about a variable in terms of how it relates to other variables. If the researcher hasn't done that, you need to think about other variables which might be related to what was reported. Then you have to ask yourself whether the interpretation would be the same if these other variables had been included in the analysis. While it may not be possible to know for sure how other variables would affect the results, merely raising the possibility that something might change in the bivariate analysis is useful.

2 What about "third" variables?
This is really two questions in one: (a) Did the researcher consider the possible effects of third variables? (b) Can you think of any other variables, not considered by the researcher, which may affect the relationships? Third variables can have a variety of effects on relationships. Some will not affect the relationship at all, suggesting that they don't play a role and need not be considered further. Others will, when explicitly considered, make important changes in the relationship, changing a moderate one to a weak one or a weak one to a strong one. It is difficult to really understand a relationship until the effects of plausible third variables have been included in the analysis.

3 Is the level at which the relationship was determined the same as the level at which the conclusions are drawn?
We must be sure that the interpretation of relationships occurs at the same level the data were collected. If the researcher did cross levels, remember that the reported relationship is rarely (if ever) close to what the relationship really is at the level of the conclusions.

4 Was each variable free to vary to its full extent?
If it wasn't, then the relationship reported by the researcher will be less than would have been found if full freedom had existed.

5 Was a causal relationship stated or implied?
If the researcher interprets the results in terms of causality, three ingredients must be included in the argument. First, there has to be a relationship—that's what most of this chapter is about. There must also be some consideration of the sequence of the two variables and of whether other third variables could have been the cause.

PRACTICE EVALUATIONS

Reminder: Answering the above questions yourself is good practice. Chapter 18 provides guidelines for you to follow in doing that. Chapter 19 provides two articles along with our evaluations of them. Chapter 20 provides two additional articles for you to practice on.

FOR FURTHER THOUGHT

1 For each of the following items, state the possible relationship and then identify a third variable which is likely to affect that relationship.
   (a) The degree to which people wear bifocals and their marital status
   (b) The infant mortality rate and the average life expectancy
   (c) The amount of formal education people have and the intelligence of their in-laws
   (d) The percentage of college graduates living in the local congressional district and the average price of homes in that district
   (e) How much electricity is used per day in homes and the number of cars per day which break down and require highway assistance
   (f) The degree to which housing is segregated in a community, and the quality of the public school system in that community
2 What, if anything, is the causal connection between the two variables in each of the above relationships?
3 Reconsider the preceding list of relationships. For each, invent a plausible way in which there could be a "crossing of levels."
4 Which relationship in each of the following pairs of relationships is likely to be stronger? Why?
   (a-1) The relationship between beauty and intelligence among those entering the first round of a beauty competition
   (a-2) The relationship between beauty and intelligence among those competing in the final round of a beauty competition
   (b-1) The relationship between SAT scores and college grade-point average at the end of the freshman year
   (b-2) The relationship between GRE scores and college grade-point average at the end of the first year of graduate school
   (c-1) For new cars, the relationship between their cost and the degree to which they are judged safe by an independent laboratory
   (c-2) For cars seven years old, the relationship between their original cost and the degree to which they were judged safe

FOR FURTHER READING

1 H. Zeisel. *Say It with Figures,* 5th ed. New York: Harper & Row, 1968.

   An introduction to the study of relationships with lots of examples which are as delightful to consider as they are constructive.

2 S. K. Campbell. *Flaws and Fallacies in Statistical Thinking.* Englewood Cliffs, NJ: Prentice Hall, 1974.

   See Chapter 13 on relationships.

3 E. Babbie. *The Practice of Social Research,* 7th ed. Belmont, CA: Wadsworth, 1995.

Pages 63–79, "The Nature of Causation," offer a more developed, but still introductory, discussion of understanding what social researchers are supposed to be thinking about as they try to construct a causal argument.

12

CONTROL: RIVAL EXPLANATIONS . . . IS SOMETHING ELSE AT WORK?

Most people don't wear garlic cloves around their necks to cure a cold. But some people do, and they believe it works. Rather than casually dismissing this belief as a case of simple superstition, let's take a closer look at why it might be believed. Presumably, the type of supporting evidence that is used comes from experience. A believer might argue as follows: "I had a cold, I wore garlic cloves around my neck, and then the cold got better." Taken quite literally the statement could easily be correct. The next time you get a cold, wear garlic cloves around your neck, and we would predict that your cold will get better.

Of course, you are not fooled by this. The facts as reported by the believer may be true, but the implication is not. Clearly the believer's experience with wearing garlic is not strong enough evidence to conclude that garlic helps cure colds.

In Chapter 11 we pointed out that to determine a causal relationship, the researcher must eliminate from consideration all other potential causes. To show that wearing garlic does relate to curing a cold, a researcher needs to identify other variables which might cure the cold and find a way to eliminate them from consideration. If no other possible variables could have cured the cold, then the researcher is left with only one possible cause, the garlic.

Underlying Patterns of Thought

What is important is the underlying pattern of thought. Although the pattern is common in both everyday situations and in research settings, it has serious shortcomings. Consider the following vignettes:

1 A teacher believes that the students are not doing well in spelling. A new spelling program is initiated and later testing shows that spelling has improved. Therefore, the teacher concludes that the new program caused the improvement.

2 A manager wants to improve employee morale. A series of discussion groups are formed to promote interaction among the workers. Sometime later the manager re-assesses the morale and believes it has improved. Therefore, the manager concludes that the discussion groups caused the improvement.

3 A therapist works with a client with emotional problems. The client is asked to do a variety of exercises at home as well as in the therapist's office. The severity of the client's problems decreases. Therefore, the therapist concludes that the exercises caused the change.

What's Wrong with A . . . B . . . C?

The same general pattern of thought runs through each of these examples. We can diagram this pattern using Ⓐ as a symbol for the original situation; Ⓑ as a symbol for the change in practice, or the treatment, or anything done to change the situation; and Ⓒ as a symbol for the new version of Ⓐ.

If Ⓐ came first, and then Ⓑ and then Ⓒ, and if Ⓒ is different from Ⓐ, then it is concluded that Ⓑ caused this difference.

In the garlic example, Ⓐ is having a cold, Ⓑ is wearing garlic, and Ⓒ is no longer having the cold.

While we may doubt the efficacy of garlic as a cure, a possibility exists that the new spelling program did cause the improvement in pupil spelling, or the group discussions did raise morale, or the specific type of exercise did help the client. Unfortunately, the pattern of thought underlying these situations is the same as in the garlic example and does not by itself strongly support the conclusions of the teacher, manager, or therapist. The weaknesses of this pattern of thought and what clues you should look for to see if the researcher has overcome them are discussed in this chapter.

Possible Rivals to B

In each of the preceding examples Ⓑ represents a variable[1] which is a possible cause of the difference between Ⓐ and Ⓒ. In each case, other variables, called "rival explanations," could also be suggested as possible causes. In the garlic "theory" of curing colds, the obvious rival explanation is that the cold got better because of normal bodily reactions to the cold virus. Medical science may not know exactly what these reactions are, but garlic as a factor can be ruled out; curing a cold without garlic takes seven days, with garlic it takes only a week. In the other examples, numerous rival explanations can be offered. A plausible one suggests that additional attention is the cause. For the teacher, the manager, and the therapist the extra attention and time devoted to the problem produced the change rather than the specific spelling program, the type of group instruction, or the kind of exercises employed.

The Hawthorne effect is not the only possibility. To begin a more thorough list of rival explanations which are viable in these examples, we need only to reconsider the biases due to the researcher and the biases due to the people being studied (see Chapter 6). This chapter will add still other possible rival explanations, and even then the list will not be complete. Clearly, this particular pattern of thought (or research design) which underlies these examples does not, by itself, make a strong methodological case for factual accuracy.

All the possible explanations are competing with one another, including **(B)**, the explanation given by the researcher, and alternative explanations you as a reader can think of. The winner of this competition would be that explanation that has the most support and makes the most sense. Sometimes several rival explanations are equally plausible. For readers of research, knowing which of these rival explanations is correct is of paramount importance. It would be a mistake and waste of time and money to adopt a new practice or implement a change and later discover that a rival explanation was the correct one.

Different patterns of thought permit a different number of rival explanations. A good social researcher will plan a study so that the underlying pattern of thought allows very few rival explanations. The better the research, the fewer alternatives possible, and the more trust a reader can place in the explanation given by the author. Your goal as a reader, then, is to be able to determine if rival explanations are possible.

LOOKING FOR RIVAL EXPLANATIONS

Asking what rival explanations are possible is always worthwhile. The more that's known about the subject matter of the study, the easier it will be to suggest alternative causes for what has occurred in an investigation. Over and above your knowledge of the subject matter you should look for three important *sources* of bias that may produce viable rival explanations: time, measurement, and people.

Time

The first of these sources is time. Time itself is rarely a rival explanation, but it is often a source of many rival explanations. In principle, anything occurring in time after Ⓐ but before Ⓒ could be considered as a possible cause of Ⓒ—a cause that rivals Ⓑ, the explanation offered by the researcher. Of course you can quickly eliminate earthquakes in China, the birth of a baby in Paris, or other seemingly irrelevant events. But other events that affect the people or objects being studied cannot be so easily dismissed. Often these events are clear-cut and pronounced, such as taking a drug, being fired from a job, or getting married. However, at other times the events are more diffuse, gradual, and less apparent—including the effects of decay, wear, aging, and growth.[2]

Some of the problems people have seem to get better or resolve themselves, even if nothing unusual is done in the interim. These "spontaneous" solutions occur for some medical and psychological problems as well as for all sorts of common everyday problems. So be wary about interpreting the outcomes of individual case studies in the therapeutic or human services situation—a person may have improved regardless of the services or treatment given. To ascribe the improvement to the services provided may be justified only if other possible causes can be discounted. The longer the time interval between Ⓐ and Ⓒ, the greater the opportunity for rival explanations to occur. But even in studies of short duration, rival explanations are possible.

Consider the situation facing a town's board of education. It wants to get support from the community for a bond issue. However, its initial survey of eligible voters indicated that the referendum will fail. To increase chances for success, members of the board decide to broadcast a series of TV spot announcements to present their appeal directly to the community. Two weeks after the TV spots are shown, the bonding referendum is approved in the vote. Can the board of education be confident that the TV spots helped?

No, it can't. This example is another instance of the Ⓐ then Ⓑ then Ⓒ thought pattern. The time interval between Ⓐ and Ⓒ should be searched for possible rival explanations. Perhaps other influencing activities took place during this period—editorials in the newspaper, PTA meetings, a phone-a-thon by concerned parents, and so forth. Before the board members accept the importance of TV spots, they need to be able to discount the effects of other sources of information and influence.

Process of Measurement

The second source of rival explanations is the process of measurement. In order to determine the existing conditions at time (A), the researcher needs to observe or measure them, and may inadvertently change those conditions to produce (C). That is, the process of determining (A) may be the cause of (C).

This "testing effect" happens often in studies of what people know or believe. If the researcher asks people about their attitudes, the very act of asking may change their beliefs by stimulating them to seek additional information or to think about the issue. They may become more aware of an issue that was previously dormant or unimportant. At time (C) these people are changed, not because of variable (B) as the researcher would have you believe, but solely because of the researcher's intervention at time (A).

Consider again the problem of the board of education and its attempt to get a bonding plan supported. The board members used a telephone survey to determine (A), the amount of support they could expect from the community. That survey may have gotten the members of the community interested and concerned about the future of the school system. By itself, the survey may have triggered enough of a reaction to pass the referendum even if no TV spots were shown.

People Being Studied

The people (or the groups, things, or objects) being studied are the third source of rival explanations. Since the researcher's conclusions depend upon an analysis of people, any distortion caused by the people could lead to incorrect results. People distortions can occur whenever there is something unusual about the makeup of the individuals who participate in the study. What we mean by "unusual" will become clearer after some examples.

Suppose people are chosen to participate in a study in the following way. All the people are measured or observed initially at time (A). But only those who score above (or below) a certain level remain in the study; the others are excluded. This practice is much more common than it may first appear. Remedial education uses some diagnostic tests to classify students, and only those with low scores are given special attention. For gifted children the criterion level is the high end of the scores. Medical treatment, psychological counseling, or social services are often given or available only to people who exceed a certain threshold as determined by measurement or observation. Administrators may wait until things get very bad before taking corrective action. The same is often true of parents—children will not get reprimanded until the disturbing behavior becomes intolerable.

All these cases involve some measurement or observation at time (A) to select those who will be given (B), the additional attention or treatment. Later, at time (C), the researcher (or teacher, therapist, administrator, parent, and so on) measures these people again to see if the treatment had any effect. If the results at time (C) differ from those at time (A), the researcher would like to believe that the additional treatment produced the change. And indeed it might; (B) could have produced the change.

Unfortunately, whenever people are chosen to participate in a study according to their scores at time (A), there is a rival explanation for the results. This rival explanation could account for all or part of the reason why Ⓒ differs from Ⓐ. To understand why, recall our discussion of reliability presented in Chapter 9. Random error is the cause of unreliable measurements or observations. Random error may decrease a person's score at one time and increase it at another time.

All measures or observations are to some degree unreliable, and this fact alone causes researchers enough headaches. But if people are initially chosen to participate in a study (or to receive any kind of special attention) because of scores obtained from unreliable measurement procedures at Ⓐ, then the researcher also has to worry about the possibility that the change observed at time Ⓒ may be due to nothing more than random error fluctuations.

A Classroom Test Example

As an example consider a classroom test given to 12 students. The purpose of the test is to identify those students who would profit from additional practice and attention. The six lowest-scoring students are to be given the extra tutoring. To begin with, suppose the test were perfectly reliable; no random error components are present in the scores. These reliable scores are given in the first column in the table below.

The second column contains the random error component, which will make the obtained scores somewhat unreliable. These can rarely be known; we've just invented them for this example. To keep the example simple, three points will alternately be added and subtracted from the scores in column 1. The third column contains the scores actually obtained by each student. They are the unreliable measures the teacher used to identify the six lowest-scoring students. Those six are D, F, H, J, K, and L; the average score for these six students is 82.5.

Student	1 Score on test with perfect reliability	2 Random error component	3 Actual score obtained on test
A	92	+3	95
B	92	−3	89
C	90	+3	93
D	89	−3	86 — low
E	87	+3	90
F	87	−3	84 — low
G	87	+3	90
H	86	−3	83 — low
I	84	+3	87
J	83	−3	80 — low
K	81	+3	84 — low
L	81	−3	78 — low

Take a minute to study the numbers in the table—don't skip over it, because the rest of this example depends upon your understanding of it.

After the test the six low-scoring students are given tutoring and extra work in order to improve their performance. Suppose for the moment that the tutoring did *not* help—the treatment given by the teacher had absolutely no effect on the students. What scores would these six students get on later testing at time Ⓒ?

Each student would be expected to obtain the same score after tutoring as at time Ⓐ (before tutoring)—except for the random error component. If the tutoring had no effect, the student's score should not change except for lack of reliability. The random error components of the scores at time Ⓒ ought to be like those at time Ⓐ. All this is shown again in the table below. The first-column scores for these six students are copied unchanged from the preceding table. Then, to illustrate the effect of random error, three points are again alternately added and subtracted, resulting in the actual scores these six students obtained after *ineffective* tutoring. The average obtained score for these six students at time Ⓒ is 84.5. Notice what has happened. Before tutoring, these students scored an average of 82.5. After tutoring, their average was 84.5. A reasonable improvement.

Student		Obtained score
D	89 + 3 =	92
F	87 − 3 =	84
H	86 + 3 =	89
J	83 − 3 =	80
K	81 + 3 =	84
L	81 − 3 =	78

For this example we assumed that the tutoring did not affect the students at all. The scores at time Ⓐ and at time Ⓒ are identical except for random error. While the teacher would like to believe that the improvement was due to the tutoring, the rival explanation in this case is the correct one. The improvement in test scores is due simply to the fact that the six students were chosen on the basis of an unreliable test— random error produced the apparent change in performance.

In real situations you cannot know for certain that the treatment at time Ⓑ had no effect. If the treatment had no effect, all change in performance may have been due to random error. If Ⓑ had some effect, then only some of the change in performance may be due to random error. The key to this rival explanation is not simply unreliable measurement. All measurements are to some degree unreliable. The key is the choice of people to be given treatment at time Ⓑ. If only some people are chosen at time Ⓐ, and they are chosen because they scored very low (or very high) as determined by an unreliable test, then some of the change observed at time Ⓒ is not real.[3]

Dropout Bias

A slightly different, but related, kind of rival explanation occurs when all the people begin the study at time Ⓐ but some of them drop out before time Ⓒ. In contrast with the preceding situation, Ⓐ is not used to select those people who will be given the treatment. All people are given the treatment or the special attention. But for a variety of reasons, not all the people complete the study. Only some are observed at time $\bigcirc$. If people choose to leave the study for reasons unrelated to the goals of the study, there is no problem. Personal illness, forgetfulness, moving out of town, or a family crisis are usually inconsequential reasons for not completing the study. But if people do not finish because of what occurs in the study, then an alternative explanation for the findings may be possible.

That alternative explanation has been called the "dropout bias" or, more grimly, the "mortality effect." Let's consider an example of this effect which is in keeping with its name. Suppose a researcher is studying the effect on rats of a new appetite-suppressing drug. Throughout the study, the rats are allowed all the food they want. At time $\bigcirc$ the researcher determines how much each rat eats. The rats are then given the new drug. Later, at time $\bigcirc$, the researcher again figures out the amount consumed. The difference between the amounts eaten before and after the drug was administered is supposed to indicate the effect of the drug. But if some of the rats died as a result of the drug, then a rival explanation is possible.

If some rats died, then the rats at time $\bigcirc$ are unusual in the sense that they are not all of the rats that were measured at time $\bigcirc$. A difference in the amounts eaten may be more of a reflection of the rats that died than of the drug. Death by starvation or by digestive or metabolic disorders will exclude from the study those rats whose appetites were affected in some extreme manner, and the measurement occurring at the end of the study will be distorted because of this exclusion.

For this potential source of rival explanation to be present, three events must take place: (1) some people dropped out during the study and were not observed or measured at time $\bigcirc$; (2) these people dropped out because of something related to the special treatment given at time $\bigcirc$; and (3) the researcher compared the measures of all the people at time $\bigcirc$ with the results of only some of the people at time $\bigcirc$. If the third component is not present, there is no source of rival explanation. These conditions frequently exist—particularly in studies in which the researcher is interested in the average performance of a group of people. In a school setting, measures are taken at the beginning of the year and an average for the classroom (or for the school or school district) is computed. At the end of the year another measure is taken and a second average is computed. If students left the classroom or were not present for reasons related to the treatment (presumably classroom activities), then those students' scores should be removed from the first set of measures collected at the beginning of the year, and a new average computed.[4]

The task of detecting rival hypotheses to $\bigcirc$ is only part of the evaluation process. You also need to judge whether the researcher adequately prevented or somehow eliminated the viable rival explanations. That is, you need to be able to recognize those research procedures that control rival explanations.

CONTROLLING RIVAL EXPLANATIONS

Astronomers have an interesting problem: how to recognize intelligent life in the universe. Suppose there is some reason to believe that a certain star system is transmitting a message. A radio telescope on Earth may pick up that message, but it would be hopelessly mixed up with other sounds that occur naturally in space. Before scientists can translate the message, they need to identify it. How can they isolate the message and separate it from the other sounds?

One possibility is to use two radio telescopes. The first is focused directly on the target star system—the one thought to be sending the message. The second radio telescope is focused on an area next to that star system, but far enough away so as to miss the message. Under this plan both telescopes will receive the same extraneous signals emitted from that portion of space, but only the first telescope will receive the message. With the help of a computer the extraneous signals received by the second telescope can be subtracted away from the signals received from the first telescope— exposing the message.

Using Two or More Groups

A similar approach is used in social research to eliminate potential rival explanations. Instead of having one group of people, two or more are used. The study is designed so that at time C all the groups have been affected similarly by the rival explanations, but only one of the groups was affected by the treatment, B. By comparing the results of the different groups, the rival explanations can be accounted for and the role of B can be determined.

Whenever feasible, a researcher will use at least two groups that are identical in all respects save one. Only one group (called the experimental group) is given a special treatment or attention at time B. Such a procedure will account for most of the rival explanations mentioned earlier. In order to be sure that the TV spots helped win the referendum, the board of education should compare the votes of those people who saw the TV spots with the votes of those who did not. If these two groups of people voted similarly, then the TV spots probably did *not* cause the outcome. Some other rival explanation was the cause. But if the group that saw the TV spots supported the referendum more than the group that did not see them, then the spots probably had an effect on the vote. But why have the rival explanations been nullified or counteracted?

Time is eliminated as a source because it should affect both groups equally. If both groups are identical and exist at the same time, then any differences between the groups at the end of the study cannot be due to any time-related differences. Using two groups also eliminates the effect of A as a rival explanation. If both groups are measured similarly at time A, then A cannot have produced the differences between the groups at the end of the study. People are also eliminated as a source for rival explanations as long as the people in both groups are treated in the same way except for seeing or not seeing the TV spots.

Note that the presence of more than one group is not enough. The groups must be identical in all respects except for B. Being identical means that the people have to be very similar and have to be treated in the same way (except for B)) at the same time. Treating groups in the same way at the same time is understandable, though often hard to achieve. But how does a researcher form groups that are composed of similar individuals?

One approach is to find people who match one another—to make sure that the same percentage of females are in all groups, that the groups are close or equal in terms of the average socioeconomic status, number of siblings, height, knowledge of Greek, age, and so on. As you can imagine, matching people on each of these aspects would be difficult; matching on all possible aspects would be impossible.

Random Assignment to Groups

Luckily for the researcher, this kind of matching is not always needed. A simple technique eliminates the need for matching and makes the groups as similar as possible. That technique is called "random assignment" or sometimes simply "randomization."[5] Randomization indicates that a flip of a coin, or something equally random, determined which group each person is assigned to. This procedure is an example of the "mixing" process described in Chapter 7, which allows a researcher to turn unknown biases into noise. If nothing but a coin flip determines group membership, then it is unlikely that the groups should differ initially on any variable. By chance alone we would expect some tall people to be put into both groups. And the same quality would be true for socioeconomic status as well as the other aspects.

Randomization causes the groups to be similarly composed by removing any unknown biases. To be a bit more precise, randomization cannot guarantee that groups are equivalent; in fact, there is nothing any researcher can do that will guarantee this. There are three points to keep in mind when thinking about randomization. First, randomization is a process that can "mix up" thousands of unknown biases to help researchers deal with what they cannot control or do not know about. Second, this "mixing" has a better chance of working the larger the sample size, so as readers of research we need to pay attention to how many people (or objects or events) were being randomized.[6] Third, and perhaps most importantly, the researcher can often calculate the probability that the groups differ because of chance alone—so that the researcher will be able to figure out if randomization fails to mix up all the unknown biases.

For these reasons, researchers will use randomization if it is at all possible. We as readers ought to be on the lookout for the use of randomization because it is a strong indication that many rival explanations cannot occur. Randomization is not always possible, however. Researchers often have to study groups that already exist; membership cannot be rearranged to meet the desires of the researcher or the whims of a coin flip. Studies in education may use intact classes or schools or school districts. Investigations of personality traits, abilities, biological attributes, or demographic characteristics cannot usually employ randomization. If schizophrenics, or overachievers, or males need to be in one group, while nonschizophrenics, or underachievers, or females need to be in a second group, there isn't any way a coin flip (or anything else) can make these groups equal.

Just because randomization is not possible, the study is not worthless. Far from it— a study may possibly be as good as or even better than one employing randomization. What matters in this situation is how the researcher copes with the problem. Since randomization is not used, other evidence will need to be given showing that any differences existing between the groups did not affect the results. The point is that you must always be on the lookout for possible rival explanations and the controls used by the researcher to prevent them.

One last caution before ending this discussion. The groups need to be similar *throughout* the study, with the sole exception of $\textbf{B}$. Randomization makes them similar at the beginning of the study. If for any one of a variety of reasons people drop out of one group more than from another, then the groups at time $\textbf{C}$ may be different because of the dropout and not because of $\textbf{B}$.

Other General Remedies

Employing more than one group of similar people is the most general remedy for rival explanations. Other practices will also help. For example, to be able to discount the measurement process, several things can be done. If the measurement at time $\textbf{A}$ is the problem, then the researcher may choose a plan of attack that doesn't require any measurement at time $\textbf{A}$. Or if the measurement is required, techniques can be employed in ways that do not affect the people being studied.

Sometimes the $\textbf{A}$ measurement already exists. Demographic information can often be found in personnel files or official records. In educational studies, measures of aptitude, achievement, and intelligence are frequently available in a school office. In service profession studies, budget or staffing changes may indicate changes in requests for service; so might applications, phone queries, circulation records, or equipment usage. In general population studies, a lot of information can be obtained from public documents—voting registrations, phone books, tax and property rolls, automobile registrations, and other official records. Even when the needed information is not already in existence, it may sometimes be collected in ways that are unobtrusive and do not impinge upon the people being studied. Researchers can often acquire the information in a manner that is both ethically and experimentally acceptable.

If the researcher is concerned that fluctuating measurement standards may be the source of rival explanations,[7] other corrective procedures are applicable. Training judges and standardizing criteria will certainly help. Long, detailed measurements or evaluations of people should be handled so that fatigue or boredom does not unfairly affect those considered first or last. For instance, in grading essay exams, a teacher should evaluate one question completely for all the students before looking at the next question. Shuffling the exam papers before starting a new question also helps. When these steps are followed, distortions due to fatigue or boredom may still occur, but will affect the grading of a particular question in about the same manner for all students—no one student will be disadvantaged.

SOME REMAINING PROBLEMS

The drunk didn't mind the drinking, but the hangovers were unbearable. To relieve his discomfort, he tried to discover the cause of his morning-after agony. One night he drank only scotch and soda and got his usual hangover the following morning. On his next drinking bout he stuck to bourbon and soda, but the morning after was just as painful. Finally he tried limiting himself to brandy and soda. Again he woke up in agony. But he learned his lesson; he vowed to give up soda.

Admittedly the process isn't a very good piece of research. But it does illustrate a problem that confronts researchers and affects you as a potential user of research— what is the precise cause of what happened? In the drunk's case the precise cause of his hangovers was not the totality of what he drank, but only the alcohol part of it. Unfortunately he zeroed in on the wrong part.

Identify the "Precise" Cause

In the preceding chapter we looked at causality in the context of a discussion about relationships. Relationships are but one of several important factors which need to be considered whenever a researcher claims that one variable caused another. One of these factors involves rival explanations.[8] In well-conducted studies the researcher will be able to eliminate rival explanations for what occurred and conclude that (**B**) was the cause. But that is true only in a general sense. The precise cause for what happened is probably only a part of (**B**).

At the beginning of this chapter we described the situation facing the teacher whose pupils were having trouble with spelling. Reconsider that situation, but this time assume that a better research design was used, one that successfully eliminated most of the rival explanations. The teacher, then, can conclude with some degree of justification that the new spelling program caused this improvement. But what precisely is the spelling program and are all parts of it necessary?

The spelling program could include any number of components: new workbooks, slide or tape self-instruction, teacher demonstrations, spelling bees, and so on. Each of these components can be broken down into numerous subcomponents. The workbook has text, colored illustrations, and an underlying logic. Are all of these aspects necessary to the improvement of spelling, or only some? Further study is needed to dissect this educational package to identify the necessary parts. But what should a reader of the study do until then? To improve spelling in your classroom, do you need to apply the entire program, or will some key parts or substitutes work as well?

The problem of identifying the precise cause also arises whenever a treatment occurs over time. As the example below illustrates, causes can regress indefinitely.

Why are Robert and Jane getting divorced?
Because they fight a lot.

Why do they fight a lot?
Because Robert had a poor role model for a husband.

Why does Robert have a poor role model?
Because his father was rarely home.

Why was his father rarely home?
Because . . .

What is the precise cause or causes of the divorce? Probably a combination of many things. Each of the items above may have been necessary for the divorce, but none of them was probably sufficient to cause the divorce by itself.

A prolonged discussion of this topic will lead into a philosophical jungle of questions such as "What is really meant by cause?" and "How precise is precise?" That is not our intent. The issue was raised because of some very real consequences for potential users of research. While the researchers try to narrow down the cause, a reader can try some other avenue of approach. Chapter 15 discusses some of these alternatives.

Discounting Rival Explanations

One last point. To present a strong case that Ⓑ is the cause of something, potential rival explanations need to be discounted. Sometimes other kinds of methodological arguments are given to make this case. When used by themselves, these arguments are not strong enough to prove causality. Because they occur rather frequently—particularly in popularized writings—watch out for them.

The first uses time order alone to show causality: if Ⓑ precedes what happens, then Ⓑ must have caused what happens. When the problem is stated directly, Ⓑ obviously has not been shown to be the cause. But as described in the beginning of this chapter, this pattern of thought is very common, occasionally disguised, and often convincing.

The second kind of argument is based solely on the existence of a relationship to show causality: if Ⓑ is related to what happens, then Ⓑ caused what happens. But, as we've seen in the previous chapter, relationships by themselves are not necessarily causal. Often relationships exist, where it doesn't make sense to think about causality: does height cause weight? But sometimes, researchers use the existence of a relationship as their main (or sole) justification for believing that one of the variables caused the other.

One reason why these two arguments are so believable is that they exist whenever causality has been shown. If we know that Ⓑ caused something, then it must also be true that Ⓑ preceded it and that Ⓑ is related to it. Both of the arguments are necessary, but neither of them is sufficient—either singly or together. The missing ingredient is the elimination of those variables which could function as rival explanations. Without that, an author may hint at causality, a reader can infer causality, but the arguments given do not present a convincing methodological case for causality.

The search for causes is a very important goal in all sciences. It is not the only goal, however, and in some situations it may not be the most appropriate goal. It would be a mistake, therefore, to construe our emphasis on cause as indicating that we believe it to be the only valid goal of social research. Sometimes a careful description of the situation is needed. Other times the most useful goal might be to identify relationships that have been previously unknown. What matters, in general, is that the goal (whatever it is) was achieved competently and that the research results are useful to you.

SUMMARY

This has been a long chapter. Without some prior knowledge about something called experimental design, you probably found the chapter complex. As more and more details were presented, you may have lost sight of the overall logic. So a brief, very general, summary is in order.

Researchers and readers of research are very often concerned with causes. They want to know what improved or changed a person's behaviors or feelings. To discover the cause, researchers conduct a study, evaluate the evidence, and posit an explanation as the cause for what occurred. If the researcher is correct, something important has been learned. If the researcher is wrong, you would like to know it before you try to use the reported (but incorrect) findings.

The main defense you have as a reader is to intellectually challenge the researcher's explanation by suggesting alternative explanations as the cause. As the number of the plausibility of these rival explanations increases, the author's findings are less justified. The researcher may still be correct, but the explanation has not been sufficiently proved.

Good researchers will design studies to minimize the number of rival explanations. One technique that helps is the use of more than one group. Much better still is the use of two or more groups that are similar in all important respects except one—the alleged cause, Ⓑ. Random assignment helps make the groups similar at the beginning of the study, but the researcher also needs to ensure that they remain similar at the end. Groups have to be treated similarly and studied during the same time period. Other techniques were mentioned that can decrease rival explanations due to measurement. Unobtrusive measures are always preferable. So is the use of measurement standards and trained judges. Any deviation from these practices allows for rival explanations.

Eliminating rival explanations is only a beginning. Many studies are needed if a specific cause is to be discovered. Even then, some difficulties exist in knowing when to stop. That does not minimize the importance of knowing that Ⓑ is necessary for the results to occur.

In terms of error, this chapter has been concerned solely with biased rival explanations— especially those due to time, measurement, or people. If a study were conducted over and over again, each time with different groups of people, then a biased explanation is one that would affect all the studies in the same way. Research findings can also be incorrect because of noise. Accounting for chance as a rival explanation—or more precisely, the error arising from the short-run effects of noise—is the topic of the next chapter.

QUESTIONS TO ASK

1 **On the basis of your knowledge of the subject matter, can you think of any explanation for what happened in the study other than the one given by the researcher?**
External criteria as well as methodological criteria should always be applied. Use your understanding of the field to know what to look for and to know how serious each rival hypothesis may be.

2 **Did the researcher eliminate potential rival explanations in the design of the study?**
Uncontrolled rival explanations compete with the explanation given by the researcher. The fewer rival explanations possible, the more likely the researcher's explanation is correct.

Continued

3 **Was more than one group studied so that a comparison can be made?**
  With only one group, time, measurement, and people are viable sources of rival
  explanations.
4 **Were the groups identical in all essential respects except for the proposed cause?**
  Random assignment is the best way to achieve equality. If randomization was not used,
  what evidence is presented that the groups were identical? With two identical groups
  being studied, most other rival explanations are accounted for. Even so, question each of
  the three sources of rival explanations.
  (a) Were the groups studied simultaneously?
  (b) Was the measuring procedure biasing?
  (c) How were the people selected and treated?
5 **Are all parts of the proposed cause needed to produce the effect?**
  For theoretical as well as practical reasons it is often helpful to tease (**B**) apart to
  determine a more precise cause of what happened.

PRACTICE EVALUATIONS

Reminder: Answering the above questions yourself is good practice. Chapter 18 provides guidelines for you to follow in doing that. Chapter 19 provides two articles along
with our evaluations of them. Chapter 20 provides two additional articles for you to
practice on.

FOR FURTHER THOUGHT

1 Explain how medical charlatans get rich and get vocal supporters even though their cures do
  not work.
2 Look through the self-improvement ads in the back of many popular magazines. For each,
  try to identify one or more plausible rival explanations that could produce the results
  claimed for what is being sold.
3 In Chapter 6, the Hawthorne study was described. Can you classify this study in terms of the
  primary source of rival explanation (time, measurement, or people)?
4 Review this chapter, but substitute the words "teacher" or "manager" or "therapist" for "researcher." Do any of the problems of rival explanations affect practitioners as well as researchers? If so, what can the practitioners do to protect themselves?
5 Go through the glossary to find other rival explanations which are viable in the three examples given at the beginning of this chapter.
6 Interpret each of the following in terms of the content of this chapter.
  (a) A researcher trained a common flea to jump upon hearing the command to jump. When
      one leg of the flea was removed, the flea still jumped on command. A second leg was
      removed and the flea jumped as usual. Each of the remaining legs was removed and the
      flea continued to jump, until the last leg was removed. Then the flea did not jump. The
      researcher concluded that removing all of the legs from the flea made it deaf.
  (b) "The fact that John Doe, suffering from a phobia, gets better four years after psychoana-
      lytic treatment has been initiated is not proof that John Doe has got better *because* of
      such psychoanalytic treatment." (H. J. Eysenck)
  (c) "If an instance in which the phenomenon under investigation occurs, and an instance in
      which it does not occur, have every circumstance in common, save one, that one occur-
      ring in the former, the circumstance in which alone the two instances differ, is the cause,
      or an indispensable part of the cause of the phenomenon." (J. S. Mill)

FOR FURTHER READING

1 D. H. Fischer. *Historians' Fallacies.* New York: Harper & Row, 1970, pp. 146–86 (Chapter VI).

An interesting and well-written presentation of nine common causal fallacies. Some are semantic and complement the procedural concerns given in our chapter.

2 E. J. Webb; D. T. Campbell; R. D. Schwartz; and L. Sechrest. *Nonreactive Measures in Social Sciences,* 2nd ed. Boston: Houghton-Mifflin, 1981.

An important, often entertaining account of how researchers can be more creative about finding measures that do not affect the people being studied. Chapter 1 is particularly recommended as it also presents a different introduction to rival explanations.

3 H. W. Riecken and R. F. Boruch (Eds.). *Social Experimentation.* New York: Academic, 1974.

The book discusses the management of experiments that are conducted in everyday settings and how to detect their major weaknesses and strengths. The Appendix contains detailed examples of social change programs such as criminal reform, rehabilitation programs in mental health, and fertility control.

4 T. Pettigrew. *How to Think Like a Social Scientist.* HarperCollins, 1996.
5 M. R. Leary. *Introduction to Behavioral Research Methods,* 2nd ed. Pacific Grove, CA: Brooks/Cole Publishing, 1995, pp. 175–207 ("Basic Issues in Experimental Research").

These two readings present complementary views about the issues of comparison and control. Pettigrew's short and delightful book is worth reading completely, but it is included here for its presentation of comparisons and control in nonexperimental types of research. The chapter in Leary's text uses an error model as it considers the same issues from a more experimental viewpoint.

13

INFERENCE: ARE THE RESULTS REAL . . . OR COULD THEY HAVE BEEN CAUSED BY NOISE?

What's your reaction to these examples?

Example 1

This difference is significant beyond the .01 level ($\chi^2 = 9.59$, df $= 1$).

Example 2

	Vertical leadership		Horizontal leadership			
	$\bar{X}$	S.D.	$\bar{X}$	S.D.	t^*	p
Measure 1	50.78	7.20	39.98	9.90	3.29	<.01
Measure 2	8.55	3.39	6.85	2.26	1.29	NS

*Two-tailed t test for correlated measures; df $= 9$.

Example 3

Correlations among variables.

	Mass media use	Use of friends	Education	Age
Mass media use		.17	.47*	.06
Use of friends			.41†	.39†
Education				−.22
Age				

*$\alpha = .01$; †$\alpha = .05$.

Many people, including many professionals, are stymied when confronted by tables such as these. Our students report that they quickly skip over statistical tables and continue reading the text of the article. Such a reaction is unfortunate because readers cannot completely understand what is reported in the literature if they do not carefully consider tables like these. Beyond the matter of understanding, there are several important decisions you need to make when you read statistical results. And, as might be expected, these decisions require some minimal knowledge of the process of statistical inference.

What you need is enough of an understanding of statistical inference so you do not have to skip over the statistics and can intelligently make decisions about the results. In this chapter we will explain what statistical inference is about, and along the way you can become familiar with many of the common statistical symbols. While this chapter cannot be a complete course in statistics, enough is included so that you will be able to understand most of the statistical information you will come across in your professional reading. And, as a result, we hope that your initial negative reactions to statistics will be somewhat lessened.

STATISTICS AND RIVAL EXPLANATIONS

As you know from Chapter 7, random errors cancel out. But that is true only in the long run. In the short run practically anything can happen. A fair coin, for example, when flipped a few times may not seem fair; the number of heads and tails can turn out to be very unequal. Only when the coin is flipped a great many times should you expect the proportions of heads and tails to be close, and even then they are not likely to be exactly the same.

The same possibility is true in research. In the previous chapter we described the process of randomization as one that is supposed to eliminate any remaining unknown biases by mixing them up. As with the coin, how well randomization works depends upon the number of people or objects. If there are few, randomization may not work. If there are many, the process is more likely to work, but even then it is doubtful that the remaining biases will balance out exactly. So there is always a possibility that incomplete randomization will produce the results, rather than the cause posited by the researcher. That is, random error is a possible rival explanation. Like other possible rival explanations, it needs to be discounted before you can accept the author's explanation.

Discounting Random Error as Explanation

By using statistical inference, researchers can tell if random error may be discounted as a possible explanation. They do this taking sample size into account. Whether the number of people studied is small or large, if the sample is chosen properly, statistical inference helps distinguish between "real" research findings (assuming proper control has eliminated potential biases) and those likely to be caused by random error.[1]

One of the more common mistakes made by readers of research is to assume that the findings must be corrected if random error can be eliminated as a rival explanation. To avoid this error you need to remember that statistical inference helps to discount only one particular rival explanation: the short-run effect of random error. The other rival explanations must be dealt with by other means, as shown in Chapter 12. But the combination of randomization followed by statistical inference is quite valuable and will be used by researchers whenever possible. Randomization accounts for many rival explanations other than random error, and inference handles the random error.

An Example of Statistical Inference

An example would help. Suppose medical researchers want to compare two drugs in terms of the relief they bring from the symptoms of head colds. They design the study carefully using randomization to assign cold sufferers to one of two groups. They then administer drug A to one group of patients and drug B to the other group.

After the test period of use, the researcher finds that the people using drug A had more relief from the symptoms of head colds than did the users of drug B. Counting the number of sneezes per hour, the researcher discovers that the average for the group using drug A was 1.46 sneezes per hour, while the average for those using drug B was 3.13 sneezes per hour. Before the researchers publish these findings, they should determine that the difference between the groups' sneezing (that is, between 1.46 and 3.13) is due to the drugs and not to some rival explanation. Since a large number of people were randomly assigned to each group, the researchers can be confident that the obtained results could not be due to unknown biases. The remaining rival explanation that needs to be discounted is the effect of random error. That is, the researchers need to determine if the results are real and not due to chance.

To obtain a better understanding of the researcher's problem, think about a hypothetical case where both groups of people were administered the identical drug. In such a situation, would you expect any difference in the average number of sneezes between the two groups? Even though the same drug was used for both groups of people, the researchers know that they cannot expect to obtain the exact same sneezing scores. Why? Because randomization is not perfect. The people in the two groups will differ in their natural (untreated) sneezing rate and in their receptivity to the drug. By chance alone, one group will probably have a lower sneezing score than the other.

The problem facing the medical researchers is to distinguish between two possible causes of the findings. The first would be real differences in the effectiveness of the drugs, and the second would be no differences in the effectiveness of the drugs. Now there isn't any way the researchers can solve this problem for certain, but statistical procedures can tell them if the differences in sneezing scores obtained in their study $(3.13 - 1.46 = 1.67)$ could have easily occurred by chance alone. If a difference of 1.67 is unlikely to be caused by chance factors, the researchers can discount random error as a rival explanation and conclude that the differences are real and that the drugs really do differ in their control of sneezing.

Differences that researchers, with the help of statistical inference, consider real are said to be "statistically significant" or sometimes simply "significant." Differences that could easily be caused by chance are not considered real and are called "nonsignificant."

Determining "Significance"

How do researchers decide if the results are significant or not? By using inferential statistics they can determine the probability of various outcomes that could occur if the drugs were equally effective.[2] With equal drugs, no difference between the sneezing scores would be expected in the long run. But in any one study, chance alone would probably cause some differences. Some of these differences would be large and some small. But if the drugs were identical, small differences between the groups would be more likely to occur by chance alone than would large differences. Statistical procedures tell researchers the probability of chance alone determining any of these differences. The table below shows some differences that could occur between the groups' sneezing scores and the probability of that difference occurring by chance alone.

If the drugs are identical, . . .	
then a difference between the groups' sneezing score of . . .	would occur approximately this often* . . .
bigger than 1.20	less than 50%
bigger than 1.40	less than 18%
bigger than 1.60	less than 5%
bigger than 1.67	less than 3%
bigger than 1.80	less than 1%

*and since the drugs are identical, the differences must be due to nondrug (chance) differences between the groups.

Reading from the table, you can see that a difference between the sneezing scores of 1.60 or higher could be caused by chance *alone* about 5 times in 100. In the sneezing study a difference of 1.67 was obtained. That difference could occur even if the drugs were equally effective in treating head-cold symptoms; in fact, a difference that big or bigger would occur under "equally effective" conditions about 3 percent of the time.

As the table suggests, any difference no matter how large could occur by chance alone—though very large differences would be very unlikely. How then do researchers decide if the results are real? How do they divide the continuum of all possible differences into two categories, the significant and the nonsignificant? Where do they put the cutting line? The answer to these questions may be quite disconcerting to readers of research. For though there are some norms that guide researchers, there are no hard-and-fast rules. The decision is entirely up to the researchers. They can decide upon any cutting line. This freedom immediately suggests that different researchers could decide upon different cutting lines, and a reader of research could decide that the results are statistically significant when the researcher concluded otherwise, or vice versa. We will consider the implications of this a bit later in the chapter. For now, what's important is to try to understand the researchers' reasoning when they decide the results are statistically significant.

The Researcher's Reasoning

In making the decision, researchers pay more attention to the probability of the result occurring than to the actual result itself. If the same study comparing the two drugs were repeated a hundred times using *equally* effective drugs, a difference of 1.67 or larger would occur in about three of those studies. But the researchers did not conduct hundreds of studies; they conducted only one. And it seems unlikely that in that one study they would get the "3 percent" result. That would be a rather unusual situation. Since unusual events rarely happen, how can the researchers make sense out of this situation? Well, they are sure about the result of 1.67. But the probability of its occurrence was based on the assumption that the drugs were identical or equally effective in treating head-cold symptoms. If that assumption were false, then the result of 1.67 would be very reasonable. If the two drugs differed in their effectiveness, then the result of 1.67 would occur more than 3 percent of the time. So, in order to avoid the conclusion that an unusual event happened in this one study, the researchers simply reject the no-difference assumption and conclude that the drugs really differ. They say that the results are statistically significant.

THE NULL HYPOTHESIS

This somewhat complicated logic is sometimes formalized as a test of the "null hypothesis." "Null" in this case refers to no "real" effect; or more generally it refers to the status quo. The null hypothesis for the above example would be

H_0: There is *no difference* between the average sneezing scores due to the administration of the different drugs.

Of course, the researcher hopes that the null hypothesis is not true and that an "alternative hypothesis" is true. In this case the alternative would be

H_1: There is a difference between the average sneezing scores due to the administration of the different drugs.

It is important to realize that statistical inference is a procedure for rejecting the null hypothesis, but not a procedure for accepting the alternative. The alternative can only be accepted if the null is rejected *and* there is no better alternative. Inferential statistics is helpful for the former but useless for the latter. All uncontrolled biases are possible alternative hypotheses. You must reject them, in addition to rejecting the null hypothesis, in order to accept the alternative hypothesis that the researcher posits.

This approach to hypothesis testing is a part of a hotly debated philosophy of research methods. Under contention are issues such as:

• How does the researcher (or reader) decide how small the percentage must be in order to conclude that the findings are significant (or that the null hypothesis can be rejected)?

• Shouldn't we be equally as concerned with failing to reject the null hypothesis when it should in fact be rejected as we are with wrongly rejecting it?

Discussing these issues is beyond the scope of this book, but it is important to know that the role of the null hypothesis in research is debatable. It is not a God-given necessity.

REPORTING THE RESULTS

Deciding that the findings are significant or that the null hypothesis can be rejected is not enough. The researchers also need to report how wrong such a statement could be. From the preceding table they know that approximately 3 percent of the time a difference of 1.67 will occur and be caused by chance factors not associated with any real differences between the drugs. So, 3 percent of the time the researchers conclude that the findings are significant (due to uncontrolled biases or real differences between the drugs), they will be wrong. This percentage from the table tells how wrong their conclusion can be—it is a measure of the accuracy of their findings.

There are a few common ways in the research literature of reporting this belief. It could be reported as a level of significance.

". . . and the findings were significant at the 3 percent level"

or

". . . and the null hypothesis was rejected at the 3 percent level."

Or it could be reported as a probability value, using the letter p to mean probability.

". . . and the findings were significant ($p = .03$)"

or

". . . and the null hypothesis was rejected ($p = .03$)."

Or an alpha level could be given, where the Greek letter alpha (α) refers to the probability of being wrong when the researcher claims significance.

". . . and the results were significant ($\alpha = .03$)"

or

". . . and the null hypothesis was rejected ($\alpha = .03$)."

Though statisticians often differentiate among these, for our purposes you can consider them equivalent ways of reporting the factual accuracy of the findings. All of them tell you the percentage of time that researchers will be wrong when they conclude that the results are real and are not due to chance.

Now you can take a second, hopefully longer, to look at the three examples presented at the beginning of this chapter. Parts of them are probably still unknown to you, but you should now be able to interpret both significance and the degree of factual accuracy.

Example 1

This difference is significant beyond the .01 level ($\chi^2 = 9.59$, df = 1).

In Example 1, you are being told that some difference is significant beyond the .01 level. The rest of the line may still be unclear, but whatever difference the researchers studied, it is judged to be real because it could only occur by chance alone in fewer than one time out of a hundred such experiments.

Example 2

	Vertical leadership		Horizontal leadership			
	X̄	S.D.	X̄	S.D.	t^*	p
Measure 1	50.78	7.20	39.98	9.90	3.29	<.01
Measure 2	8.55	3.39	6.85	2.26	1.29	NS

*Two-tailed t test for correlated measures; df = 9.

Example 2 presents the results of comparing "horizontal" versus "vertical" leadership. We would need to read the author's operational and conceptual definitions of these terms to interpret them. But we still can interpret the statistical findings. The two types of leadership were compared using first the mean score ($\overline{X}$), and the standard deviation (S.D.), a measure of how scores are spread around the mean. Using measure 1 in the first row, a significant difference was found at the .01 level or less, as shown in the last column for the p value. With measure 2 in the second row, the difference between the two leadership measures is not significant.

Example 3

Correlations among variables

	Mass media use	Use of friends	Education	Age
Mass media use		.17	.47*	.06
Use of friends			.41†	.39†
Education				−.22
Age				

*$\alpha = .01$; †$\alpha = .05$.

In Example 3, two of the correlations indicated by the asterisk (*) were significant at the .05 level. One was significant at the .01 level, as shown by (†). In this case the asterisks refer to the alpha (α) levels given at the bottom of the table. By elimination, we assume that the author does not consider the other correlations (.17, .06, and −.22) to be significant. In other words, they are so small that they could really be zero, and the actual values obtained were most likely due to chance differences among the people and not any actual correlation between two variables.

Now that you've been able to gain a beginning understanding of the idea behind statistical inference and some of the ideas researchers attempt to convey in statistics, you need some general guidelines for evaluating inferential statistics.

READING AND UNDERSTANDING INFERENTIAL STATISTICS

Our major recommendation with regard to reading statistical information is

IF IT'S IMPORTANT, GET EXPERT ADVICE

By important we mean that there's a chance that some decision or some action will be taken based on findings in a research report. If you decide to use some new product, process, or idea that will have a big impact on yourself or your organization in terms of time, money, or effort, seek expert advice in interpreting the statistical findings.

Statistical significance, alpha, and p are only a very few commonly used statistical terms and symbols found in the professional literature. Since it is impossible to identify every term, we will select the most common ones and classify them according to the role they play in statistics; other statistical terms are described in the glossary. This may be enough for you to decide if more help is needed. While we cannot turn everyone who reads this into a statistical expert, our objective in this section is to try to make the information presented in reports and articles understandable.

When using statistical inference, researchers tend to follow a generally accepted series of steps in reaching their conclusions. By understanding this process in general, you can learn to pick out the most important elements of the process and evaluate them for yourself. Table 13–1 has been constructed to help you understand this process.

As you can see in the first column, we have divided the statistical part of research into six major steps. Although the order of some parts may change in different research situations, the steps themselves remain fairly constant. They are at the heart of what researchers do when they present inferential results in articles or reports. Read them over to get them clearly set in your mind.

As an evaluator of statistical results, or even as a user of those results, you must first and foremost be aware of ways in which the researcher could err in each of these steps. In the second column we indicate the errors you should watch out for in each of these steps. For example, in obtaining the data the researcher could err in many ways, such as choosing the wrong people, using improper, unreliable, or invalid measures, or even collecting the wrong data.

Once you have identified the errors that *can* exist in the statistical aspects of research, your next task is to discover *if* they exist in the research you are evaluating. Column 3 helps you do just that.

Finally, to help you wade through the baffelgab of symbols and jargon, in column 4 we present some of the terms and abbreviations commonly associated with each of the steps. Keep in mind, however, that these symbols are only a small portion of those commonly used. Unfortunately, the same symbol can sometimes stand for different things.

TABLE 13–1
A READER'S GUIDE TO INFERENTIAL STATISTICS

Major steps in inference	Some ways in which the researcher could err	How you, the reader, can discover the error	Commonly used symbols or jargon*
1. Obtain data from the people or objects selected.	Data could be in error—collected wrong data, chose incorrectly, used poor measurement.	Sections Three, Four, and Five of this book are devoted to these concerns.	Percentage (%) Mean ($\overline{X}$) Standard deviation (s, S.D., σ) Frequency (f) Scale value of dependent variable
2. Choose statistical procedure.	The wrong procedure could be chosen—one that doesn't answer the question desired, or doesn't handle the type of data found in this study, or has underlying assumptions that are not met.	We cannot help you here. If the article you are reading seems potentially important, get advice.	Chi square (χ^2) Analysis of Variance (AOV, ANOVA) Nonparametric statistics Regression or least squares t test Factor analysis Multiple discriminant analysis Correlation coefficients (r, ρ, λ)
3. Do calculations to come up with a figure.	Arithmetic mistakes.	If arithmetic is presented, you can check it. If it isn't presented, a statistician can often detect major errors. If the article is very important you could write to the author for a copy of the data.	Intermediate numbers arising from calculations are often reported, e.g., sum of squares (S.S.), expected value (E), regression coefficients (b, B, β).

154

4. Look up this number in a table of probabilities.	The wrong table could be used, or the wrong part of the correct table, or a simple error of recording the number from the table.	With very little instruction anyone can learn to look up these values. Or get some help—a student in a statistics class can do this.	Degree of freedom (df) Sample size (n, N) One-tailed, one-alternative Two-tailed, two-alternative The above are needed to find the right part of the table. The tables themselves have unusual names, such as t, F, χ^2 (chi square), and z (normal).
5. Make a statistical conclusion.	Our major concern here is not with errors but with differences in judgment. Researchers may base their statistical conclusions on criteria that are too liberal or too conservative for *your* needs.	You must determine the *significance level criterion*, e.g., .05, .01, etc., that makes the most sense for your situation, then see if you would arrive at the same statistical conclusion (i.e., significant or not) with your criterion.	Statistical significance Confidence Alpha (α) p value
6. Interpret this conclusion in a broader research context.	Again, this is not an error, though you want to watch out for nonsignificant findings being treated as if they were significant. This is a function of judgment and is justified solely by the force of the researcher's arguments.	You must determine if the results are meaningful to you. See the rest of this chapter. Also remember that statistical inference by itself accounts for only one rival explanation. Interpreting the results in a research context probably requires accounting for the other rival expectations in some way.	No special symbols are used here.

*Warning: The symbols in this column are a small portion of those commonly used and, unfortunately, the same symbol occasionally stands for different things.

You can put this information to work immediately by trying once again to understand Example 2 given at the beginning of the chapter. The research was comparing "horizontal" and "vertical" leadership. Using the table as a guide you can interpret a lot more of what is presented. The sample produced a mean ($\overline{X}$) and a standard deviation (S.D.), and the asterisk indicates that some statistical procedure called a "t test for correlated measures" was used. The "df = 9" and "two-tailed" are items of information needed to look up a number in a table of probabilities and find the level of significance. Finally, you might be able to guess that the column headed by "t" actually gives the value of t that was used to look up the resulting probability (p). Even though you still may not know exactly what these terms mean, you can make some sense out of what is reported. With some practice using actual journal or research articles, you can begin to evaluate and assess the previously unintelligible statistical results that you've seen and skipped in the past.

A MORE GENERAL DEFENSE

You need to ask three questions whenever you read any study using statistical inference. The questions will neither uncover the wrong statistical procedure nor determine whether the procedure was carried out incorrectly—only technical training or expert advice can help in these matters. But those more technical questions matter only after you decide that the statistics could help you. The three questions, which you yourself can answer, must be affirmative in order for the statistics themselves to be of any concern to you.

1. Are the Results Worth Interpreting Statistically?

There is no point in carrying out a great statistical exercise if the data being analyzed are ambiguous. Some researchers do fancy statistical analyses of data derived from a poorly conducted study. Perhaps they believe that statistics can cure a bad study or improve the data. Both beliefs are false. Statistics works only with the numbers supplied—it doesn't change their quality. Or, as they say in the computing business: "garbage in—garbage out (GIGO)." Statistics cannot salvage a poorly conducted study. While some researchers unfortunately act as if GIGO were not true, the fact remains doubly unfortunate that many readers of research let the mystique of statistics cloud their judgment of the entire piece of research.

Throughout most of this book we have identified many of the major flaws possible in research. If any one of these flaws actually occurred in a given study, you would have to determine if the data were good enough to warrant statistical analysis. As a reader you must decide if the study produced numerical data that are unambiguously interpretable. If the data are inadequate then the statistical analysis may be irrelevant—even though the author presents it.

What kinds of flaws in the drug study described earlier would make a statistical analysis irrelevant? We can list some possibilities:

- What if the two groups understood their job differently (lack of proper control over directions), and one group included in its sneezing totals those done at

night while the other group assumed that daytime sneezing was all that mattered?
- What if one group was selected from a list of hospital patients already receiving another drug, and you have reason to believe that the second drug (or the interaction between the two drugs) may also affect sneezing?
- What if the groups were told the nature of the drugs they were taking and the expected effect of each drug?
- What if . . . ?

The key point to all this is that the purpose of research is to answer a question about the nature of the world. Statistics may be needed to help do this job, but they can never do the job alone. Some nonstatistical procedures still must be employed to remove the effect of other possible rival explanations. Statistics deals with numbers, and statistical conclusions are conclusions about numbers. Only if the numbers themselves are meaningful (in other words, the study was well planned and conducted) will the statistical conclusions help in drawing a research conclusion about the nature of the world.

2. Do You Judge the Results to Be Real?

Once you have satisfactorily come past our first question you can turn attention to statistical inference. Again you have to assume or find out by other means that the researcher used the appropriate statistical procedures and used them properly.

The question being asked here is, "Do you think the results are likely to be due to chance?" Another way to get at the same question is to ask, "Are the results statistically significant?" or "Are the results real?" If results are not significant, they may be caused by chance differences among the items studied (people, books, events, and so on) and there is little justification in the data to pursue these findings any further.

Notice that we began the question with "Do *you* judge. . . ." You, the reader, must make an extremely important decision. Suppose a researcher reports that findings are significant with $p = .25$. This researcher is concluding that the findings are real because they could be caused by chance (that is, not real) only about 25 percent of the time. That is, 1 out of 4 times when the author makes this kind of statement it will be wrong.

Both authors and readers have a responsibility to specify a criterion for accepting a finding as real. But there is no reason why authors and readers must agree on the criterion. Practicing professionals decide on a criterion based on the risk and consequences of being wrong—if lives are at stake or if it takes a lot of money or energy, one may want to be more critical in the findings. For example, if a new drug were to be marketed, you would want to make sure that the claimed effects were real. If research on the drug indicated results were significant at the .10 level, you would still stand the chance of the drug not producing the intended effects. That kind of chance might be enough to lose customers and, more importantly, claim an effect when none would be produced. You might market the drug only when the p level was as low as .001. That is, 1 in 1,000 was the maximum risk you could tolerate of being wrong. On the other hand, if the advocated change is easy to implement and its failure (if it is wrong) is almost risk-free, then you could be rather liberal in your criterion and .25 might be acceptable.

A related concern is the number of statistically significant findings that may occur by chance alone. A researcher who is using the .25 significant level is willing to say something is significant and know that this may be wrong approximately 1 time out of 4. So if you read a study containing 10 statistical tests each employing that 25 percent significance level, neither you nor the author should be excited if 2 or 3 of these statistical tests identified significant findings. Similarly, if the .05 significance level is used, about 1 statistical finding out of 20 would be significant because of chance alone. So if many statistical tests are reported in a study, you should use the stated significance level to determine how many of these tests may be significant by chance. And unless many more than this number turned out to be significant, you ought to be very cautious in accepting the genuineness of the statistical findings.

Finally, we need to point out that statistical decision making is one-directional. If a finding turns out to be significant, the author may argue that the finding is real. If, however, the finding is not significant, the author should not argue the opposite. Researchers cannot use their findings as proof of "nonrealness." In statistical inference, it is easy, especially for untrained researchers, to get nonsignificant findings. Mistakes made by the researcher push the statistical result toward nonsignificance. This one-directional aspect of statistical inference is necessary if the conservative nature of science is to be followed. In general, science makes it very difficult to produce proof; it screens out a lot of untested and poorly thought out ideas. Thus, findings of nonsignificance cannot generally be used to conclude anything. All that can be said when the findings are nonsignificant is that there is no evidence that the results are real—they may be, but this study didn't determine that.

3. Are the Results Meaningful to You?

After all this discussion about statistics and statistical significance, you need to remember what you are about. Presumably one reason why you read journals and books is because they might help improve job performance or somehow impinge on the real world. Statistical significance states only that the findings are probably real, that they will affect the real world. Statistical significance does not state *how much* the findings will affect the world. This is an important distinction. Frequently, we have noticed among our students a tendency to equate statistical significance with meaningfulness or what is sometimes called "social significance." A simple example will demonstrate the error of such a position.

Suppose you are responsible for choosing textbooks for a third-grade reading program. Reading is a very important part of primary education, and any textbook that can help would be worth considering for use throughout the school district. Each month you receive in the mail a couple of new reading textbooks to review. One of these textbooks came with a brochure comparing it with the textbook your school system is currently using.

As you read the brochure, you notice that the study is well conducted. Rival explanations have been controlled, and there are no major flaws that you are aware of. That is, all known potential biases have been adequately treated. Furthermore, the statistical procedures are correct. The major finding reported in the brochure is that third-graders read better after using this textbook than the other textbook. This result is statistically significant at the .001 level.

Now, if you were to recommend this new textbook for general use because of this study, you would be basing that decision on insufficient information.

Suppose everything reported in the brochure is correct. All that statistical significance means is that the results are not likely to be due to chance. A study with results significant at the .001 level can be truthfully described as different from one with results significant at the .05 level. In the former case you can have more confidence that the results are not due to chance. But you cannot tell from the statistical significant levels the meaningfulness of the findings. In this case you do not know how much better students will perform using the new textbooks; that is, you need some measure of effect size. For this you have to go back and look at the original data.

The original data in the book study might be in the form of average reading scores of third-graders on a standardized reading test. Suppose the third-graders using the new textbook were tested as reading on the 3.7 grade level, but those using your current textbook were reading at the 3.6 reading level. Since the results are statistically significant, we know that the differences in performance between these groups (3.7 − 3.6 = 0.1 grade level) is real. But is it important or meaningful to your situation? Is an average improvement of 0.1 grade level enough of an improvement to warrant changing textbooks? Or would such a change be justified only if the average improvement were more—say at least one-half a grade level?

Because one cannot often judge meaningfulness in a vacuum, budget considerations should be included in this decision. Raising the average reading level of third-graders by one full grade level would be remarkable—and socially significant. Any textbook that could produce that increase regularly would have to be considered for possible adoption. But suppose such a textbook uses individualized stories and pictures taken from the actual life situation of each student. Such a book might be just too expensive for your district. So even though the book produces real effects (it is significant statistically) and even though the results are meaningful (the rise in reading levels is large enough), the book will not be adopted for use because of cost.

Only you can ascertain the meaningfulness of a study's findings. You cannot give that responsibility to the author of the study or to a statistician. Only you know the specifics of your situation; you must make the decision.

In many ways the question of the results being meaningful goes beyond the scope of this chapter and of this entire section of the book. In these six chapters our primary concern has been with the factual accuracy of a researcher's results. Have possible sources of distortion been adequately prevented or controlled? Are the findings correct? Can you believe the findings to be true? And so on. We've devoted a lot of pages to helping you answer these questions. They are important questions, and they ought to be among the first ones you try to answer when you evaluate a research report.

But once you get beyond this hurdle, your job is not done. Learning factually accurate information is often worthwhile for its own sake. But frequently, readers of research want to make use of these findings, to apply them to some school project or some job-related activity. Applying research results requires more than accuracy. In the next section of the book we identify those clues you should look for in a research report to determine whether the findings can be and ought to be applied to your particular situation.

QUESTIONS TO ASK

1 **Are the data good?**
   If the study was poorly conducted, the resulting data will not be unambiguous. In such a situation, statistics cannot help improve the data, and statistical conclusions, even if significant, must be suspect.

2 **Was the statistical inference needed?**
   Inference is not required when the results are so plainly obvious that there could be no question as to whether they were due to chance.

3 **Were the statistics correct?**
   This is a two-part question. First, were the proper statistical procedures employed? And second, were they employed correctly? There is no way one can answer these questions without some training in statistical inference. So if the study is important, get some expert to judge the adequacy of the statistics employed.

4 Could the findings have occurred by chance?
You probably should focus attention only on those findings that are statistically significant—all others are more likely to be chance occurrences. Not all significant findings may be acceptable to you—it depends on the level of significance. While you can enlist the aid of statisticians, they can only help you identify the significant findings. You must determine whether the level of significance (risk of being wrong) is acceptable for your situation.

5 How important are the findings?
Given statistically significant findings at an acceptable level of significance (or an acceptable confidence level), you must decide whether the findings are meaningful. Are the results large enough to warrant further interest on your part?

PRACTICE EVALUATIONS

Reminder: Answering the above questions yourself is good practice. Chapter 18 provides guidelines for you to follow in doing that. Chapter 19 provides two articles along with our evaluations of them. Chapter 20 provides two additional articles for you to practice on.

FOR FURTHER THOUGHT

1 Discuss the possible role of statistical inference in the following story.

A Modern-Day Parable

Once upon a time, a highly respected and revered psychometrician of a great university was sailing about from sea to sea enjoying a well-deserved vacation. On a fine sunny day, his ship put in at a very small harbor of a very small atoll where, the crew informed him, they occasionally stopped to leave food for three hermits who were the only inhabitants. Sure enough, there they were standing on the sand to greet the professor, their long white beards and their white lab coats blowing in the breeze, looking exactly as hermits should look, and their delight in seeing him was gratifying. For, they explained, they had come out to this solitary archipelago long, long ago, in order to enter into pure animal behavior research, and not be interrupted by the cares of the world, such as teaching, faculty meetings, and the myriad of other distractions. But, during these many years, they had forgotten a good deal of the proper statistical methods taught them at the University and were most eager to refresh themselves at the fount of the professor's wisdom.

So the wise doctor spoke with them for many hours, reviving their memories of simple and complex designs, of methods and techniques necessary for publications, and instructed them so they could recognize the proper statistical test for their data once more. Feeling that he had done a fine day's work, the psychometrician returned to his ship and sailed away.

At dawn—for he was ever an early riser—he was sitting in his deck chair when in the clear light and against the bright horizon he saw a strange—an unbelievable—sight. After trying for some time to identify a boat, or a canoe, or a kayak, or even a raft, the professor sent for the captain, and they stared through the binoculars and soon had to admit the impossible, for a rhesus monkey was riding on the back of a large porpoise. So there seemed nothing to do but lean over the rail as the monkey and the fish guided to below it. The monkey cried out, "Dear and wise Professor, we have been trained in the laboratory of the hermits, and they crave your forgiveness for sending us to trouble you with their difficulty, but none of them can remember how you said to determine the denominator degrees of freedom, and since they must know this in order to get their results published. . . ."

2 Interpret the following quotations in terms of the materials in this chapter.
   (a) "The purpose of computing is insight not numbers." (R. Hamming)
   (b) "Researchers have repeatedly shown the advantages of transforming a research problem in human behavior into a complex statistical exercise. These advantages increase geometrically from M.A. thesis to Ph.D. dissertation to post-doctoral research." (From an anonymous list of poor, but pervasive, habits in research)
   (c) "Criteria of significance should not be methodological, but substantive in nature. They should always be grounded in the nature of the problem itself and not in the tools of problem solving." (D. H. Fischer)
   (d) "Chance /is/ the ever-present rival conjecture." (G. Polya)
   (e) "Since no scientific hypothesis is ever completely verified, in accepting a hypothesis on the basis of evidence, the scientist must make a decision that the evidence is sufficiently strong or that the probability is sufficiently high to warrant the acceptance of the hypothesis. Obviously, our decision with regard to the evidence and how strong is "strong enough" is going to be a function of the *importance,* in the typical ethical sense, of making a mistake in accepting or rejecting the hypothesis." (R. Rudner)

FOR FURTHER READING

1 F. Williams. *Reasoning with Statistics: How to Read Quantitative Research,* 4th ed. Fort Worth: Hardcourt, 1992.

This short book attempts to introduce major statistical concepts with a minimum of mathematics.

2 E. Minium; B. King; and G. Bear. *Statistical Reasoning in Psychology and Education,* 3rd ed. New York: Wiley, 1993.
3 R. P. Runyon and A. Haber. *Fundamentals of Behavioral Statistics,* 8th ed. New York: McGraw-Hill, 1996.

Two easily readable beginning textbooks on inferential statistics. Good texts to consult if you wish to obtain discussions of topics referred to in this chapter.

USEFUL INFORMATION

Should you apply it?

Factual accuracy and usefulness are very different attributes of information. Just because you believe the results of research does not mean that you can use them. They may not apply to you or there may be practical limitations. This section discusses these issues.

Researchers probably have a greater responsibility to provide factually accurate information than useful information. Many times there is little the researcher can do to ensure that the results will apply to you. In this section we discuss how to evaluate what the researcher has done to make the results useful, and the decisions you must make largely from your knowledge of your own situation and your own needs.

14

GENERALITY: DO THE RESULTS APPLY TO YOU?

WASHINGTON 3/15 (UPI)—Rep. Andy Jacobs, D-Ind., yesterday introduced legislation that would allow the sale of saccharin in the United States, but each saccharin container would have to carry this warning:

"Warning: The Canadians have determined saccharin is dangerous to your rat's health."

The Food and Drug Administration has proposed a ban on the artificial sweetener because Canadian researchers have discovered that massive doses cause tumors in rats.

At one time, there was a great outcry against a proposed ban on saccharin. Much of the clamor was generated because the public did not see a relationship between massive doses of saccharin given to rats and the much smaller amounts taken by humans. Do rat facts apply only to rats, or can they be generalized to people? This example may seem extreme, but it poses the same question as most research findings—to whom do they apply?

Researchers seldom study anything of interest to you as a reader. It's true. A study may have been conducted in March 1969 on methods of teaching algebra to seventh-graders in School No. 86 in Chicago. You, however, are teaching algebra to eighth-graders in Syracuse several years later. Or a survey of 350 members of the American Management Association obtains their views on some issues. But you want to know how all the members feel. Or, to take an example from Chapter 2, a colleague uses a trained social worker to handle the reception desk at a hospital's outpatient clinic, while your situation involves a university's guidance center.

None of these situations makes clear whether the results apply to you. And, in principle, that will always be the case. Because no two situations are ever exactly the same, how can you determine whether the findings of a study generalize to your situation? Answering this question is what this chapter is about. Our emphasis here is with assessing the strength of a researcher's methodological arguments for generality. You should not forget, however, to also evaluate those arguments based on reasoning and replications.

Examining the Differences

To begin with, let's take a closer look at how "your situation" differs from the ones reported in the journals. Certainly the people (or the objects being studied)[1] are different, but so also are the times, the environments, and the initiators (the researcher in the journal article and now you). Operational definitions, measurements, or other aspects of the procedures may also possibly differ. Ideally you would like to know the extent to which the research findings generalize across all these differences to your particular situation. This concern for what has been called ecological representativeness is important because the majority of studies in the social sciences that actually deal with generality tend to explicitly deal only with the people dimension.

For example, a typical library-user study will obtain a sample of adults in the library's community to determine their attitudes toward the library, its services, and its policies. If a carefully drawn representative sample of adults is used, we can have some confidence that the findings apply to all adults in the community, not just to the ones questioned. The results can be generalized over the people dimension. Yet there are other dimensions to the study that have to be considered when evaluating generalizability. Would the same results have occurred if different instruments were used— say, a personal interview rather than a mailed questionnaire? What would happen if the question wordings were changed slightly, or if the survey took place during summer vacation periods rather than at another time of the year? These are the types of questions that a reader needs to ask regarding the generality of a study's findings along nonpeople dimensions. The researcher, by carefully choosing a representative sample of adults, has tried to account for the people dimension, but you as a reader must worry about the other dimensions as well—the ones that make your situation different from the one reported.

Because no one study can be designed to generalize across all dimensions, a researcher has to choose which dimension is most important. In the social sciences it is probably best to worry about generalizing over people first because that dimension is the most difficult to deal with. Many times the other dimensions don't matter that much—the environments are essentially the same, the measurements are sufficiently alike, and so on—but the people are guaranteed to be different. So if the researcher can ensure through the research procedures that the people dimension is covered in terms of generality, you have an easier time accepting the applicability of the study's findings to your situation. At times, of course, the other dimensions do matter a great deal, particularly when some obvious changes have been made. In these cases you need to pause and take stock of the situation. Even though the researcher didn't directly worry about the other dimensions, you have to. So, what kinds of clues should you look for or think about in order to determine the generality of research findings?

Discounting Important Differences

The key to generality is eliminating or discounting all potentially important differences between the situation described in the research report and the situation the results are to be applied to. If the differences between the research situation and your situation are minor and do not affect the findings, then it is reasonable to generalize across these differences. In other words, the research situation and your situation must be alike in *all essential ways.* But what differences are important and what ways are essential?

Sometimes the relevant differences seem clear-cut. In the case mentioned earlier of teaching algebra to seventh-graders, you probably would not be concerned that the students in 1969 had longer hair than your students do today. You probably don't have any reason to believe that length of hair has anything to do with responsiveness to different methods of teaching. That is, length of hair is not an essential difference.[2] You would, however, want to be sure that they had about the same intelligence as your students—teaching methods demonstrated on bright students may not work at all or as well on a more general group of students. Motivation, parental encouragement, and many other variables would also be potentially important differences between the students studied and your students.

Most of the time the situation is not clear-cut because it isn't obvious which differences matter and which are irrelevant to generality. In these cases you need to judge the adequacy of the evidence or arguments offered by the researcher (or constructed by yourself). In principle, any part of the research procedures, or anything the researcher does, could affect the generality of the findings. But because generalizing over the people dimension is often the most important to a reader, as well as to a researcher, we will look closely at how a researcher chooses people to study.

CHOOSING PEOPLE

To "generalize over the people dimension" means that the results of a study that used a relatively small group of people are applicable to a larger group of people. In order to base this generalization on a methods argument, the researcher would have to choose people to study who are like the larger group of people in all essential ways. Or to say it a bit more formally, the sample of people used in the study (the small group) must be chosen so they are representative of the population (the large group) the researcher wants to generalize to. How can that be done? That is, what *procedures* produce representativeness?

Just One? Or Everyone?

One obvious way to solve this problem is to study everyone. Because the entire population is being studied, it is clearly representative of itself. But studying everyone is usually too costly. It may be impossible to study everyone; it can be counterproductive to study everyone; and because of available research procedures it is unnecessary and inefficient to study everyone. Some group of people comprising less than 100 percent of the population will do; if properly chosen, they will be a representative sample of that population.

Let's look at the other extreme. What about a sample of one person? Studies with a sample of one are frequently reported in the applied social sciences. The social worker or psychiatrist reports on an individual case study, the journalist interviews one person for a story, and a manager tries to learn from another manager who reports unique experiences. When reading about a single person (or group, or event, and so on), you always need to ask: why that person? Why should this one person be representative of the larger group you are interested in—especially if you know that other people you're interested in are different in essential ways from the one discussed in the article?

When there is no justification for choosing that one person (and that's most of the time), additional case studies should be sought as replications. When there are enough of them reported you can have some confidence in the generality of findings common to most or all of them. Until you have enough replications, however, studies based on a sample of one must be used cautiously. There is no method known that will identify a single representative person for a researcher.

There are methods, however, for identifying a representative group of people (more than one, but less than the entire population). Unfortunately, these methods are not always used by researchers. When they aren't, the question asked of one-person samples is just as applicable in this situation: why *this* group of people? What reason is there to believe they are representative of the large group you are interested in?

Representativeness and Bias

This concern for representativeness comes from the more general concern for bias in studies. An unrepresentative sample is biased because it contains too many of one kind of people and not enough of another kind. It will give systematically incorrect findings. A good example is the selection of a sample of registered voters to determine the percentage of all voters who will support each candidate. A TV reporter interviewing people on the street may select the first fifty who are available. There is no apparent planning in how these fifty were selected, but a bias is likely. To decide for yourself you need only to ask if the poll would have produced a similar result had it been conducted at another place or without the presence of a TV camera. Clearly, a poll in a rundown shopping district in the inner city would produce different findings than one in a new suburban shopping mall. Moreover, some types of people probably steer clear of a TV camera, whereas others are attracted by it.

Volunteer samples are just as troublesome. Many times those who volunteer are different from those who do not volunteer. As we noted in Chapter 6, volunteers tend to be brighter and to be less authoritarian than nonvolunteers. They often have a high socioeconomic status, and they seem to need more approval. If any of these differences affect what is being studied, the use of volunteers will bias the findings—the results cannot be generalized easily to a population that includes nonvolunteers.

Volunteer samples and accidental (or available) samples are commonly used, perhaps because they are the easiest to get. But in general, these samples should be suspect. They may be biased. To generalize from them requires some reliance on replications (which may not exist) or on reasoning alone (which is weak)—a "methods" argument is not available.

Random Sampling

There is only one generally acceptable method of choosing a sample that is unbiased and therefore representative of the larger population. That method depends on some form of random sampling.[3] In random sampling every person in the population has an equal (or known) chance of being chosen for the study. Thus, by chance alone, the sample should be unbiased—there should be approximately the same percentage of males in the sample as there are in the population, the same percentage of Republicans, introverts, Lithuanians, senior citizens, and so on. It is important to say "approximately the same" because no method of sampling will guarantee that the percentages will be equal. What's special about random sampling is that it allows the researcher to use statistical inference (see Chapter 13) to figure out the probability of whether the random process did or did not work. Readers of research can then interpret that probability to decide if they want to believe that the random sample is "approximately the same" as the population.

There are many kinds of random sampling; a research study may use one rather than another for reasons of cost or efficiency. The most common types are simple random samples, stratified random samples, and clustered random samples. Sometimes two or more of these are combined in some "multistage" sampling plan. The distinction among these is not important here. It is important, however, to be able to recognize their names so that you will treat them as varieties of random or probability samples.

Given a random sample, how large should it be? Well, it depends on so many considerations and technical matters that we cannot help you as a reader to determine if the researcher used a reasonable sample size. We only can give a couple of rules of thumb to guide you in your evaluation.

How Many? Rule of Thumb 1

First of all, random samples depend upon chance or probability to remove biases. Probability "works" only in the long run. A fair coin should come up heads and tails in about equal proportions, but you shouldn't be too surprised if three flips of the coin resulted in three heads. You would probably be quite surprised, however, if 100 flips of the coin resulted in 100 heads. In the long run, things ought to balance out. The same principle applies to random sampling. A small sample, even if chosen randomly, may by chance alone result in an atypical (that is, biased) result. So the first rule of thumb suggests that too small a sample, even if randomly selected, may not be representative.

How Many? Rule of Thumb 2

The second rule of thumb is more difficult to understand and therefore is viewed with some mistrust by nonstatisticians. To state it very simply, the actual size of a large population has little to do with determining the proper sample size.[4] Or to put the idea another way, what matters is the actual size of the sample, not its percentage of the population. If 1,000 people selected from the city of Syracuse are enough to generalize to all the inhabitants of Syracuse, then that same number of people selected from the whole state of New York will suffice to generalize to all the inhabitants of New York State. This rule of thumb is true even though the sample consists of 0.6 percent of the Syracuse population, but only 0.001 percent of the New York State population. Accordingly, if you discover a researcher who determines sample size primarily by taking some percentage of the population, you may want to question that researcher's understanding of the principles of sampling.

How Many? Rule of Thumb 3

For the third rule of thumb let's consider a simple example. Suppose the state legislature is considering enacting a law requiring automobile drivers to retake the license examination every ten years. The legislature would like to know how many drivers do not have up-to-date knowledge of traffic regulations. With the aid of a sampling expert, a representative sample of licensed drivers is asked a series of questions about traffic laws. Approximately 43 percent of those questioned did not know the answers and would have failed the examination.

Good sampling techniques assure you that the sample of people is representative of all licensed drivers in the state. But since the results are based on a sample, there is no reason to believe that the percentage obtained (43 percent) would be exactly the same if a different sample were used. Another sample, also representative, might come up with 46 percent. A third representative sample might produce a finding of 42 percent. If the results of different representative samples vary, the reader or decision maker needs to know how much they might vary. Certainly a decision maker would behave differently if the maximum range was plus or minus 3 percent (that is, 40 to 46 percent) as compared with a possible range of 25 percent (that is, 18 to 68 percent).

A researcher can control the range of error by adjusting the sample size. In fact, except for practical or financial limitations, the main consideration in choosing a sample size is to limit the possible error to some acceptable level. The researcher wants to control how wrong the results can be. In general, the larger the sample size, the smaller the possible error. This third rule of thumb leads directly to our next topic.

CONFIDENCE INTERVALS

Using a form of random sampling removes biases, but introduces noise in its place. And, as we mentioned in Chapter 7, the researcher is fortunate to have a tool for seeing through the noise. That tool is inferential statistics. With random sampling, inferential statistics are used to tell researchers how wrong they can be when they try to generalize the results to the total population. Or saying it another way, inferential statistics tells researchers how confident they can be that the findings from the sample are good estimates of what exists in the population.

If a researcher has used inferential statistics in this way, the statistics usually take the form of a "confidence interval" and ought to be included in the journal article. Confidence intervals may be stated in a variety of ways—here are some common ones.[5]

1. The poll showed that the percentage of people who will vote for Jones is 70 percent ± 6 percent (95 percent level of confidence).
2. The poll showed that the percentage of people who will vote for Jones is between 64 percent and 76 percent (95 percent confidence level).
3. The probability is .95 that between 64 percent and 76 percent of the people in this district will vote for Jones.

What Confidence Intervals Tell You

Each of these says the same thing. The researcher's best guess as to what percentage of all the people in the population will vote for Jones is 70 percent. But the result is unlikely to be exactly 70 percent, so an interval or range is put around that guess. In this case the range is 6 percent in either direction. But even with an interval, researchers know that sometimes the actual percentage in the population will be outside that interval, so they tell their readers how confident they are that the results will be in the interval. In this case they know that 95 times out of 100, the actual percentage will fall somewhere between the interval of 64 percent and 76 percent.[6] Confidence intervals can be constructed for all kinds of estimates, not just percentages. Averages are frequently used: "And the median income in the city is $10,400 (± 1,250 at 90 percent confidence)." In translation this means that the researcher is 90 percent sure that the median family income in the city is somewhere between $9,150 and $11,650.

Notice that there are two parts to a confidence interval—the range and the confidence level. Both of these can be controlled by the researcher. If it is important to have a tighter estimate (say ± 3 percent instead of ± 6 percent) or more confidence (99 percent instead of 95 percent), or both, the researcher will need a larger sample size. If a wider estimate or less confidence is acceptable, fewer people will do. No matter what options the researcher chooses, as a reader you need to determine if the range and level of confidence are acceptable for your needs.

How Wrong Can the Findings Be?

With a random sample, a confidence interval can usually be computed. In many cases research is reported that didn't or couldn't use random sampling. Sometimes there is no way to identify the entire population; other times the use of a random procedure for drawing a sample is impossible. In these situations, like all others, there is no doubt that the researcher's estimates may be wrong. But because the researcher cannot compute a confidence interval with a nonrandom sample, you as a reader are not given any help in determining how wrong the findings may be. Even so, it is important to remember that researchers can be wrong and the size of the possible error should affect your interpretation and use of the results. You must make some estimate of how wrong you think the findings might be.

Related to this problem in surveys is the problem caused by loss of subjects in experiments. A bias may creep into the study if people drop out before the study is completed. Usually, not all subjects who start a study complete the entire study. Having some subjects drop out is not a critical concern if there is no systematic connection between the study and the reason why they dropped out. That is, if the people dropped out for a variety of different reasons not due to the study itself, there's no problem. However, if noncompletion occurs because of some particular condition in the study, generalizing the findings may be impossible.

Questionnaires sent through the mail often have a very low response rate: having more than 60 percent of the questionnaires returned without a lot of prompting is unusual. A dropout bias (that is, a distortion caused by nonreturned questionnaires) is always possible, but is even more likely with a low response rate. If people who returned the questionnaire differ in some systematic way from those who did not, a bias may have crept into what was originally a representative sample. This potential bias is the reason why researchers work so hard to get a high response rate. For the same reason, this is why readers of research need to ask hard questions of studies that base results on a low rate of response.

If bias is present, the researcher (and sometimes the reader) can correct for it if the direction and extent of the bias can be determined. Suppose a questionnaire were sent to a sample of members of some organization. If demographic questions (age, sex, position, years in the organization, and so on) are asked, the distribution of these variables on the returned questionnaires can be compared with other sources of the same information—say a published membership directory. If those who replied are similar to the full membership on the demographic variables, you may feel more comfortable believing that those who replied are similar to the full membership on all the questions asked.

If the replies differ systematically from the full membership, the study, though biased, can still provide some useful information about the group that replied. Thus, if a large percentage of senior members of the organization replied, you can identify the nature of the bias and interpret the results as representing mostly senior members' views.

If you cannot determine the nature or extent of the bias, you may have to disregard the study. In cases like this, no information is often safer than information that is biased in an unknown manner.

OTHER CONSIDERATIONS

Even with a representative sample and no dropouts there still may be problems. Anything the researcher does to the people that makes them different from other people in the population may affect the generality of the findings. For example, if the people realize that they are in a study of some kind, the results may not be generalized to people who don't have this awareness. This isn't always the case, or else the great majority of studies would have limited generality. But if the participants in the study act differently in any way related to the purpose of the study, then there is a problem.

A group of first-year college students who know they are in an investigation of sexual habits may respond and act far differently than those outside of the study. If the responses of these people are hedged, incomplete, or exaggerated, the results will not represent the sexual habits of the population of all first-year students.

A similar threat to generality is found many times in educational studies. Schoolchildren are extremely sensitive and aware of changes in their class routine. Even if a child is not consciously aware of being in a study, changes such as a different lunch hour, a different order of classes or topics, or even a different room may be enough of a disruption to change normal behaviors. In situations like this ask yourself whether the results would have been the same if the members of the sample did not know they were in a study.

Being tested or measured at the beginning of a study may change people. They may respond differently from people who have not been previously tested. Findings from this kind of study may very well be right, but they could generalize only to people who had also been previously tested. For example, think about a study in which tests of anti-Semitism were first given to individuals. After the test, they were given training sessions dealing with sensitivity to religious ideologies. Because the pretest sensitized the people, they reacted to the training sessions differently than they would have if no pretest had been used. The researcher would like to make some conclusions about the effect of the training session on the general population. But all that can be justified in this situation are conclusions about the combined effects of the pretest and the training sessions. The researcher does not have any solid evidence about how training sessions alone would work on the population.

In the anti-Semitism example, a pretest reacted with the training sessions. Sometimes the pretest doesn't affect anything but the final testing or measurement at the end of the study. In such a case, as in the previous one, there still is a problem with generality. Would the same results occur if there were no pretest?

Finally, don't forget our concern about "all essential ways." If anything important— including things other than people—is changed, a subsequent investigation may not get the results found in the original study. When a new paperback reading program for retarded teenagers is begun, other, normal teens may be hired to talk with the book recipients to see how the program was being received. The program may work well, and a decision could be made to institute it statewide. However, if adults rather than teenagers are used to distribute the books, the results may not be the same as in the first study. Perhaps the retarded teenagers will react differently to adults than to those in their own age group. The point is that anytime you make use of a study's findings you need to itemize *all* the differences between your situation and the one described in the journal. You have to decide if each of these differences is important and could affect the generality of the results to your situation.

A QUICK REVIEW

Think back to our example at the beginning of this chapter of teaching algebra to seventh-graders. Do the results from that study generalize to your eighth-graders in Syracuse? Well they may, but not because of anything done by the researcher. First of all, it does not look like any form of random sampling was used. More likely, the researcher simply made use of an available sample of some seventh-grade class in school No. 86 in Chicago. So a method argument cannot be used to support the generality of findings to your situation.

But even if a random sample were used, could you generalize the results to your Syracuse eighth-graders? Again, the answer is no. Random sampling, if properly done and if there are no further biases due to dropouts, reactions from pretests, and so forth, means that the results may be generalized only to the population the sample was drawn from. If a random sample were taken of all seventh-graders in the Chicago school district, then the results strictly apply only to that population. To go beyond that population and argue that the results are applicable to eighth-graders in Syracuse requires a reliance on reasoning (discounting essential differences) and replications.

Let's forget the Chicago study and suppose that a comparable study were done with a random sample of all eighth-graders in Syracuse, New York. Would the results of this study apply to you? For your current class, the answer is yes. The applicability gets weaker if you also want to apply the findings to next year's class and classes thereafter. Ultimately the argument for generality comes back down to reasoning and replication.

It is easy and somewhat reassuring for nonresearchers to place the responsibility for showing generality on the author—particularly so when some form of random sampling is used. In addition, an overreliance on sampling may lead researchers to ignore the other methodological considerations that weaken generality. Remember to search for the sample actually used, not the sample selected. Also watch for any procedures, such as pretests, which may make the people being studied respond differently and as a result limit the generality of findings only to those other people who have been similarly pretested. Good methods help, but only you know your situation and therefore only you can identify essential differences and judge if they have or have not been dealt with sufficiently.

Our emphasis in this chapter has been on the principles of generality. Do the results apply to your situation? How can you make that determination? What kinds of arguments can be raised? What sorts of clues can you look for in an article? These are very important questions to consider and should always be asked. But as our friends in the working world point out, if you *stop* here and make a decision to use research results after considering only these questions, you are being impractical and unrealistic, and are almost sure to fail. The next chapter goes beyond the theoretical aspects of generality and introduces you to some of the other practical considerations that matter.

QUESTIONS TO ASK

1 **Are the results factually accurate?**
First know the strengths and weaknesses of the results, then concern yourself with their generality.
2 **What are the dimensions over which you need to generalize the findings?**
Each of the dimensions you are concerned about needs to be supported separately.
3 **Did anything happen to the people during the study that made them less representative?**
Watch out for excessive dropouts, low completion rates, and pretests that change the people and their reactions to the rest of the study.
4 **If confidence intervals are used, are the range and the confidence levels acceptable for your use?**
You must decide for your own situation.

PRACTICE EVALUATIONS

Reminder: Answering the above questions yourself is good practice. Chapter 18 provides guidelines for you to follow in doing that. Chapter 19 provides two articles along with our evaluations of them. Chapter 20 provides two additional articles for you to practice on.

FOR FURTHER THOUGHT

1 In Chapter 2 we discussed some of the problems of using experience as a way of knowing about the world. Consider experience again, but this time from a generality point of view.

   (a) Are one's experiences representative? If so, of what?

   (b) In what ways do you think a person's experiences may be biased? What items are more likely to be remembered?

2 In everyday conversation, people use examples to support the positions they take. How good are examples when used in this way? Why? (*Hint:* consider sample size.)

3 What are the major uses of inferential statistics in the social sciences? Review Chapters 7, 12, and 13 as well as this one to see if you can find a common thread running through the major uses of statistics.

4 Interpret the following quotation in terms of the material in this chapter.

"Those who refuse to go beyond the facts rarely get as far as the facts." (T. H. Huxley)

5 To what degree do you agree with the following advice concerning political polls?

"Ignore polls. If you see a story about a poll, turn immediately to the end. If the actual questions asked aren't listed, if the sample size isn't stated, if the margin of error isn't stated, if those polled aren't likely voters—forget it. It's probably meaningless at best, biased at worst." (M. Gartner, *USA Today,* December 26, 1995.)

FOR FURTHER READING

1 A. Wolff. "Of Rats and Men." *The New York Times Magazine,* May 15, 1977, p. 90.

A brief review of the FDA's decision to ban saccharin, along with a discussion of the research and statistical principles that allowed the researchers to generalize from megadoses given to rats to the smaller amounts consumed by humans.

2 D. Huff. *How to Lie with Statistics.* New York: Norton, 1954.

3 S. K. Campbell. *Flaws and Fallacies in Statistical Thinking.* New York: Prentice Hall, 1974.

Both the Huff and the Campbell paperbacks deal with sampling and the notion of generality in easy-to-read texts. Amusing examples and illustrations.

4 E. R. Babbie. *Survey Research Methods,* 2nd ed. Belmont, CA: Wadsworth, 1990.

An introduction to the problem of generalizability from the perspective of survey research.

BEING PRACTICAL:
GOING BEYOND ERROR

Research has clearly shown that "programmed instruction" allows students to learn at their own pace. Lockstep progress can be minimized. Optimal learning conditions can be developed for each student, and no one is penalized for being too slow or too fast.

Since many educators agree that students should be allowed to learn at "their own pace" and since research has shown that programmed instruction can meet this goal, the approach is frequently adopted. But do students actually learn at their own pace in schools using programmed instruction?

A study of Pittsburgh City Schools in the early 1960s showed that in at least this one case some teachers resisted not being able to continue their traditional role as liaison between knowledge and the student. In a short time, the teachers began to—intentionally or unintentionally—subvert the system.

Students who were progressing at a slow rate were encouraged to continue their work at home. Faster students were restricted to using materials only during school hours. And in a variety of other ways, teachers were taking actions to force the students back into the very lockstep progress that programmed instruction was supposed to avoid.

The seemingly short step from research findings to the use of that research is sometimes a long and tortuous journey. The previous 14 chapters were written to help you determine the factual accuracy, generality, and applicability of published research findings. They do not, however, deal with how to make use of the findings, which is often the reason for reading the research in the first place.

Not all accurate and generalizable findings have implications for action. Furthermore, for those which do, the action needs to be carefully planned with as much regard for social and psychological factors as for the intrinsic truth of the findings themselves.

This chapter goes beyond evaluation. It is included primarily to remind you that evaluating information, though important, is often only the first step in applying research findings. We wish to caution you not to fall victim to a common form of excessive rationalism that assumes that truths will be seen as such by everyone, that their implications are unambiguous, and that they will be readily accepted by all people involved.

Differences among Readers' Objectives

Until now we have not distinguished among readers of research according to their objectives for reading. Criteria for evaluating research are relatively independent of one's objectives. However, objectives matter a great deal once evaluation is completed and the reader is considering making use of part or all of the study.

At one extreme, a reader's objective may be the pursuit of "truth"—the gathering of factually accurate knowledge that holds up under careful scrutiny by many qualified experts in a wide range of settings. Students and scientists often have this objective for their reading. They want to get a more accurate, more complete understanding of the world—knowledge for its own sake. These readers usually make use of knowledge to advance their field of study or their own understanding. They may want to posit a theory, suggest a study to explain anomalous observations, or resolve conflicting points of view.

At the other extreme, a reader's objective may be to have an immediate impact or effect on some new or ongoing event. Practicing professionals frequently have this as their objective. They are confronted by problems needing an acceptable solution and decisions needing a workable resolution. The key words here are acceptable and workable. While the practitioner would like to be just as sure of the information as the student or scientist must be, the practitioner is constrained by realities that do not affect the latter as much, if at all.

Most readers of research fall between these extremes. In some situations you may need to act like a practitioner when you read a journal article, while in other situations you will behave more like a scholar. The words "scholar" and "practitioner" are not used to identify your career; rather, they refer to your purpose at any particular moment. Practicing professionals have legitimate scholarly objectives, and university professors and students have practical concerns.

Because time is a major constraint, "practitioners" often have to make use of information before the "scholar" would be convinced that the information is correct. Scholars can, and should, suspend judgment if they are not reasonably sure of things. Practitioners do not have this luxury. Making a deliberate decision based on acceptable information is many times better than suspending judgment. To defer a decision often means that the decision will be made by default through the passage of time, rather than by the practitioner.

Consequences of Being Wrong

The consequences of being wrong also affect practitioners differently from scholars. When scholars err, the error usually appears on paper first, permitting others to discover the mistakes before much damage is done. In contrast, when practitioners err, people, services, and organizations are often immediately affected. So practitioners are in a double bind—not only do their decisions have immediate real-world consequences, but also their decisions may be based on information that is not yet fully substantiated.

A further complication arises because there are two ways in which one can be wrong in the use of research findings. The first is using the results inappropriately; the second is not using the results at all. And, there is a "cost" associated with each of these.

Accepting research results that turn out to be false may result in using evidence inappropriately. The claims of a potential lifesaving drug are the most dramatic example. The cost of using the drug when the evidential claims are not true may be catastrophic if lives are lost. On the other hand, evidence may be rejected even though it actually is true. Rejecting the use of a drug that can save lives can have equally catastrophic costs.

The real-world consequences of these two costs are often immediate for the practitioner. Yet, for the scholar faced with the same problem, the consequences may not be seen right away because many replications are needed to winnow out the truth.

The objective of the scholar is neither more nor less legitimate or valuable than that of the practitioner—it is just different. Because both types of readers begin in the same way we haven't differentiated between them until now. After an article is read, there are seven major (and many minor) decisions that the potential user of research needs to consider. The first two of these fall within the scope of the earlier chapters and are included here for the sake of completeness. Both scholars and practitioners need to make these two decisions—though in terms of applying the results, the scholar may require more evidence of the factual accuracy and generality of the findings than the practitioner has time to wait for. The other five decisions occur after the results have been judged acceptable. They are concerned with those practical matters which distinguish good ideas that may work from "merely" good ideas. They are, therefore, more useful to the practitioner than the scholar.

Major Decisions for Research Users

1 Are parts, or all, of the findings factually accurate? Answering this question is what most of this book is about. The rationale and criteria throughout, but especially Chapters 8 through 13, were written with this question in mind. There is no need to summarize those chapters here. Notice that the decision does not have to apply to all the findings. Articles are often not implemented or of interest as a totality. If only some of the findings are interesting, you will want to determine the factual accuracy of those specific parts and the entire article should be evaluated accordingly.

If the answer to this question is positive, you can proceed to the next step without worry. If the answer is negative, we would ideally recommend that you stop here, particularly if you are not a practitioner—but occasionally risks have to be taken, and in such cases you will need to go on but more cautiously.

2 Do the findings apply to your situation? Chapter 14 deals with this question. You need to determine if the evidence is strong enough for your purposes. Were there enough successful replications in enough settings? Was a representative sample employed—were the conditions of the study similar to the people, objects, groups, or events you are concerned with? If neither representativeness nor replication was achieved, what arguments can be raised to support the applicability of the results to your situation? Are they valid arguments?

As before, proceed to the next step cautiously if you are not satisfied with your answers to these questions.

3 Do you need to take action now? If you haven't already done so, this is the time to consider your objectives. Why did you read the article? If you wanted to "keep informed" or to make some scholarly use of the research you can stop here, though we recommend that you remember the strengths and weaknesses of the study as well as the findings.

If your goal is to apply the study in your professional practice, how long can you wait? The longer you wait the more opportunity you have to collect other information from the literature or from colleagues, staff, and clients that may help you reach a better or more secure decision. Waiting, of course, has its risks. If you wait too long, a decision may be made for you by default, or, as in the case of medical treatment, the action you take may be less effective. So you need to balance your need for collecting information with the need to make a decision.

4 What actions are "suggested" by the findings? The link between findings and actions is extremely weak. Rarely will the results suggest a single action. Different readers interpret findings from different perspectives, and each may see different actions justified by the article, even when the readers are all in the same profession and are confronted by the same problem.

In one investigation of this kind of diversity of interpretations, students and professionals were given a description of the situation facing a product manager and a copy of a new market analysis for that product. The students and professionals were asked to use the results of the analysis to plan a marketing strategy. Not only did they come up with widely different strategies, but some were in direct conflict with others. Each was cogently defended by data from the study's results.

Perhaps the best you can do is to get additional inputs from others. A listing of many plausible actions will prevent a premature commitment to the first one you thought of. You can also use help to pare down the list of actions to those which appear to be most strongly supported by the findings.

5 Which of these actions is best? There are two aspects of best that need to be considered. The first deals with desirability—should the action be taken? Questions of ethics, policy, and standards need to be answered. Under all but the most extreme circumstances you would remove from consideration any action that failed this test even though it would solve the problem. Burglarizing a competitor's research laboratory, for instance, might unquestionably solve your problem of a need for information about competition over the next few years. But many businesspeople would reject the solution on ethical grounds.

If more than one action is judged desirable, the second concern is to choose the one with the best chance of succeeding. Decision theory is concerned with precisely this type of situation. Each alternative action has several outcomes, and you may not know which of these will occur. Furthermore, each outcome has associated with it some risk and some potential benefits. Making a choice in these circumstances will be easier if you follow the procedure given in an introductory decision-making textbook. In so doing, you may actually identify the best action to take, but even if the exact textbook procedures are not used, the time devoted to considering risk, uncertainty, consequences, and benefits will be well spent.

6 How should the chosen action be implemented? If the proposed action is minor, only affecting yourself, this may not be a serious problem, though some personal changes, like dieting, are not that easy to carry out successfully. In all other situations the change ought to be planned.

All changes affect people, even technological changes. Because people are different, they react differently to change. Unless a great deal of training or publicity preceded the change, some of their reactions will be negative—even if the change is beneficial. Whether you are dealing with the general public or your fellow workers doesn't matter; the safest way to proceed is to expect resistance, confusion, and fear and to plan accordingly. Negative reactions occur for voluntary changes as well as mandatory ones. In most cases you would prefer acceptance and support, not merely compliance.

You also need to plan strategies and tactics for implementing change. There are many, and the most effective combination depends upon your particular situation.

Some general approaches are listed here to give you a better idea of the options a change agent has to work with and the complexities involved.

Political approach: Including lobbying, use of mass media, compromise

Interpersonal approach: Including use of norms, asking favors, persuasion

Reinforcement approach: Including rewards and punishments

Modeling approach: Including demonstrations and "setting a good example"

Educational approach: Including training, giving facts, providing a rationale

Compliance approach: Including giving orders and making whatever changes you can without consulting others

Much has been written about effecting change, and you may want to review some of that material if you are not already familiar with it.

7 Was it successful? After the change has been implemented and has had an opportunity to work for a while, a wise practice is to evaluate its effectiveness. For some changes, it doesn't matter much if they don't work out as planned. For other changes, the consequences are serious and some assessment is needed so that corrective action can be taken.

Evaluating change is a form of research and is subject to many of the problems and errors that have been detailed throughout the book. Depending upon the seriousness of the situation, you may want to use outside help to assist in the evaluation.

This has been a short chapter; so short, in fact, that it might be better as a checklist for applying research findings. We cannot do much more in one chapter. Many factors are involved, they are complex factors, and much has already been written about them. Using the checklist requires judgment. While the seven steps or decisions were presented in order, you may need to proceed to a subsequent step even though you are not completely satisfied with an earlier one. The best we can do for you in such a situation is to remind you to estimate the consequences of being wrong and to remember that estimate as you go on to later steps. There are no hard-and-fast rules. Practitioners and scientists need to do the best they can in whatever situation they find themselves, but they also need to have a realistic understanding of that situation.

QUESTIONS TO ASK

Throughout this book we have used questions in this section to summarize the advice we gave in the chapter. This chapter is little more than a summary itself. So, maybe you could just reread the chapter.

FOR FURTHER THOUGHT

1 Think of situations where information was put to use. Were the seven questions we asked considered seriously? What were the consequences of doing so or not doing so?

2 Other than this chapter, only Chapter 2 has had anything to say about value judgments. Review our statements about what we believe about what we know in Chapter 2. Who can you

think of that would not agree with what we believe? How might those people affect your actual use of factually accurate information?

3 How do your values and other people's values, in addition to your objective evaluation of information, influence how you will use that information?

4 Relate the discussion of dogmatism in Chapter 5 to people's willingness to evaluate the success of a change they themselves introduced.

5 Interpret the following quotations in terms of the materials in this chapter.

    (a) "If science is primarily concerned with moving from facts to *understanding,* program evaluation, in the present context at least, is mainly concerned with proceeding from facts to *decisions.*" (A. A. Lumsdaine and C. A. Bennett)

    (b) "A manager is concerned with arriving at a decision (good or bad) on the basis of the information available, whereas a scientist is concerned with determining the information necessary to make the decision (which is always more than what he has)." (A. A. Lumsdaine and C. A. Bennett)

    (c) "Success for the researcher depends upon being first with a discovery or a proof. But, success in the bureaucracy often means never doing anything first." (Anonymous)

FOR FURTHER READING

Evaluation

1 C. H. Weiss. *Evaluation Research: Methods of Assessing Program Effectiveness.* Englewood Cliffs, NJ: Prentice Hall, 1972.

A short but thorough coverage of what is involved in evaluating how well a program succeeds in accomplishing its goals. The issues she considers are equally important in evaluating any change implemented to achieve some goal.

2 C. H. Weiss. *Evaluating Action Programs: Readings in Social Action and Education.* Boston: Allyn and Bacon, 1972.

Primarily relevant to evaluation in the specific settings mentioned in the subtitle. Some readings cover broader issues such as methodology.

3 R. L. Schalock. *Outcome-Based Evaluation.* New York: Plenum Press, 1995.

Another, more recent, look at how to evaluate whether a program accomplishes its goals.

4 P. H. Rossi and H. E. Freeman. *Evaluation: A Systematic Approach,* 5th ed. Newbury Park, CA: Sage Publications, 1993.

A more comprehensive description of how evaluations of social programs should be conducted.

Implementing Change

5 W. G. Bennis; K. D. Benne; and R. Chin (Eds.). *The Planning of Change,* 2nd ed. New York: Holt, 1969.

A good sourcebook that includes articles by some of the major thinkers in the change field.

6 R. G. Havelock. *Planning for Innovation through Dissemination and Utilization of Knowledge.* Ann Arbor: University of Michigan Press, 1971.

An integration of findings with an organized approach to the study of innovation. Produced through work at the University of Michigan's Center for Research on Utilization of Scientific Knowledge (CRUSK).

7 E. M. Rogers. *Diffusion of Innovations,* 4th ed. New York: The Free Press, 1995.

A cross-cultural approach to the study of innovations. Presents Rogers's four-part model of the adoption of innovations by individuals. Especially useful is Chapter 11 on "The Consequences of Innovations," from which the example at the beginning of this chapter was taken.

8 W. D. Coplin and M. K. O'Leary. *Everyman's Prince: A Guide to Understanding Your Political Problems,* 2nd ed. N. Scituate, MA: Duxbury Press, 1976.

A humorous, but very practical step-by-step guide for influencing political and regulatory bodies specifically, and for effecting social or organizational change in general.

9 J. McCalman and R. A. Paton. *Change Management: A Guide to Effective Implementation.* London: Paul Chapman, 1992.

An up-to-date summary of how to apply your knowledge of change management to the actual task of implementing changes in an organization.

Decision Theory

10 G. S. Fulcher. *Common Sense Decision Making.* Evanston, IL: Northwestern University Press, 1965.

An easy-to-read introduction to the topic of decision making. A good starting point for beginners or those who want a nonmathematical treatment.

11 W. Lee. *Decision Theory and Human Behavior.* New York: Wiley, 1971.

An introductory-level book on decision theory at a level somewhat more advanced than the Fulcher work. Presents formal theories of decision theory without mathematical treatment of the topic.

12 J. G. March. *A Primer on Decision Making.* New York: The Free Press, 1994.

A more recent introduction to the state of our understanding of the process of making decisions.

APPLICATIONS

How to do evaluations

Our ideas on the evaluation of research were summarized in the questions found at the ends of the chapters throughout the book. The only thing you have to do to evaluate an article is simply to answer these questions. Right? Wrong! No one does it that way. Besides, it would be inefficient and unnecessary.

The purpose of this section is to tell you how actually to tackle a research report. We've boiled it down to six steps. Before you jump ahead, remember that even a step-by-step guide to evaluation isn't the same easy process as making instant rice. Evaluation is more complicated. Some of the complexities you face are as follows.

No "Correct" Process

First, there's no one correct way to do an evaluation. The process is much more of an art than a science simply because the evaluator's judgment is such a large part of the evaluation. You will be limited because you almost always know far less than you would like about the research. Information is likely to be missing from an article. In addition, you may use different personal standards than another evaluator. There's just no one correct way.

No "Correct" Questions Set

Also, there's no one correct set of questions for all journal articles. The Questions to Ask, reprinted in the next few pages, give you a place to start. Your knowledge of the subject area and the research methods used will often suggest different questions that are more useful in evaluating any particular article. And once you identify a potential error, you will probably call on more specific questions to explore the error in depth and its possible consequences. It is impossible, therefore, to specify the complete set of questions ahead of time; too much depends on you and on the article you're evaluating.

No "Correct" Results

Finally, there's no one correct result to an evaluation. The standards you apply depend on your purposes, as Chapters 1, 14, and 15 pointed out. Readers with different purposes can't be expected to come up with similar evaluations. Even when evaluators have the same purposes, reconciling differences in their judgments is difficult if not impossible. While we expect some degree of overall agreement among different evaluations of the same journal article, complete agreement should not be expected.

In the pages that follow, we will outline a six-step guide to evaluation. It is a beginning. There isn't any easy way to do an evaluation. Carrying out the six steps completely is an arduous process. In practice, many people will skip steps or do them incompletely because they don't have the time that is required. We recognize that there is almost never enough time. However, to do the evaluation job right requires that *all* the steps be carefully followed.

16

A STEP-BY-STEP GUIDE FOR EVALUATION

Step 1 Clarify your purposes for reading and evaluating.

Why are you evaluating this journal article? As Chapter 15 asked, are your needs more like those of a scholar or a practitioner?

Step 2 Skim the article.

Read the title, abstract, summary, conclusions, and headings to determine (1) the topic being researched, (2) the more important findings and conclusions, (3) the author's method, and (4) the findings and conclusions that are of interest to *you.*

Step 3 Review your general orientation.

Before beginning the evaluation you need to know where you stand as a judge. Will your opinions toward this topic, or toward this type of research, systematically bias your evaluation of the report? Some of the Questions to Ask are given below. The numbers in parentheses identify the chapter and question number in case you want to refer back to our original discussion of the question.

- What is your mental set when you read an article? (5–2)
- Are you too optimistic about the factual accuracy of this research report? (1–1)
- Are you too quick to condemn all aspects of the report because of some detected shortcomings? (1–3)

Step 4 Marshal your external knowledge relevant to this article.

Research does not exist in a vacuum, and evaluators often have some prior understanding of the topic, the research traditions, the personalities, and the journals in the field. These should not be ignored in any evaluation. Some of the Questions to Ask are:

- How important is this problem to your more general concerns? (8–3)
- What do you already know about this topic—firsthand knowledge as well as the results of other research? (1–2)
- What do you already know about the methods the author used to study the topic? (1–2)
- How much influence should the credibility of the author and the journal have on your judgment of the article? (5–1)
- Are purposeful distortions a possibility? (4–4)
- Who did the observation? (3–4)
- What additional sources of knowledge should you consider? (2–1)

Step 5 Evaluate the article.

There are three components to the evaluation. First you need to review the Questions to Ask. Then you should read the article and try to answer each of these questions. Finally, you need to assess the consequences of your answers.

Step 5A Review the Questions to Ask.

Actually, only one question needs to be answered: Are the results factually accurate and useful for your purposes? But that's so abstract as to give you no guidance. The following questions may be more helpful because they summarize the general goals of an evaluation:

- What kinds of errors are present? (Chapters 6 and 7)
- How important are the consequences of these errors for your purposes? (Chapters 6 and 7)
- Do the findings and conclusions follow from the data? (Chapters 3 and 4)
- Are the findings and conclusions generalizable to your situation? (Chapters 14 and 15)

Even though these questions give you some broad evaluation criteria, they still give too little specific guidance. The Questions to Ask from the ends of the chapters are more detailed and should be used here. They have been reorganized to assist your evaluation efforts and are reprinted beginning on page 190. Remember to add additional questions as necessary and to probe further whenever a potential error is uncovered.

Step 5B Read the article and answer each question.

These questions apply to all types of research. Researchers and readers in specific subject areas tend to concern themselves with only some types of errors. For example, psychology's experimental tradition places great weight on the control of extraneous variables and less on the generalizability of the findings. In survey research the emphases are usually reversed. Your evaluation, however, must be concerned with all possible errors, regardless of the research traditions in the discipline.

Step 5C Determine the implications of your answers to the questions.

A researcher can never control or eliminate all possible sources of error in a single study. But not all uncontrolled error will adversely affect the findings in an important way. You need to estimate the effect or the consequences of the errors on the findings themselves and on your possible use of those findings.

Step 6   Summarize Your Evaluation in an Abstract.

The abstract you find at the beginning of an article usually states the topic goals, what the researcher did, and the findings and conclusions. Your abstract should also include this information, but in your own words. More importantly, it should also contain your assessment of the actual accuracy of the findings and their generalizability to your situation. We will call your summary a Reader's Abstract.

A Reader's Abstract, then, is a review and an evaluation of the researcher's work—expressed to reflect your purposes. Some of the Questions to Ask are:

- What are the dimensions over which you need to generalize the findings? (14–2)
- Do you need to take action now? (15–3)
- What actions are suggested by the findings? (15–4)
- Which of these actions is best? (15–5)

FOR FURTHER READING

You might want to compare our approach with evaluation strategies suggested by other authors.

1 T. Tripodi; P. Fellin; and H. J. Meyer. *The Assessment of Social Research: Guidelines for the Use of Research in Social Work and Social Sciences.* Itasca, IL: Peacock, 1969.

2 J. Millman and D. Bob Gowin. *Appraising Educational Research: A Case Study Approach.* Englewood Cliffs, NJ: Prentice Hall, 1974.

3 P. C. Stern. *Evaluating Social Science Research,* 2nd ed. New York: Oxford University Press, 1996.

4 E. R. Babbie. *Social Research for Consumers.* Belmont, CA: Wadsworth, 1982.

5 T. R. Black. *Evaluating Social Science Research.* Thousand Oaks, CA: Sage Publications, 1993.

6 J. R. Fraenkel and N. E. Wallen. *How to Design and Evaluate Research in Education.* New York: McGraw-Hill, 1993.

7 E. R. Girden. *Evaluating Research Articles from Start to Finish.* Thousand Oaks, CA: Sage Publications, 1996.

8 P. C. Stern and L. Kalof. *Evaluating Social Science Research,* 2nd ed. New York: Oxford University Press, 1996.

17

QUESTIONS TO ASK

Reprinted below are those Questions to Ask taken from the end of each chapter in this book that are specific enough to actually be useful when evaluating a research report. They are to be used in Step 5 of the Step-by-Step Guide for Evaluation. Remember that the first four steps are essential prerequisites for their use.

WARNING: The Research General has determined that using these questions without understanding the rest of the book can be dangerous to your intellect and to the authors' reputations.

The questions are arranged according to that part of a journal article most likely to contain the information needed for their answers. This classification scheme will be helpful, but it is not foolproof. Many times, the information needed to answer a specific question will be found in other parts of the article. You need to respond to each question regardless of the location of the information.

1 *Framework questions* You are likely to find answers to these questions in the beginning of most journal articles. The *framework* consists of everything prior to the detailed description of the researcher's methods—including the problem statement, the literature review, the hypotheses, and the definitions.

Problem Statement

• Is the problem stated so that it can be solved? (8–1)

A problem may be simple or difficult depending on the way it is stated.

• Is the problem open-ended and nonbiasing? (8–2)

Some ways of stating a problem can restrict the scope of a study and eliminate useful alternatives from consideration.

• What is the effect of the language used in the article? (4–3)

Did the author maintain neutrality in the choice of words, or are emotionally laden terms employed? Do the language and style reveal or conceal what occurred? This question obviously applies throughout a journal article, not just to the beginning.

Definitions

• Are definitions sufficiently specific? (8–7)

Definitions are arbitrary; you don't know what is meant unless the author takes some pains to tell you. If definitions are not sufficiently specific, your meanings and the author's meanings may well be different.

• Are the definitions fruitful? (8–9)

Definitions should build on the research traditions in a field, and they must be useful to you.

• Are circular definitions used? (8–6)

It will not always be obvious that a word is just being defined by itself. Sometimes questionnaires or other procedures must be examined in detail to discover whether the concept is linked to anything besides itself.

Literature Review

• What was included in the literature review? (8–11)

The selection of articles should be based on relevance. Articles should be recent and should not exclude disagreeing or contradictory findings. Ideally, the review should be evaluative, but it should also include enough descriptive information for you to completely understand the research cited. If a review is missing, it does not mean that the research findings are not factually accurate or generalizable; there is just less information on which you can base your evaluation. See also Question 8–10.

• Did the author thoroughly consider what might be found and the corresponding implications prior to gathering the data? (8–12)

"Interesting" findings can be gleaned from almost any research study after the data have been collected. "Conclusive" findings are much more likely, however, to come from a prior commitment about what will be learned from specified findings. Justification for this prior commitment often exists in the literature review.

2 *Method questions*   You are likely to find answers to these questions in the middle of most journal articles. The *method* consists of a detailed description of how the data were obtained—including data collection techniques, subjects or objects studied, experimental design, sampling procedures, and instrument construction and use.

Observation

• What is left out? (3–1)

Since the world cannot be completely described, an observer intentionally or inadvertently selects a very small part of the world to observe. What is omitted may not be useful to that individual, but it may be extremely important to you.

• Did the observer control for possible distortions? (3–6)

If the observer did not attempt to control for distortion, it does not guarantee that the observations were in error; they may be, but we have no way of knowing. If the observer did attempt to control distortion, it does not prove that there was none, but it does lend weight to our confidence in the observation. Not only do observations occur directly, but in many cases "aids" to observation are used such as questionnaires, instruments, tests, and so on. Each has its own limitations and vulnerabilities in terms of possible distortions. See also Question 3–3.

• In what context was the observation made? (3–5)

Knowing something about when and where an observation was made may help. What wasn't observed may have affected what was.

Measurement

• Are operational definitions used and are they adequate? (8–8)

Operational definitions are to help ensure that you know what the researcher is talking about in terms of the real world. However, they are seldom wholly adequate for the concepts they define. They may include something not included in the concept, and they may miss something that should be included. You must decide to what extent they are on target. More than one operational definition for each concept helps ensure that the conceptual target is hit.

• Is the researcher trying to measure more precisely than the instrument allows? (9–1)

A ruler calibrated in sixteenths of an inch cannot be used to measure to 1/64 inch. The instrument just doesn't have that degree of precision. Very precise measurement is a goal in all scientific fields, but you can't let researchers imply they have achieved a finer degree of measurement than their instruments allow.

• Is some measure of reliability given? (9–2)

With such a measure your job is easier; you get not only an estimate of the reliability, but also a clue about the researcher's concern for careful measurement. If no measure is given, you may want to estimate the amount of noise present. Once you have a measure of reliability you need to determine if it is sufficiently high for your purposes, and if it represents the kind of reliability you need. See also Questions 9–3 and 9–4.

• What is really being measured? (9–5)

In general terms a measure is valid to the extent it measures what it is supposed to measure. Could the instrument be measuring something other than what the author indicates? One clue is its predictability. Does the measure predict well enough, and predict what you are interested in? A second clue is the number of different components or dimensions being measured at one time; it is usually safer to measure each independent dimension separately. See also Questions 9–6 and 9–7.

Control

• Did the researcher eliminate potential rival explanations in the design of the study? (12–2)

Uncontrolled rival explanations compete with the explanation given by the researcher. The fewer rival explanations possible, the more likely the researcher's explanation is correct.

• Was more than one group studied so that a comparison can be made? (12–3)

With only one group, the three sources of rival explanations (time, measurement, and people) are viable. When more than one group is used, they need to be identical in all essential respects except for the proposed cause. Look for random assignment or some other evidence that the groups were identical. See also Question 12–4.

Generality

• How strong are the arguments that are used to support generality? (2–4)

Combine those given by the author (reasoning, method, or replication) with your assessment of them and your knowledge of the subject matter.

• Did anything happen to the people during the study that made them less representative? (14–3)

Watch out for excessive dropouts, low completion rates, and pretests that change the people and their reactions to the rest of the study.

3 *Results/Conclusions questions* You are likely to find answers to these questions toward the end of most journal articles. The Results/Conclusions consists of what the researcher discovered and how the discoveries were interpreted—including summaries and analyses of the data, the findings derived from the data, and the conclusions and the interpretations reached from the findings and other sources.

Fair Summaries

• Are the summaries fair? (10–2)

Fairness in terms of summaries is a relative notion. All summaries must leave something out and reflect someone's viewpoint. You need to decide if a fair picture is given for your purposes. To help evaluate a summary, ask (1) how it was computed, (2) what alternatives are there, and (3) what was left out. Averages and percentages are two very commonly used summaries. Each can be judged by asking the three questions above. See also Questions 10–3 and 10–4.

Interpretations

• Is there anything missing that might be important? (4–1)

It is difficult to evaluate what isn't there. Search for possible missing assumptions, hints that bad results were not included, and the presence of all necessary parts of a journal article. You will need to make use of your knowledge of the subject matter, the author, and the journal.

• Are all interpretations acceptable to you? (3–2)

Even direct observation includes interpretation. You must decide whether you, or another researcher, might interpret differently at this very basic level. In addition, findings are reported on the basis of the observations. They also involve interpretations. Finally, authors frequently interpret the findings in order to draw conclusions. You need to pay careful attention to the interpretations involved in each step.

• Does the researcher answer the question asked? (8–4)

Make sure the researcher's interpretations deal with the question the research answered. Remember: the question answered may not always be the same as the question asked.

• Do the findings make sense in terms of the literature cited? (8–13)

If the current findings agree with those of earlier studies and your own experiences, you will probably want to trust them more than if they are clearly at variance with the earlier work. The major exception to this is when the researcher predicted a contradictory result before the data were collected.

Relationships

• Was the analysis or the conclusion based on a single variable? (11–1)

Rarely will this type of simple analysis be sufficient. Usually, to understand what's occurring, you will need to think about a variable in terms of how it relates to other variables.

• What about "third" variables? (11–2)

This is really two questions in one: (1) Did the researcher consider the possible effects of third variables? and (2) Can you think of any other variables, not considered by the researcher, which may affect the relationships?

• Is the level at which the relationship was determined the same as the level at which the conclusions are drawn? (11–3)

We must be sure that the interpretation of relationships occurs at the same level the data was collected. If the researcher did cross levels, remember that the reported relationship is rarely (if ever) close to what the relationship really is at the level of the conclusions.

- Was each variable free to vary to its full extent? (11–4)

If it wasn't, then the relationship reported by the researcher will be less than would have been found if full freedom existed.

- Was a causal relationship stated or implied? (11–5)

If the researcher interprets the results in terms of causality, three ingredients must be included in the argument. First, there has to be a relationship. There must also be some consideration of the sequence of the two variables and of whether other third variables could have been the cause.

Explanations

- On the basis of your knowledge of the subject matter, can you think of any explanation for what happened in the study other than the one given by the researcher? (12–1)

External criteria as well as methodological criteria should always be applied. Use your understanding of the field to know what to look for and to know how serious each rival explanation may be. See also Questions 12–2 and 12–3.

- Are all parts of the proposed cause needed to produce the effect? (12–5)

For theoretical as well as practical reasons it is often helpful to know a more precise cause of what happened.

- Are definitions being misused as explanations? (8–5)

Definitions tell us how to label things, but labeling does not explain anything.

Inferences

- Was statistical inference used correctly? (13–3)

This is a two-part question. First, were the proper statistical procedures employed? And second, were they employed correctly? There is no way one can answer these questions without some training in statistical inference. So if the study is important, get some expert to judge the adequacy of the statistics employed.

- Could the findings have occurred by chance? (13–4)

You probably should focus attention only on those findings that are statistically significant—all others are more likely to be chance occurrences. Not all significant findings may be acceptable to you—it depends on the level of significance. You must determine if the level is acceptable for your situation. Remember, however, that statistical procedures work on numbers—even unreliable, invalid, and ambiguous numbers. Statistics cannot improve a poor study and statistical findings, even if significant, are suspect if the data are not accurate. See also Question 13–1.

- If confidence intervals are used, are the range and the confidence levels acceptable for your use? (14–4)

Confidence intervals are a form of statistical inference and you must decide this question in terms of your own situation.

- How important are the findings? (13–5)

Given statistically significant findings at an acceptable level of significance (or an acceptable confidence interval), you must decide if the findings are meaningful. Are the results large enough to warrant further interest on your part?

18

PRACTICING

DO I REALLY NEED DIRECTIONS ABOUT HOW TO PRACTICE?

That seems like a reasonable question. Some of our readers are eager to get started doing evaluations; they want to jump immediately to Chapter 19 to see if their evaluations match ours. But, before you begin, we think it is important to understand what kinds of help we can give and what kinds of help we can't. So, take a few minutes to read this very short chapter, and then you'll be better prepared for the evaluations in Chapter 19.

To start with, we want to point out that the Questions to Ask at the end of Chapters 1 through 14 are really of two types. Some pose questions about the content of the article. Other Questions to Ask are aimed at you, the reader. While our evaluations can provide answers to the former type of question, they can't answer any questions about you. We've marked the latter type of question with an asterisk so you will understand why they have not been answered.

Questions Focusing on the Evaluator

For practice with this type of question, read one or more of the two articles that we evaluate (pp. 202–207 and pp. 216–24 and the two additional articles that we do not evaluate (pp. 231–37 and pp. 238–55). Then, write out your answers, present them to other readers of this book, and get their feedback on how honestly and thoroughly they believe you answered the questions.

Questions Focusing on the Article

The other type of question focuses on the article. Prepare your own answers to those questions for the two articles that we evaluate (pp. 202–207 and pp. 216–24). Then, compare what you wrote with our evaluations using the table below to find where we answer each question.

You can also prepare answers to the questions for the third and fourth articles (pp. 231–37 and pp. 238–55), but we do not provide evaluations for those articles. You are on your own.

See Chapters 16 and 17 for a thorough approach to evaluating articles. Here you are applying the questions in isolation for practice. When you have finished the book, you can combine your answers to the questions into coherent evaluations of the two articles and compare your work with ours.

Question Number	Our Evaluations	
	First Article	Second Article
1–1	*	*
1–2	*	*
1–3	*	*
2–1	*	*
2–2	*	*
2–3	*	*
2–4	p. 212	p. 227
3–1	p. 209	p. 226
3–2	p. 214	p. 228
3–3	none explicitly, but see our reference to 3–6	
3–4	none explicitly, but see our reference to 3–6	
3–5	p. 210	p. 226
3–6	p. 210	p. 226
4–1	p. 213	p. 228
4–2	*	*
4–3	p. 208	p. 225
4–4	None, we did not answer this question for these articles. There are no obvious reasons to suspect purposeful distortions, but you might want to speculate on what some obscure reasons are that might exist.	
5–1	*	*
5–2	*	*

Chapters 6 and 7

The questions in this chapter are relatively theoretical, and we don't address them directly in our sample evaluations in Chapter 19. The more detailed questions from other chapters cover these broader issues. Thus, you won't be able to compare your answers with ours, but for practice in spotting bias and noise you can write out your answers and compare them with the answers of other readers of this book.

8–1	p. 208	p. 225
8–2	p. 208	p. 225
8–3	*	*
8–4	p. 214	p. 229
8–5	p. 214	**
8–6	p. 208	p. 225
8–7	p. 208	p. 225
8–8	p. 210	p. 226
8–9	p. 208	p. 225
8–10	none, the answer is simply "yes" which is implied by our answering the following three questions	
8–11	p. 209	p. 225
8–12	p. 209	p. 226
8–13	p. 214	p. 229
9–1	p. 211	p. 226 & 227
9–2	p. 211	p. 226
9–3	*	*
9–4	none explicitly, but see our reference to 9–2	
9–5	p. 211	p. 226
9–6	*	*
9–7	none explicitly, but see our reference to 9–5	
10–1	none, this is a rhetorical question	
10–2	p. 213	p. 228
10–3	none explicitly, but see our reference to 10–2	
10–4	none explicitly, but see our reference to 10–2	
11–1	***	p. 228
11–2	p. 211	p. 228
11–3	***	p. 228
11–4	***	p. 228
11–5	p. 211	p. 228
12–1	p. 214	**
12–2	p. 211	p. 227
12–3	p. 211	p. 227
12–4	***	p. 227
12–5	p. 214	p. 227
13–1	none explicitly. This is a very abstract question. We evaluate the quality of the data at various points in the evaluation with answers to other more specific questions.	
13–2	none explicitly, but the answer is "yes" and we evaluate the authors' use of inferential statistics in both articles.	
13–3	p. 214	**
13–4	p. 214	**
13–5	p. 214	**
14–1	none explicitly. This is a very abstract question. We evaluate factual accuracy at various points in the evaluation with answers to other more specific questions.	
14–3	p. 212	p. 227
14–4	****	**

*These questions focus more on you, the evaluator, than on the article. See our comments at the beginning of this chapter about how to practice answering these questions.

**Our answers to these questions for the second article are scattered throughout the evaluation. We refer to this on page 229, but you will have to read the previous pages of the review carefully to find our specific comments.

***Not relevant since this article reports on a field study.

****Not relevant because confidence intervals are not used.

19

SAMPLE EVALUATIONS

This section contains reprints of two articles. The first is from the *Journal of Social Psychology;* the second is from *Contemporary Education.*

The evaluations were added to illustrate how our criteria apply to a wider variety of methodologies. The *Journal of Social Psychology* article uses a quasi-experimental design and direct observation methodology. The *Contemporary Education* article uses a survey research design with a mail questionnaire.

Following the reprint of each article is our evaluation of it. Each evaluation is the direct result of following Steps 5 and 6 of the step-by-step guide. The first four steps in the guide affect the written evaluations only indirectly. They are an important part of what an evaluator does, but they do not usually receive specific attention in a written evaluation.

In our evaluation, a purpose (Step 1) is not explicitly mentioned since we have a very general one—namely, to learn something about human behavior. We are not, at this time, interested in applying these results to any particular group of people or in designing buildings, sidewalks, or services on the basis of these findings.

The facts that we skimmed the article (Step 2) and that we reviewed our general orientation toward research (Step 3) do not need to be mentioned. External knowledge (Step 4) appears at various places in the evaluation when it is relevant.

Thus, our sample evaluation is primarily an example of how the questions could be answered and the consequences assessed. Complex and detailed aspects of statistical analysis, experimental designs, and technical problems of reliability have not been analyzed in depth. As you gain knowledge about these more complicated issues, you will have additional questions to apply. We have evaluated the article as though our only knowledge of research methods and statistics was from this book and maybe an introductory research course.

Since these are sample evaluations, we have included, in brackets, explanations of what we were thinking at various points. We also refer to our Questions to Ask by number. So as not to contaminate our example, we clearly distinguish these bracketed comments from what would normally appear in an evaluation.

Determinants of Nonstationary Personal Space Invasion*

Robert S. Sobel and Nancy Lillith

Hunter College of the City University of New York

SUMMARY

The personal space of 116 pedestrians in midtown Manhattan was violated by a male or female experimenter. The subject population consisted of predominantly middle-class adults of all ages. Fifty-three percent of the subjects were male, and 27 percent were black. The experimenter walked toward a target subject in an unwavering straight line. Subjects and experimenters approached and passed each other in a section of the street where a measurement grid had been drawn on the sidewalk. Observers measured the point at which subjects initially deflected from the collision line, and the distance between subject and experimenter at the point at which they passed each other. The results indicated that males were given less frontal space than females ($p < .01$). About 40 percent of the trials resulted in mild *brushes* even though the line of vision between the experimenter and subject was always clear. The male experimenter was brushed more often than the female experimenter ($p < .05$). These results differ markedly from the findings of laboratory experimenters.

A. INTRODUCTION

Experimental investigations of the effects and determinants of personal space invasions have become increasingly popular in recent years (4, 14). Perhaps the most consistent finding in the area concerns the relationship between physical distance and psychological distance. A variety of studies have demonstrated that less personal space is maintained for friends (9), peers (8), and people with whom attitudes and political and cultural orientations are shared (1, 12, 15). The interaction between personal space and spatial relationships between people and objects has also received considerable attention. Systematic effects have been produced by varying such factors as the angle and position of chairs (3, 5, 13) and the angle at which one person approaches another (7, 11). The least consistent findings in the area concern the effects of the sex of the person being approached and the sex of the approaching person on the amount of personal space that is ultimately obtained. The experimenter (E) in these laboratory studies is either the person being approached or the approaching person. In the former case, the subject (S) is told to walk toward the E and stop at a comfortable distance. In the latter, E walks toward the subject and the subject tells E when to stop. The distance between S and E in either case defines the amount of personal space that S gives E, or that E receives from S. Dosey

*Received in the Editorial Office, Provincetown, Massachusetts, on October 29, 1974, and given special consideration in accordance with our policy for field research. Copyright 1975, by The Journal Press.

Source: The Journal of Social Psychology 97:39–45 (1975). Reprinted with the permission of The Journal Press and Robert S. Sobel.

and Meisels (2) found that females approached closer to other females than to males, while the personal space given by males did not differ as a function of the sex of the person approached. Kassover (6) found that both male and female subjects stood closer to a female E than to a male E. In a study in which the subjects were stationary, Pederson and Heaston (10) found that in both simulated and experimental conditions closer frontal approaches were permitted by males than by females. Although it is difficult to derive any clear-cut conclusions from these limited data, one interpretation is that although American females prefer to be given more personal space than American males, they in fact are given less.

An important limitation in all but a few of the personal space experiments has been the artificiality of the experimental situations and the overreliance on static conditions in which at least one of the observed persons is stationary. This limitation has been particularly evident in the studies in which the sex of the Es and Ss has been an experimental variable. In many real life situations both persons are nonstationary and presumably carry their personal spaces around with them, like protective screens. Violations of nonstationary personal space and the behavioral effects of such violations may depend upon a somewhat different set of norms than we find in the traditional laboratory setting.

The purpose of the present study is to examine the determinants of nonstationary space invasions in a field-experiment format. The strategy of the study is to have a male and a female E approach solitary pedestrians by walking toward them in an unwavering straight line. Observers then record the distance at which the subjects first deflect from the line of contact and the distance between the Es and the Ss at the point at which they pass each other.

B. METHOD

1. Subjects

One hundred sixteen adults who were walking on 34th Street between Madison and Fifth Avenues in New York City on a Saturday afternoon in April 1974 served as experimental subjects.

2. Location

The 34th Street location was chosen for two reasons. First, the flow of pedestrian traffic was constant but not so heavy that the Es would have difficulty in maintaining a straight-line approach toward the Ss. In addition the flow of pedestrians was light enough so that the subjects could easily see the approaching E. Second, the location provided an ideal hiding place for the observers. The display windows of a major department store were indented between pairs of structural columns. Each window had a small concrete lip where the observers could unobtrusively sit and record data. Subjects were unlikely to notice the observers in the first place, and if they did, there was no cue as to their function; the observers appeared to be casually lounging in front of the display windows.

3. Procedure

Two observers (O_1 and O_2) stationed themselves in front of the display window, sitting about 10 feet apart. Directly in front of them a measurement grid was drawn on the street in light blue chalk. The grid was barely noticeable to passing pedestrians and seemed to draw virtually no attention throughout the day. The dimensions of the grid are presented in Figure 1. The grid was 8 feet wide and 25 feet long. It was drawn in the center of the sidewalk. Marks were made at 30-inch intervals lengthwise, and at 6-inch intervals from side to side.

The male E was 5'10" tall and of medium build. The female E was 5'7" and also of medium build. Both Es wore casual, middle-class, sport clothes. The Es practiced walking together at a uniform speed, and the walking speed of the Es was later measured during each experimental trial. Throughout the experiment, the male and female Es alternated trials.

Each trial began as an E stationed himself (herself) at the corner of Madison and 34th Street, about 100 feet from the measurement grid. The E picked as the target S the first person walking alone at a normal pace toward the grid at about 100 feet in the opposite direction. Only a few choice conflicts arose and these were resolved by choosing the person who would arrive at the most central portion of the grid. Having picked the target S, E walked toward him (her) in a straight line, at constant speed, avoiding direct eye contact. Es were directed to stop only if a direct frontal collision was imminent, a situation which never occurred. Slight collisions or *brushes* were allowed to occur.

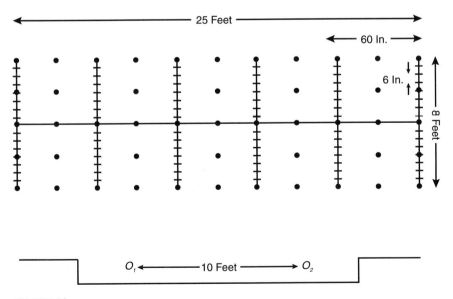

FIGURE 1
Sidewalk measurement grid and observation positions.

For each trial, the observers independently recorded the distance at which the S first began to deflect away from a collision with E. The observers also recorded the distance between the S and E at the point at which they crossed paths. After noting these distances, the observers also noted the S's race (black, white, other), socioeconomic status in terms of general appearance and apparel (low, middle, high), and age group (young—18 to 34 years; middle—35 to 49 years; old—50+ years).

On those trials where *brushes* occurred, it was very difficult for the observers to estimate accurately the point of first deflection because of the closeness of the Ss to E. It was generally agreed that Ss had to begin to move from the collision line when they were about 15 inches from E. Therefore, when *brushes* occurred, the initial deflection distance was uniformly set at 15 inches. Of course, the side deviation distance was set at zero inches whenever brushes occurred.

C. RESULTS

Fifty-three percent of the Ss were male, 69 percent were white, 27 percent were black, and 4 percent were Oriental. In judging the age category of subjects the Os disagreed 28 percent of the time. In those cases where the Os did agree, 40 percent were judged to be young, 39 percent were considered middle aged, and 20 percent were placed in the old age category. Clearly, there was sufficient variance in the sex, age, and race ratings to permit additional analyses. In 94 percent of the cases where the observers agreed as to the socioeconomic status of the subjects, they were judged to be middle class. As a consequence no further analyses could be conducted with these data. The lack of variance in this category is probably due more to the difficulty of judging SES on the basis of general appearance and attire than to the lack of true variance in the population.

Forty-six of the 116 trials resulted in *brushes*. Since the distance in these cases were uniformly set at 15 inches, they were excluded from the calculation of interrater reliabilities. The interobserver reliability coefficient for the judgment of frontal deflection was .83, and the coefficient for side distances was .49. Typically, side distances were relatively small, and the difficulty in judging distances at the crossing point, as well as the O's poor angle of vision, served to reduce the reliability of side judgments.

With sex of E and the sex of Ss as factors, a 2×2 analysis of variance was performed on the frontal deflection distances. There was a significant main effect due to sex of E ($F = 6.28$, df $= 1$, 112, $p < .05$). Male Es were given an average of 37.1 inches of frontal personal space, while females were given an average of 55.9 inches. There were no differences in the amount of space given by male ($\overline{X} = 46.4$) and female ($\overline{X} = 46.5$) subjects. The interaction term was not significant ($F = 2.40$, $df = 1$, $p = .12$), though there seems to be a tendency for males to give one another the least space ($\overline{X} = 31.2$), and females the most space ($\overline{X} = 61.6$). This interaction is significant, however, when only those subjects who did not brush the Es were used in the analysis ($F = 4.76$, $df = 1.62$, $p = .03$). There were no significant effects when the distance between E and S was the dependent variable. Separate, nonparametric tests were performed for those subjects who brushed the Es, to assess whether or not there was a relationship between *brushing* and sex of *E* or sex of *S*. When sex of *E* is used, the association is significant ($\overline{X}^2 = 3.88$, $p < .05$). The association is not significant when sex of *S* is used ($\overline{X}^2 = 2.6$). Thus, the results for the subjects who brushed the *E*s is consistent with the overall findings.

A 2×2 analysis of variance was performed with race of subject as the third factor. Race was not significantly related to frontal or side distances. Another analysis of variance was performed with age as the third factor. Only *S*s whose age category was agreed upon by both observers were used in the analysis. There was no main effect due to age, but there was a significant age × sex of subject interaction for both frontal and side distances (frontal: $F = 4.32$, $p = .01$; side: $F = 5.76$, $p < .01$). This interaction was caused by the difference in personal space given by old men compared with the amount given by old women. Old men gave almost three times as much space as old women, but generalizations from these data should be restricted because it is based on a relatively small sample size ($N = 17$).

D. DISCUSSION

1. Sex Effects

The results of this field experiment are clearly at odds with the findings of laboratory experiments of stationary personal-space invasion. We found that, regardless of the sex of the *S*, females were given more personal space on the street than males. Dosey and Meisels (2) found an interaction between sex of *S* and sex of *E;* females approached closer to other females than to males. Our results indicate no such interaction, and the means are in the opposite direction. Kassover (6) found that all *S*s gave less personal space to females than to males. Our results indicate exactly the opposite. Apparently the norms governing the limits of personal space in stationary laboratory situations may be different from the norms of the street. It may be more permissible to move close to a stationary female than a nonstationary female. Of course, the difference between the present findings and laboratory results could also be due, in part, to differences in the type of subject tested (i.e., New York City pedestrians versus college students).

2. Proportion of Brushes

The most surprising experimental finding was the high percentage of brushes that occurred. In spite of the fact that all *S*s had a clear line of vision in the direction of *E,* and in spite of the fact that a trial started when the *E* and the *S* were approximately 200 feet apart, 42 percent of the trials ended with some physical contact. In these cases *S*s refused to give up unilaterally their right of way until the very last moment. This phenomenon suggests the presence of a strong norm of bilateral accommodation in street behavior. We recommend that the skeptical reader try walking straight at people, at a constant rate of speed, on any moderately active street and record the proportion of brushes.

3. Implications

If the norms of the street differ so dramatically from the norms of more static environments, it seems reasonable to assume that other situations will produce still different effects. Some interesting locations for further study of nonstationary personal space include department stores and other retail establishments, sports events, and highly active work settings such as construction sites and busy offices. As an unobtrusive, manipulable, and easy to measure construct, personal space may prove to be a highly effective variable for the study of comparative norms with the use of a nonquestionnaire methodology.

REFERENCES

1 Baskett, G. D., and Byrne, D. Seating choice as a function of attitudinal similarity-dissimilarity. Paper presented at the annual convention of the Southwestern Psychological Association, Austin, Texas, 1969.
2 Dosey, M. A., and Meisels, M. Personal space and self-protection. *J. Personal. & Soc. Psychol.* 11, 1969, pp. 93–97.
3 Felipe, M. J., and Sommer, R. Invasions of personal space. *Soc. Prob.* 14, 1966, pp. 206–14.
4 Hall, E. T. The Hidden Dimension. Garden City, NY: Doubleday, 1969.
5 Hare, A. P., and Bales, R. F. Seating position and small group interaction. *Sociometry* 26, 1963, pp. 480–86.
6 Kassover, C. J. Self-disclosure, sex, and the use of personal distance. Unpublished doctoral dissertation, Department of Psychology, University of Texas, Austin, 1971.
7 Lewit, D. W., and Joy, V. Kinetic versus social schemas in figure grouping. *J. Personal. & Soc. Psychol.* 7, 1967, pp. 63–72.
8 Lott, D. F., and Sommer, R. Seating arrangement and status. *J. Personal. & Soc. Psychol.* 7, 1967, pp. 90–95.
9 McDowell, K. V. Violations of personal space. *Can. J. Behav. Sci.* 4, 1972, pp. 210–17.
10 Pedersen, D. M., and Heaston, A. B. The effects of sex of subject, sex of approaching person, and angle of approach upon personal space. *J. Psychol.* 82, 1972, pp. 277–86.
11 Rawls, J. R., Trego, R. E., and McGaffey, C. N. A comparison of personal space measures. A report of NASA Grant NGR-44-009-008, Institute of Behavioral Research, Texas Christian University, Fort Worth, Texas, October 1968.
12 Sandler, S. B. Physical distance as a function of psychological distance. Paper presented at the annual convention of the Eastern Psychological Association, Atlantic City, New Jersey, 1970.
13 Sommer, R. Studies in personal space. *Sociometry* 22, 1959, pp. 247–60.
14 _____ . Personal Space. Englewood Cliffs, NJ: Prentice Hall, 1969.
15 Thayer, S., and Alban, L. A field experiment on the effect of political and cultural factors on the use of personal space. *J. Soc. Psychol.* 88, 1972, pp. 267–72.

Department of Psychology
Hunter College of the City University of New York
695 Park Avenue, Box 1511
New York, New York 10021

EVALUATION

Overview

This study was an investigation of several factors that might be related to the way in which people react to invasions of their personal space. "Invasion" consisted of having an assistant walk straight at subjects on a New York City sidewalk. The researchers recorded the distance at which the subjects first turned away from the collision course, the distance apart the subject and assistant were when they passed, and the number of subjects who brushed against the assistant in passing. They examined the relationship of these variables to the sex of the assistant and to the sex, age, race, and socioeconomic status of the subjects.

> [This sort of introduction has always seemed to us to be necessary even though it only repeats some of the information given in the article. What is said here strongly reflects the purpose of the evaluator. We mostly want to remember what the study was about. Other evaluators might include mention of how the study was conducted if they had particular methodological concerns. For others, the fact that the subjects were pedestrians on New York City streets might be important.]

The Framework for the Study

The researchers state that their purpose was to "examine the determinants of nonstationary space invasions in field-experiment format." This wording and their review of the literature suggest that they have a theoretical interest in "personal-space invasion" and that they would like to use a "field-experiment" format for the research.

It should be noted that the researchers wanted to limit the scope of the study to this particular methodology and to the particular variables and related factors mentioned above. Their approach to the problem makes it eminently researchable and there is no apparent bias. However, findings will be subject to the strengths and weaknesses of that methodology and will be limited to the variables and related factors which were chosen. [Questions 8–1 and 8–2 answered.] In particular, the language used in the article is descriptive, not emotionally laden, and gives the impression that the researchers arc careful and competent. [Question 4–3 answered.]

Nonstationary personal-space invasion is not conceptually defined in the article. The ordinary meanings of the words probably suggest about the same things to us as they do the authors. However, since we know little about specifically what the authors mean [Question 8–7], we cannot assess the fruitfulness of the definitions for the field or possible circular uses of the definitions [Questions 8–9 and 8–6]. Also, we will not be able to assess how well operational definitions used later match the target concept. The implication of this lack of information is that we will consider the findings in terms of the particular operational definitions used in the study; we will not be able to conclude much about the relationship of the findings to the concepts.

> [Our approach in the above paragraph is similar to that which any "naive" reader would have to take. Someone who knows the previous research on this and related topics could bring external knowledge to bear on these definitional issues. Such an evaluator could probably make good guesses about what the authors had in mind conceptually and could certainly assess the adequacy of the operational definitions in terms of conceptual definitions currently in use.]

The literature review is helpful in identifying other work that has been done. Also, the descriptions of the other studies help in understanding what the authors mean by "nonstationary" and "personal-space invasion." However, the review of the literature is not helpful in determining the factual accuracy or generality of the findings because there is no indication that the strengths and weaknesses of the methodologies used were taken into consideration. Also, no indication is given of what criteria the authors used in deciding which studies to include, but we suspect that they included *all* relevant studies since this is usually the practice in the better journals. [Question 8–11 answered.]

The authors list a number of findings concerning how the sex of the interactants affects personal-space invasion. However, it is difficult to interpret them without at least knowing more precisely how "personal-space invasion" was operationally defined in each of the earlier studies and the actual distances involved. These findings are not crucial for the evaluation of this study, however, since the authors apparently did not make firm predictions of what they expected to find. Doing so can strengthen findings through agreement with theory and with previous research. This study stands on its own, and for that reason alone we will retain some skepticism about the factual accuracy and generality of the findings until we see theory or replications that also support them. [Question 8–12 answered.]

> [The limitations noted above for the review of literature are very common in this type of journal article. Authors are frequently very careful about describing the research, using proper statistics, and drawing only warranted conclusions, but they give less consideration to the more theoretical aspects of their research. Sometimes space limitations in journals also make it difficult for authors to include a thorough literature review.]

Methods

Turning now to the methods used by the researchers, we note that what was actually observed was the distance between the assistant and the subject when the subject first turned away from the collision course, the distance between the assistant and the subject when they passed one another, and the sex, race, age, and socioeconomic status of the subjects. The first distance assumes in its definition that assistant and subject are headed directly toward each other until the subject turns in order to avoid a collision. We wonder how well this condition was met. It would seem that subjects would sometimes change their course for other reasons, but maybe not. Since the authors did not comment, we have a small lingering doubt. Other information that might have been included would be any insights the researchers may have had that were not formally recorded. For instance, were there any characteristics of subjects, other than those they set out to observe, that seemed to be related to how pedestrians responded to almost being walked over on a New York City street? [Question 3–1 answered.]

Judging distances under these circumstances is obviously difficult. The use of the grid drawn on the sidewalk and the use of two independent observers were attempts to control for errors in observations. Reliability data discussed later gives us some indication of how successful this attempt was. Sex, race, age, and socioeconomic status were noted by observers. Accurate observation of sex should not have been a problem, but there is certainly the possibility of questionable decisions as to age and race. The authors do not indicate what, if anything, they did to improve the accuracy of the observers' judgments, but having two independent observers is an excellent precaution. For socioeconomic status the authors report that it was probably not judged accurately, and the researchers correctly decided not to pursue analysis of that variable. [Question 3–6 answered.]

> [We do not see any notable effect of context on the observations made in this study (Question 3–5), probably because the authors were careful to choose variables that could be observed relatively objectively. Thus, we would not normally make any mention of it.]

The operational definition of personal-space invasion is very clear: "*E* walked toward him (her) in a straight line, at constant speed, avoiding eye contact. *E*s were directed to stop only if a direct frontal collision was imminent, a situation which never occurred. Slight collisions or brushes were allowed to occur." As noted previously, we cannot assess the adequacy of this operational definition in terms of the conceptual definition, but we do feel confident that we know what the researchers were observing.

Unfortunately, two important aspects of the operational definition are missing. We do not know the age or race of the assistants, and we do not know anything about "who" the assistants and the observers were. (We do know the height and build of the assistants.) We would guess that both assistants were white since the authors would probably have mentioned race if they were otherwise. However, we suspect that the findings might be quite different for assistants of different races, and we would definitely want to check with the authors. We can continue the evaluation since our comments will apply whatever race the assistants were, although assistants of different races would considerably complicate the statement of the findings.

Our concern about "who" the observers and the assistants were is with the expectations they may have brought to the study. Expectations of observers and experimenters can have pronounced effects on the findings through very subtle means. We would like to know what expectations these people were likely to have had. We suspect that the authors were two of the four people. Obviously, they have thought a lot about how people behave in this sort of situation, and they may have very definite expectations. In addition, at least subconsciously most researchers want their studies to provide some results so that their efforts are not wasted. There is not enough information in this article to assess the possible effects of the researcher's expectations.

We don't feel any need for operational definitions of sex, race, or age, except for what the authors tell us about the age categories used. We would be concerned about socioeconomic status, and in fact the authors dropped it from the study because of measurement problems. [Question 8–8 answered.]

Distances like 31.2 and 61.6 inches are surely misleading in indicating accuracy to a tenth of an inch. We assume that the observers did not make their estimates that precisely. The decimal probably was the result of taking the mean of several observed distances. The authors were obviously more interested in the relationships between the various factors and the distances than in the distances themselves. The use of the grid and the concern the authors showed by assigning all "brushes" as 15 inches suggest that the authors were careful about the accuracy of their measurements. We feel confident that the observed differences of about 30 inches and "three times as much space" are larger than measurement error could account for. [Question 9–1 answered.]

A measure of reliability is given for all of the measurements by comparing the judgments of the two observers. It is quite good for the distance at which the subject first "turns" (.83, which we assume is a standard correlation coefficient with an upper limit of 1.00), but not good for the side distances (.49). The lack of reliability for the side distances makes us unwilling to accept the lack of findings for this variable as accurate. Lack of findings could very well be due to noisy (that is, unreliable) measurement.

The measure of reliability for the other variables was the percentage of time that the two observers agreed. They apparently agreed 100 percent of the time on the race and sex of the subjects. They agreed only 72 percent of the time on age, but that seems high enough so that some trust can be put in the data. [Question 9–2 answered.]

[Question 9–5 asks, what is really being measured? The answer seems very straightforward in this study, and we would not include any comments on the question. We have already noted that we cannot assess the adequacy of the operational definitions in terms of target concepts.]

Because this was a field study, there was almost no control for extraneous variables. Differences that appear to be due to sex, race, or age might be due to other variables that make the males in this study different from the females, young different from old, and so on. We will have to look to other research or theory to gain confidence that these are really the causal variables. [Questions 11–2, 11–5, 12–2, and 12–3 answered.]

[This is a good place to remind ourselves that all studies have some weaknesses and that limitations of a study are not necessarily due to the depravity of the researchers. It is easy to feel that a study should provide answers to all reasonable questions. However, as we pointed out in the main part of this book, one study never proves anything. There will always be some questions left unanswered. We are sure, for instance, that the authors are well aware of the limitations of a field study for providing evidence of causal relationships. Our statements above must not be read to imply that the study should have been designed better. We simply feel that it is necessary to note that the limitation exists so that we can use the findings appropriately.]

The subjects were pedestrians on a particular New York City street. Very little is known about them or the location. Thus, as the authors state, we will have to be very cautious about generalizing to any other group of people or any other location. The subjects were not randomly chosen, but the researchers do seem to have tried to avoid any systematic selection. They say that "The *E* picked as the target *S* the first person walking alone at a normal pace toward the grid at about 100 feet in the opposite direction. Only a few choice conflicts arose and these were resolved by choosing the person who would arrive at the most central portion of the grid."

[Other considerations could well be important for some readers' purposes. For instance, might there be personality differences between people who walk down the middle of the sidewalk and those who walk along the edges, or might there be differences between people found walking alone and people who are excluded because they were with other people?]

No mention is made of attrition of subjects, but because the ability to generalize is limited, it is probably a moot point anyhow. [Questions 2–4 and 14–3 answered.]

Findings and Conclusions

All the data for sex, race, and number of brushes are given. That is, since we know that there were 116 subjects, the percentages given allow us to calculate exactly how many subjects were in each category of each of those variables. The same is true of age and socioeconomic status except that we do not know the age or socioeconomic status assigned to subjects when the two observers disagreed. They disagreed on age for 28 percent of the subjects, and only the 72 percent of the subjects for whom they agreed were included in the data analysis. Note that this is a type of attrition of subjects. Any conclusions about age as a factor in reaction to personal-space invasion are based only on a subset of all the subjects. We cannot think of any plausible reason why this subset would be different from the whole group, but there is that possibility.

The summaries of the distance measures, which are our main concerns, are scant. Some data are not summarized at all; findings are just stated. Usually only means are given; it would have helped to know how much the individual data points varied. Thus, we don't know as much about the distances observed as we would like. We are curious as to what the range of distance was and their variability (normally given as a standard deviation). What we do know can be summarized in a table. The numbers given are mean inches between the subjects and the assistants when the subjects first "turned."

[In many journals a table like this is very expensive and so, by the way, are illustrations. Authors are under pressure to report all that they can in the text. In fact, after we wrote this evaluation we sent it to Dr. Sobel, the first author. He said, in response to this section of the evaluation, that the original manuscript for the article had tables that included all the distances and standard deviations. The editors of the journal, however, asked that the article be shortened considerably. Thus, the tables were removed and only essential distances were incorporated into the text.]

		Assistant		
		Male	Female	
Subject	Male	31.2	61.6	46.4 N = 61
	Female			46.5 N = 55
		37.1 N = 58	55.9 N = 58	

That is, male subjects turned 31.2 inches away from the male assistants and 61.6 inches away from the female assistants, and the average for male and female assistants combined is 46.4 inches. We are not given the first two distances for female subjects, but we do know that the average distance of "turning" for male and female assistants combined was 46.5 inches. In addition, if male and female subjects are combined, they turned at 37.1 inches from the male assistant and 55.9 inches from the female assistant.

[Note that you cannot figure out the missing distances easily because there are more males than females in the study. We have checked some of the mathematics and found it plausible. For instance, if there were 61 male subjects and 55 female subjects, the reported percentages of males and females in the study would be correct. ($N = 116$ is reported by the authors in the abstract.) In addition, since male and female assistants alternated walking toward subjects, each should have interacted with 58 subjects, and 46.4 should be the mean of the two numbers 31.2 and 61.6 in the table, and it is. Assuming that we have figured things out correctly, we could use these numbers to fill in the missing distances in the table (but we haven't bothered to do so).]

The authors use inferential statistics to determine whether the differences among the various numbers in the table might be caused only by chance. The p associated with the differences between 37.1 and 55.9 was found to be less than .05, indicating that the authors believe this is a real difference and not due to chance alone. The numbers 46.4 and 46.5 hardly differ at all, and the only reasonable conclusion is that the difference is due to chance alone. For 31.2 and 61.6 the authors say that "the interaction term was not significant, . . . though there seems to be a tendency for males to give one another the least space ($\bar{X} = 31.2$), and females the most space ($\bar{X} = 61.6$)." We do not know for sure what the authors' criterion for "significance" was, but it is probably safe to assume that it was .05. So, the p value is probably something greater than that, but we don't know what.

The distances between subjects and assistants when they passed is described only as "relatively small." In addition, the authors state that no significant differences were found in these distances as related to any of the factors.

We don't have any summary of the data related to race except for the statement "Race was not significantly related to frontal or side distances." Since we do not necessarily ascribe to the widely used significance criterion of .05, we wonder if there might have been some interesting differences with p values around .1 and .2. The risk of being wrong is greater, but still acceptable to us, and if space were available we would have been interested in the data.

For age we know only that there was no significant difference between age groups if male and female subjects were considered together (stated by the authors as "no main effect due to age"), but that "old men gave almost three times as much space as old women." No distances were given. The finding had a p of .01 associated with it.

Thus, some potentially useful, but supplementary, information was left out by the authors. We don't know a number of things we would like to know. However, the authors appear to be accurate in their calculations, and we tend to believe that what is stated is factually accurate. [Questions 10–2 and 4–1 answered.]

[Our comments in the last few paragraphs go a bit beyond the naive user we have been trying to simulate. Some knowledge of the inferential statistics technique of analysis of variance is useful in deciphering the authors' presentation of their data.]

The authors state a number of findings based on their data, draw conclusions from
those findings, and go on to discuss implications. They made very few assumptions as
they went from step to step. We do find that our lack of information about previous research makes it difficult for us to evaluate their statement, "The results of this field experiment are clearly at odds with the findings of laboratory experiments of stationary
personal-space invasion." The authors note that the different findings might be due to
differences in the type of subject tested. The differences could also be due to differences between the types of assistants used, and we would want to examine the differences in the ways subjects' personal spaces were invaded in order to assess similarities
and differences among the studies. [Question 3–2 answered.]

[The researchers do answer the questions asked so we would not discuss Question 8–4 in the
evaluation. Similarly, because of some missing information in the literature review, we
would not try to answer Question 8–13 which asks if the findings make sense in terms of the
literature cited. Question 12–1 asks about other explanations. We can think of none, except
for the possibility of extraneous unmeasured variables, which were discussed above. Questions 12–5 and 8–5 also need no comment in the case of this study.]

The use of inferential statistics seems to be correct. Since we do not have a specific
use in mind for the findings, exact p values that would be acceptable cannot be stated.
When a particular application comes up we will look back at the p values with criteria
in mind. Differences of 18.8 inches, 30.4 inches, and "three times as much space" are
large enough to interest us. [Questions 13–3, 13–4, and 13–5 answered.]

SUMMARY

All in all, we would conclude that the results should be accepted tentatively. All studies are bound to have limitations. In this one we found some, but no major errors that
convinced us that the data were wrong. In terms of the consequences of these limitations we concluded that they allow us to accept the data tentatively. We will look for
replications of this study and for theory that reflects on this topic. We would be willing to do research to further explore the topic.

We found the authors exemplary in stating findings and conclusions based on the
data. The findings and conclusions can be no better than the data, and so they too are
accepted tentatively, but they do not become progressively less accurate because of
unwarranted assumptions introduced by the authors.

Finally, we want to know if the findings and conclusions are generalizable to our
own situation. We do not know who the conclusions can be generalized to, whether
the results would be the same in other situations, or whether the results would be the
same for other assistants. The differences that would be found in a "tough" part of

town or in a Western city are interesting to contemplate, for instance. Moreover, as the authors pointed out, the results of this study differ from those found in a laboratory. Clearly, additional research is needed before anyone is sure what caused the differences. Within the limitations of this type of study, the authors have done all that they can to help us. They have described in detail how the subjects were obtained. The subjects were not randomly sampled from a population, so the only way to support a statement about generalizability is to argue that the people you want to generalize to are similar to the people studied. The same is true of "locations" and "assistants." Since we do not wish to generalize at this time, we simply keep the characteristics of those studies in mind. [The four general questions listed in Step 5A are answered.]

READER'S ABSTRACT

This study was an investigation of several factors that might be related to the way in which people react to invasions of their personal space. "Invasion" consisted of having an assistant walk straight at subjects on a New York City sidewalk. The variables were distance at which the subjects first turned away from the collision course, distance apart the subject and assistant were when they passed, and the number of subjects who brushed against the assistant in passing. The relationship of these reactions to the sex of the assistant and to the sex, age, race, and socioeconomic status of the subjects was examined.

The main findings had to do with the sex of the assistant and the sex of the subject. Male subjects turned, when confronted by the female assistant, at almost twice the distance (61.6 inches) as when they were confronted by the male assistant (31.2 inches). Females turned at about the same distance for both male and female assistants. Combining male and female subjects, the distance given to the male assistant (37.1 inches) was less than the distance given to the female assistant (55.9 inches), but that is probably due mostly to the difference for male subjects noted above. One other finding of interest was that "old men gave almost three times as much space as old women," but only seventeen subjects were involved.

The authors note in their discussion that findings in this study contradict findings in previous laboratory studies. It appears that the exact nature of this contradiction would be worth exploring. Also, 42 percent of the trials ended with some physical contact ("brushes"). This refusal of subjects to unilaterally give up their right of way is interesting.

This article leaves a number of important questions unanswered. The race and age of the assistants are especially important, and we are interested in the accuracy and the variability of the distances observed. In general, we believe that the study has been competently carried out and that we can tentatively accept the findings, conclusions, and implications. If we needed to use the findings, we would want to obtain more information from the authors.

Faculty Perceptions of a Teacher Career Ladder Program

By Horace E. Johns*
Middle Tennessee State University

INTRODUCTION

Merit system has been defined as "a system or practice in which persons are hired or promoted on the basis of ability rather than patronage."[1]

> Merit pay is supposed to encourage excellence. "The purpose of merit pay," write Miller and Young, "is to provide a motivating force, an incentive, which results in greater productivity of the worker, whether he/she is a laborer, a government employee, or a college professor."[2]

A merit pay system has as its main objective to make reward and recognition more commensurate with productivity.[3] In American society, salary is an inescapable measure of the desirability of any job.

Many persons think that business and industry have differentiated between those who produce and those who do not.[4] Others argue, however, that private business has not "found merit pay to be widely usable."[5] Private business has found that development of objective measures of performance and maintaining the necessary record-keeping systems are too difficult, expensive, and time-consuming to be of much practical interest.[6] These have proven to be controversial factors in developing an acceptable merit rating system for the teaching profession as well. There are few, if any, objective measures of teaching effectiveness.[7]

There exist two critical problems facing the teaching profession today: (a) the lack of teachers with quality education backgrounds and (b) the lack of career incentives sufficient to retain the most talented teachers.[8] The merit rating system was originated as a possible solution to solve the teaching profession's dilemma; however, there has been much objection to it.

Carl J. Megel, former president of the American Federation of Teachers, lists nine reasons why he thinks basing teachers' salaries on a merit rating plan is both educationally and professionally unsound:

(1) merit rating cannot fairly evaluate the true effectiveness of teaching because the aims of teaching are intangible;

---

*Horace E. Johns holds both B.A. and J.D. degrees from Vanderbilt University, an M.B.A. from Syracuse University, and both an M.A. in social science education and Ph.D. in higher education from George Peabody College. Johns currently serves as director of the Business and Economic Research Center and assistant professor of Management and Business Law at Middle Tennessee State University in Murfreesboro, Tennessee. He is editor of the *Tennessee Business and Economic Review*. Johns has published in *Higher Education, Innovative Higher Education, Leadership and Organization Development Journal,* and the *Journal of the Legal Profession*. His current research interests include motivation of classroom teachers, the impact of federal laws on personnel administration, consumer's attitudes toward advertising by health care providers, constitutional limitations on attorney advertising, and current public attitudes toward labor unions.

Source: Contemporary Education 59:4, pp. 198–203 (summer 1988). Copyright 1988 by Horace E. Johns and *Contemporary Education*. Reprinted with permission.

(2) merit rating rewards conformity because the teacher who wishes to advance feels that he/she must conform to the rater's opinion;

(3) merit rating puts a premium on the absence of teacher problems, or to put it another way, most performance ratings are based on personality characteristics rather than on objective results achieved;

(4) merit rating fosters a competitive rather than a cooperative spirit because merit-pay-increase budgets presume there are as many persons performing below average as above average (however, in many organizations, there is a vast majority performing above average);

(5) merit rating strikes at the security of the teacher because the teacher fears the disfavor of the rater, thus making him/her refrain from initiative;

(6) rating systems disregard the type of environment in which a teacher teaches (e.g., a teacher can perform better in a facility with all the latest equipment while those in less fortunate circumstances are hindered);

(7) merit rating cannot improve the quality of education because teachers are almost unanimously opposed to it;

(8) merit rating, because it lowers teacher morale, is a dangerous mirage and cannot relieve the teacher shortage; and

(9) merit rating plans do not reward good teachers for superior work, or to put it another way, the difference in increases between acceptable performers and top performers is not great enough to warrant the extra effort and actually may be demotivating to employees.[9]

Despite the many critics and studies indicating the questionable influence of merit pay as a means of motivating teachers and thereby improving the quality of education, there appears to be a growing notion that there should be some means for encouraging teachers to teach high performance standards. Also, a sizable public consensus is that there must be some means of holding teachers accountable for their performance in the classroom. With this type of public support behind him, Gov. Lamar Alexander instituted a plan in Tennessee in 1984 to improve the quality of teachers and administrators by strengthening "knowledge, preparation, incentives, and rewards."[10] Governor Alexander's Better Schools Program places major emphasis on the Master Teacher Plan, with the outcome of the program being highly dependent upon the success of a merit pay system for Tennessee's public school teachers.

Tennessee's Master Teacher Plan is based on the Career Ladder Program which identifies five career stages: Probationary, Apprentice, and Career Levels I, II, and III. A teacher must have at least 12 years of experience to apply for a Master Teacher or Career Level III position. Supplemental or merit pay begins with Level I. In essence, the plan is intended to reward the most competent teachers with higher positions and accompanying higher salaries in exchange for increased responsibility on the part of those teachers.

The Career Ladder Program received legislative approval after many months of stormy political battles and intense lobbying efforts, both for and against its passage. The program is characterized by a highly structured system of evaluation of classroom teachers from kindergarten through the 12th grade. It is also characterized by considerable record keeping on the part of both administrators and teachers. In short, the program has been hailed as giving Tennessee teachers the proper incentives to become better and more accountable at their jobs, while it has been assailed as being a morass of bureaucratic paperwork which does little to motivate teachers and improve the quality of education.

Because of the controversial nature of Tennessee's Career Ladder Program and because of the considerable disagreement as to the Career Ladder's impact on teachers and teaching, a study was conducted to ascertain teachers' attitudes and perceptions toward their work and toward the introduction of a career ladder/merit pay program into their work environment.

PURPOSE OF THE STUDY

The purposes of this study were to: (a) determine the overall perception of teachers toward the Career Ladder Program and (b) determine whether any selected biographical/demographic characteristics of teachers were significant factors in the teachers' perceptions of the Career Ladder Program.

It was the researcher's hope to provide some information which would indicate how a particular managerial tool for motivation—that is, the Career Ladder Program—was being received by the public school teachers in Tennessee. Furthermore, it was the researcher's hope that this study would, in some way, contribute directly or indirectly to more effective and more highly motivated teachers. Ultimately, it is hoped that the information furnished by this study will help to improve the quality of education in both Tennessee and the nation as a whole.

PROCEDURE

The first section of the questionnaire used to collect the data concerned demographic characteristics of the respondents. There were categories within each of the demographic characteristics which are shown in Table 1.

The second section of the questionnaire included 20 questions designed to measure how favorably teachers perceived the Career Ladder Program. The respondents were asked to answer Likert-type questions in regard to their strength of agreement on a scale ranging from "strongly agree" to "strongly disagree." The individual responses were given numerical values and then summed to provide an overall index score of the teachers' perception of the Career Ladder Program. These 20 questions are contained in Table 2. The theoretical range of the perception index was 20–100, with 100 indicating the most favorable perception of the Career Ladder Program and 20 the least favorable perception. The researcher, after consultation with the Tennessee Education Association, devised the questions in the first and second sections of the survey instrument.

The relevant population for the study consisted of all public school teachers in Tennessee who taught in grades kindergarten through the 12th grade. When this study was undertaken in October of 1985, there were approximately 28,000 K–12 classroom teachers in Tennessee's public schools.

With the assistance of the Tennessee Education Association, to which belong approximately 80 percent of the total population of K–12 educators in Tennessee, the

TABLE 1
CATEGORIES OF DEMOGRAPHIC CHARACTERISTICS

Category	Demographic characteristics			
Age	20–29	30–39	40–49	50/above
Sex	Male	Female		
Race	White	Black	Other minority	
Extent of formal education	Bachelor's	Master's	Doctor's	Other
Total years of full-time teaching	0–3	4–7	8–11	12/more
Income per year from teaching	Less than $10,000	$10,000–$15,000	$15,000–$20,000	$20,000–$25,000
	$25,000–$30,000	Over $30,000		
Association status	TEA	Other	Nonmember	
Type of community in which you teach	Urban	Suburban	Small town or rural	
Major work assignment, Grades:	K–3	4–8	9–12	Other
Highest career level applied for in 1984–1985 school year, Career level:	I, Fast track	II	III	Other
Was your career level application made in 1984–1985 school year approved?	Yes	No		
Career level for which you plan to apply in 1985–1986 school year, Career level:	I	II	III	Other

researcher obtained a random sample of 1,500 teachers from the National Education Association in Philadelphia. The research instrument was mailed to these 1,500 teachers, 927 of whom returned usable questionnaires, for a 61.8 percent response rate.

Percentages of respondents were 45.6, 28.7, and 25.7 for east, middle, and west Tennessee, respectively. According to the 1980 census, actual population dispersion percentages were 38.5, 32.9, and 28.6 for east, middle, and west Tennessee, respectively.

It is important to note that the Career Ladder Program first became effective during the 1984–1985 school year. Consequently, this survey, which was conducted during the fall of 1985, reflects opinions of teachers after one full academic year's operation of the Career Ladder Program.

The level of significance for all statistical tests was set at the 0.05 level.

STATISTICAL TESTS AND FINDINGS

The mean perception of Career Ladder score was 39.957, with a high of 97, a low of 19, and a range of 79. The mean score indicates a relatively negative perception of the Career Ladder Program on the part of teachers.

From Table 2 it can be seen how negatively teachers perceive the Career Ladder Program. For example, all perceptual statements, except statements 10 and 20, had more than 50 percent respondents who answered the statements in a negative manner—for example, strongly agree and agree or strongly disagree and disagree, depending on how each statement was worded—and even statement 10 had 49.2 percent who answered negatively. Only statement 20 ("Because of the Career Ladder Program, I am considering leaving teaching in the near future") had a percent clearly under half (that is 36.4 percent) who answered negatively.

Also, Table 2 indicates that statements 2, 6, 7, and 18—have approximately 90 percent or more of the respondents expressing some degree of negative perception. To illustrate this particular finding, it can thus be said that 90.7 percent of the teachers did not feel that Career Ladder would be a significantly positive factor to keep them in teaching; that 92.0 percent of the teachers did not feel that Career Ladder had had a positive effect on the morale of the teachers in their building; that 89.9 percent of the teachers felt there were better ways than Career Ladder to motivate persons to become teachers; and that 91.4 percent of the teachers did not feel that Career Ladder had increased their enthusiasm about teaching.

The researcher also wished to determine whether the teachers' demographic characteristics were significant factors in the way the teachers perceived the Career Ladder Program. A one-way analysis of variance was used to determine if there were significant differences among the demographic characteristics (as shown in Table 1) and the teachers' perceptions of the Career Ladder Program.

It was found that there were significant differences among the independent variables of age ($p < .05$), race ($p < .001$), total years of full-time teaching ($p < .05$), major work assignment ($p < .001$), highest career level applied for in 1984–1985 school year ($p < .001$), and career level for which you plan to apply in 1985–1986 school year ($p < .001$) and that of the dependent variable—the teachers' perceptions of the Career Ladder Program. In short, these variables made a significant difference in the way teachers perceived Career Ladder.

It was found that there were no significant differences among the independent variables of sex, extent of formal education, income per year from teaching, association status, type of community in which you teach, and was your career level application made in 1984–1985 school year approved, and that of the teachers' perceptions of the Career Ladder Program. In short, these variables did not account for a significant difference in the way teachers perceived Career Ladder.

TABLE 2
PERCEPTIONS OF CAREER LADDER PROGRAMS

Perception	Strongly agree	Agree	Undecided	Disagree	Strongly disagree
1. I believe that the Career Ladder Program will improve the quality of teaching and administration	1.5	10.1	15.9	31.1	40.6
2. The Career Ladder Program will be a significantly positive factor in keeping me in the teaching profession	1.0	3.1	5.2	24.6	66.1
3. Career Ladder documentation is detracting from my instructional and preparation efforts	42.6	33.3	7.8	11.3	4.9
4. Preparation of written professional materials for evaluation has made me a better teacher	1.7	7.3	12.5	40.0	38.5
5. The Career Ladder Program has resulted in an excessive number of observations and evaluations of teachers	38.1	35.9	11.5	11.1	3.1
6. Implementation of the Career Ladder Program has had a positive effect on the morale of the teachers in my building	1.8	2.5	3.7	25.3	66.7
7. I believe there are better ways than the Career Ladder Program to motivate persons to become better teachers	66.8	23.1	7.4	1.6	1.1
8. The Career Ladder Program will hinder harmonious relationships among the faculty in my building	27.8	27.6	23.6	16.9	4.0
9. I believe the Career Ladder Program will work effectively and fairly	1.6	3.6	15.0	33.0	46.8
10. As a result of the Career Ladder Program the amount of time I spend on instruction has decreased	20.1	29.1	12.9	30.5	7.4
11. The criteria by which career levels II and III can be achieved are very strongly related to the requirements for good teaching	2.1	11.6	19.5	31.7	35.1

Continued

TABLE 2   (*concluded*)

PERCEPTIONS OF CAREER LADDER PROGRAMS

Perception	Strongly agree	Agree	Undecided	Disagree	Strongly disagree
12. Supplemental pay in the Career Ladder Program will act as a strong incentive for me to become a better teacher	2.6	7.2	8.4	38.3	43.4
13. Because of the Career Ladder Program, I have to devote too much time to nonessential, non-teaching duties	33.8	38.1	11.3	13.7	3.0
14. The Career Ladder Program requirements do not significantly detract from the time I have to prepare for teaching	1.5	14.0	10.1	43.9	34.5
15. Advancement through the Career Ladder Program will depend too much on "politics" and not enough on merit	32.4	31.0	26.9	7.3	2.5
16. Teachers who achieve career level II or III will be perceived by their colleagues as superior instructors	2.3	8.5	13.3	42.5	33.4
17. My opportunities to exercise professional judgment are being limited by Basic Skills First (BSF), Career Ladder and other reform initiatives	31.7	36.4	15.7	14.0	2.2
18. The implementation of the Career Ladder Program has increased my enthusiasm about teaching	1.8	3.3	3.5	27.3	64.1
19. The Career Ladder Program will improve the quality of my teaching	1.0	6.4	9.7	32.8	50.1
20. Because of the Career Ladder Program, I am considering leaving teaching in the near future	19.9	16.4	30.8	21.3	11.5

For those variables which accounted for significant differences in the way teachers perceived Career Ladder, Newman-Keuls post hoc multiple comparisons were conducted to locate the significant differences.

The data for age show that category one had significantly higher perceptions of Career Ladder than categories three, two, and four ($p < .05$). The data for race show that category two had significantly higher perceptions of Career Ladder than category one

($p < .05$). The data for years of full-time teaching show that category two had significantly higher perceptions of Career Ladder than category four ($p < .05$). The data for major work assignment show that categories four and three had significantly higher perceptions of Career Ladder than categories one and two ($p < .05$). The data for the highest career level applied for in 1984–1985 school year show that categories three and two had significantly higher perceptions of Career Ladder than categories four and one ($p < .05$). The data for career level for which you plan to apply in 1985–1986 school year show that categories three and two had significantly higher perceptions of Career Ladder than categories one and four ($p < .05$); in addition, category two had significantly higher perceptions than categories five and three ($p < .05$).

CONCLUSION

It was not the researcher's purpose to evaluate the educational value of Tennessee's Career Ladder Program. For this reason, I offer no evaluation or judgment of the program's value in enhancing the quality of teaching or of enhancing the quality of education in general. Rather, I merely undertook to examine Career Ladder as a managerial tool for motivating teachers, for providing them with financial as well as other incentives, and for encouraging them to do a better job.

In examining the teachers' perceptions of Career Ladder from a managerial standpoint, I discovered some alarming attitudes. I found that teachers, in impressive numbers, considered the Career Ladder Program not to be effective in (1) improving the quality of teaching and administration, (2) retaining teachers in the teaching field, (3) providing teachers with strong incentives to become better teachers, (4) enhancing teacher morale, (5) setting out specific and fair criteria for evaluation purposes, and (6) increasing enthusiasm for teaching.

Furthermore, I found that teachers, in impressive numbers, considered the Career Ladder Program to (1) detract from their instructional efforts, (2) be a burden in terms of excessive paperwork and evaluations, (3) hinder harmonious relationships with their fellow teachers, (4) depend too much on "politics" and not enough on merit, and (5) limit their professional judgment.

Finally, it should be noted that almost nine of every ten teachers believed that there were better ways than Career Ladder to motivate teachers and that over one-third of the teachers were considering leaving teaching in the near future because of the program. In short, it appears that the Career Ladder Program has a severe perception problem with Tennessee teachers.

The post hoc multiple comparisons revealed some interesting findings. For example, the youngest teachers (i.e., those in their twenties) tended to view Career Ladder more favorably than other age groups. Black teachers viewed Career Ladder more favorably than white teachers. Those teachers with 4–7 years of full-time teaching experience viewed it more favorably than teachers with the longest experience. High school teachers viewed Career Ladder more favorably than teachers in kindergarten through junior high school. Teachers who, in 1984–1985, applied for the higher levels under Career Ladder, viewed the program more favorably than those teachers who applied for the lowest level. Similarly, teachers who planned to apply for the higher levels in 1985–1986 viewed the program more favorably than those teachers who planned to apply for the lowest level. These findings could potentially have considerable meaning for policymakers and administrators charged with implementing and upgrading this managerial and motivational technique.

NOTES

1 *Random House College Dictionary* (New York: Random House, 1975), p. 837.
2 James R. Miller and Jon I. Young, "Merit Pay: An Unexplained Concept in Higher Education," in "Why Not Merit Pay?" by Lawrence J. Dennis, *Contemporary Education* 54, no. 1 (Fall 1982), p. 18.
3 Buddy Robert Silverman, "Why the Merit Pay System Failed in the Federal Government," *Personnel Journal,* April 1983, p. 294.
4 Sheldon Moore, "Administrative Problems under a Merit Plan," *Journal of Teacher Education,* March 1959, p. 28.
5 Larry W. Barber and Karen Klein, "Merit Pay and Teacher Evaluation," *Phi Delta Kappan,* December 1983, p. 247.
6 Silverman, pp. 294–97, 300–302; and James T. Brinks, "Is There Merit in Merit Increases?" *Personnel Administrator,* May 1980, pp. 59–64; Barber and Klein, p. 247.
7 Moore, p. 28.
8 Fenwick W. English, "Merit Pay: Reflections on Education's Lemon Tree," *Educational Leadership,* December 1983/January 1984, p. 73.
9 Carl J. Megel, "Merit Rating Is Unsound," *Phi Delta Kappan,* January 1961, pp. 155–56.
10 Carlton H. Stedman, "Tennessee's Master Plans for Teachers, Supervisors, and Principals," *Journal of Teacher Education* 36 (1983), p. 55.

ACKNOWLEDGMENT

Special appreciation is given to Cory O'Donnell and Hank Stephens, senior students at Middle Tennessee State University, who assisted in the research and preparation of this manuscript.

Horace E. Johns

EVALUATION

Overview

This study was a survey of teachers' perceptions of the Career Ladder Program, a system for administering merit pay, in the Tennessee Public Schools grades K through 12. It was conducted in October of 1985, one academic year after operation of the program had begun. Overall favorability of teachers' perceptions of the program was determined, and differences in favorability were analyzed in terms of several demographic characteristics of the teachers.

[In this introductory statement we chose to focus on what was studied rather than methodology in order to be sure we are clear about the topic. Also, we want readers of this review to be able to determine whether the findings are of value to them. This seems especially important since the study provides rather specific information about a particular issue in a particular educational system at a particular time.]

The Framework for the Study

The setting of this study is crucial to the evaluation of its findings and conclusions. The topic is neither academic nor theoretical. It is hotly political and probably of great importance to the teachers being studied. Most people take a lot of interest in how their level of pay is determined.

The author has, appropriately, described the political and attitudinal climate. We are alerted to the potential for strong feelings and powerful personal interests that might affect those designing the study, those carrying it out, and those being studied.

Although the setting is emotionally charged, the problem itself is clearly and objectively stated. The author wished to determine favorability of perceptions of the Career Ladder Program and to examine relationships, if any, between several demographic characteristics of teachers and favorability of perceptions. [Question 8–1 answered.]

We should note, however, that the author's own wording at the end of the introductory section could be misleading. He mentions that "a study was conducted to ascertain teachers' attitudes and perceptions toward their work and toward the introduction of a career ladder/merit pay program into their work environment." The attitudes and perceptions of teachers toward their work are studied only within the narrow focus of the Career Ladder (merit pay) Program, and it is not "the introduction" of the program that is studied. In the next paragraph, the first paragraph in the section titled Purpose of the Study, a very precise statement is given. We need to remember precisely what is being studied, as stated in our previous paragraph above.

The problem, as stated, is nonbiasing, but it is limited in scope (e.g., not open-ended). Only answers to very specific questions will be found. An additional open-ended aspect to the study might have added value, but that does not diminish the value of what was done. [Questions 8–2 answered.]

The language used is nonbiasing. The choice of works and syntax do not seem to favor any particular result. It is written in an objective, scientific manner. However, in the Introduction the balance of comments favorable versus unfavorable to merit systems, in general, leans heavily toward the unfavorable. Some readers may know whether this reflects a similar imbalance in the literature; we do not. However, we are suspicious that the author has an unfavorable attitude. We would have preferred that he explicitly discuss the balance in the literature and his own position. [Question 4–3 answered.]

[The definitions used are so straightforward and clear that mentioning them seems superfluous. Thus, Questions 8–7, 8–9, and 8–6 need not be explicitly discussed.]

In addition, we should note that the most recent citation is for 1984. We got useful information about the topic but, depending on when we were reading the article, would want to search for more recent articles and newspaper accounts. The author doesn't give us an overview of the literature or his criteria for inclusion and exclusion. [Question 8–11 answered.]

[By the way, few authors provide their criteria. We wish they would, but it is not at all common.]

We should note that this is not the type of study where the author would make prior predictions of exactly what conclusions will be drawn from what results. Its purpose is primarily descriptive. He is looking for a level of favorability and for any of many possible relationships between demographic variables and favorability. Thus, the findings "stand alone" and will not have the added credence of fitting with other findings or theory. This is an inherent limitation of this type of study which we will keep in mind. [Question 8–12 answered.]

Methods

One advantage of knowing exactly what was asked of the teachers is that we can think clearly about what was left out. Each reader will have to decide whether the specific information obtained is of interest and value. There are, obviously, many more issues related to the program than were studied. [Question 3–1 answered.]

Distortions introduced by measuring instruments are always a danger. We see no reason to suspect a problem in this study, but some possibilities include

• Wording of the twenty items could have biased the results. (Having proponents and opponents react to and evaluate the items could provide information on this. Also, half the sample could have been given items worded in reverse. This would have cost more and complicated the analysis. It would only have been worth it if this were a serious concern.)

• The political and emotional climate at the time the survey was conducted may have been quite different than a few months before or after (i.e., the context for the study may have been unique).

• If questionnaires were distributed by the administrators in their schools, teachers may have feared that their responses would not be kept confidential and they would have answered what they thought administrators wanted them to say.

Each reader will need to apply his external knowledge to decide if these or other sources of possible distortion are plausible. [Question 3–5 and 3–6 answered.]

[We're not sure if we were only nit-picking in some of the above comments or not. Maybe readers of this article can adequately assess the adequacy of the questionnaire, but we prefer to see the results of a pretest. If the author was confident of the fairness of the instrument and saw little to be gained by spending more time and effort, he was justified in not doing it. However, in general, readers do need to look out for this type of problem.]

Two issues of the adequacy of measurement have already been covered (adequacy of operational definitions and what is really being measured) except to look specifically at the measurement of the demographic variables. These operational definitions are fully and clearly presented. [Questions 8–8 and 9–5.] We know how each variable was defined and categorized.

Precision of measurement seems not to be an issue [Question 9–1], but the reliability does need to be considered [Question 9–2]. The favorability scale has apparently not been tested for reliability. We suspect that respondents would provide very similar responses if it were administered again since it is quite straightforward. However, we are not sure that it is really measuring only a *single* concept: favorability of perceptions of the Career Ladder Program. There may be several facets or aspects of favorability that are being lumped together. We need to remember that we have a broad-brush measure that might include meaningful facets or aspects.

[Since findings of causality are not sought, there is no need to address Questions 12–2, 12–3, and 12–4.]

Given the purpose of the study, we would like to know how all the approximately 28,000 teachers in Tennessee would respond. However, contacting all of them would be prohibitively expensive and might even create so much "notice" of the study as to bias the results in some way. Thus, surveying a sample is an appropriate tactic.

The author states that a random sample was drawn, and we see no errors in his approach. However, much information is left out. For instance, was the sample actually drawn from a list of all 28,000 teachers in the Tennessee Public Schools? Were the 20 percent who do not belong to the Tennessee Education Association included? Was the list up-to-date? We need to check with the author to be sure the sample actually represents the larger group that we are interested in.

We also need to note that percentages of respondents were 45.6, 28.7, and 25.7 for east, middle, and west Tennessee, respectively, whereas census data shows a general population dispersion of 38.5, 32.9, and 28.6. Thus, the eastern region may be over-represented.

If nonmembers of the Tennessee Education Association would have different views than members or if teachers in the eastern regions would have different views from teachers in the middle and western regions, we would want to examine further for any possible bias that might follow.

Finally, we need to note that 61.8 percent of the sample of teachers responded. We have no data from the remaining 38.2 percent. We will take this into account when evaluating the findings. [Questions 2–4 and 14–3 answered.]

FINDINGS AND CONCLUSIONS

Teachers' responses to the twenty items on the favorability instrument are explicitly given. We know exactly what percent gave each response to each item. Thus, we know what was left out as well as the average responses. However, for overall favorability we do not have complete information, and there is an error in reporting (though probably inconsequential). The average of 39.957 is given along with the high of 97 and low of 19. But, the minimum possible favorability score is 20. We wonder if there were missing data and how they were handled, but this is not likely to have any substantial effect.

The average, when reported as 39.957, might appear to be more precise than is warranted. "Rounded to 40.0" would seem to be a more realistic way to report it. [Question 9–1 answered.] Some additional information on the overall favorability scores would have been helpful. For instance, what is the 95 percent confidence interval for the average of 39.957, and what was the median and dispersion of the scores? In all, the summaries seem to be fair, and we can proceed to interpret the findings. [Question 10–2 answered.]

Table 2 is extremely valuable in interpreting the findings. Although 39.957 seems rather low on a scale of 20 to 100, in itself it is hard to evaluate. However, it is not at all hard to evaluate the large percentage of negative responses to eighteen of the twenty items, with a nineteenth item not very positive either. The data in the table make the case very well.

Our only lingering doubt has to do with

- the 38.2 percent of the sample who didn't respond
- the 20 percent of the teachers who do not belong to the Tennessee Education Association who may not have been included in the sample
- the possible overrepresentation of eastern Tennessee

The conclusions we must draw about the favorability of those who did respond is clear. However, we need to examine the potential impact of each of these three doubts.

With regard to the first, if those who did not respond are similar to those who did, we can be confident that our conclusions apply to all teachers in the Tennessee system. Only if we have reason to doubt this would we question the generality of the findings.

[If this had been a serious concern of the author, he might have studied the nonrespondents. For instance, he might have sent a second mailing of the survey or called a sample of the nonrespondents on the telephone in order to check whether they were similar in their attitudes and demographic characteristics to the respondents.]

Our assessment of the importance of the second and third doubts depends on external knowledge. If we believe these doubts to be significant, we would need to contact the author for further information. [Questions 4–1 and 3–2 answered for these findings.]

A second set of findings has to do with the relationship between favorability and each of the demographic variables. [Question 11–1 answered.] Inferential statistics seem to have been properly used to identify nonchance relationships. But, the author does not give enough of the statistical results for a knowledgeable reader to check their accuracy. In addition, we cannot consider the relationships meaningful until we know how big they are. Small differences, although statistically significant, might mean little for policymaking and managing the program. We would need to seek this additional information before using these findings. [Questions 4–1 and 3–2 answered for these findings.]

In addition, if we pursue additional information about the relationships found, we must be concerned about potentially important third variables [Question 11–2], and we must remember the importance of level of analysis [Question 11–3] and beware of the temptation to jump to conclusions about causality without sufficient evidence [Question 11–5]. If the sample was drawn properly, each variable was free to vary to its full extent in the population of all 28,000 teachers. Thus, the relationships reported would not be unduly restricted. [Question 11–4]

The overall conclusions that the author draws are straightforward. They are consistent with information presented in the literature review, and they answer the question asked. [Questions 8–4 and 8–13 answered.]

[Several of the remaining questions from our list have already been answered: 12–1, 8–5, 13–3, 13–4, 14–4, and 13–5. The question about causality, 12–5, is not relevant, as previously discussed. Thus, we have addressed all the relevant questions from our list.]

All in all, we find the primary finding of the study striking. Valuable information about teachers' perceptions of the Career Ladder Program in Tennessee is provided and potentially valuable relationships were discovered between favorability and several demographic variables (although we need more data to evaluate the latter).

The author clearly defined a problem and stuck with it. He answered the questions posed and did not generalize beyond the actual scope of the study. We can review much of the raw data and check most of the author's conclusions against the data. Most of the shortcomings of the article are typical of those found in many journals and can probably be overcome by seeking more information from the author. If not, we would become very skeptical.

READERS' ABSTRACT

This study was a survey of teachers' perceptions of the Career Ladder Program, a system for administering merit pay, in the Tennessee Public Schools grades K through 12. It was conducted in October 1985, one academic year after operation of the program had begun. Overall favorability of teachers' perceptions of the program was determined, and differences in favorability were analyzed in terms of several demographic characteristics of the teachers.

Data gathering was attempted from a random sample of 1,500 teachers in the system. Responses to a written questionnaire were received from 927 (61.8 percent). No information is given about the 38.2 percent who did not respond. We question whether teachers who were not members of the Tennessee Education Association were included in the sample and whether there is a significant overrepresentation of eastern Tennessee.

The items on the questionnaire are reproduced in the article along with a detailed accounting of responses. p values are given for relationships judged statistically significant, but we are not told how big or important these relationships are.

The primary finding was that teachers hold very unfavorable perceptions of the program. We see no reason to doubt the finding, but do note that there are several possible sources of error which some readers might want to investigate more thoroughly based on their external knowledge or general skepticism.

The secondary findings relate demographic variables to favorability. Although interesting, the relationships are not meaningful until their sizes are also known. Additional information from the author is needed.

Overall, the study seems to provide useful information about the topic studied. It appears to have been competently done and is well presented.

20

PRACTICE ARTICLES

The Portrayal of Children on Prime-Time Situation Comedies*

Amy Jordan

Three decades ago, Phillipe Aries argued in his social history of family life that "childhood"—a distinct and separate time of life—is a relatively modern invention (353). Using paintings and diaries as evidence, Aries showed that until the middle ages children were treated as little adults. They mingled, competed, worked and played with mature adults. The separation of children and adults came slowly and gradually as the concept of a time of life called *childhood* became accepted (46).

Though not everyone is convinced by Aries' thesis, studies of childhood as a social construct have flourished. Most prominent in the U.S. have been studies of childhood in colonial New England (Beales 7) and the development of the science of motherhood (which is easily joined with developing notions of childhood) in 20th-century America (Dally 57; and Weiss 283). These studies also point to the emergence of a larger public discourse of childhood as a time of life with unique physical and emotional needs.

Recent scholarly thinking, however, points to a *change* in the nature of childhood. Today one hears about "children without childhood" (Winn 5); "the disappearance of childhood" (Postman xiii); and a generation of children who are "growing up absurd" (Goodman 2). While no one would argue that children today are treated as they were in the middle ages, many sociologists and psychologists such as Meyrowitz and Postman see a homogenization of the ages during the 20th century. Especially persuasive on this point is Meyrowitz, who writes about the "adult-like child" and the "child-like adult" and an America in which distinctions between adults and children are becoming blurred (153). Meyrowitz gives the example of children who dress like adults and adults who dress like overgrown children (227). Postman, moreover, makes the argument that the tastes, styles, and even concerns of adults and children are merging (80).

Why is there a reversal in the earlier tendency to make the worlds of adults and children distinct and separate from one another? Why is there a homogenization of the generations? Meyrowitz and Postman argue that the media are partly to blame, especially the visual media. Television and movies, argues Meyrowitz, are socializing children to adult ways of life before their time (57). Adult interactions that were once secret and private (such as conversations about how to discipline children) are now readily accessible to children (247). What's more, children are watching media children act as if they are adults trapped in children's bodies. Meyrowitz gives the examples of Brooke Shields and Gary Coleman (229) and more contemporary examples might include Tom Hanks' character in the movie *Big* or the precocious and responsible children of the television situation comedies *Doogie Howser, M.D.* (where a 16-year-old is a practicing physician), *Full House* (where the oldest girl acts as a

Source: The Journal of Popular Culture 29:3 (Winter 1995), pp. 139–47. Copyright © 1995 by *The Journal of Popular Culture*. Reprinted with permission.

surrogate mother), and *The Simpsons* (where the middle child, 8-year-old Lisa, is wiser and more sensitive than her older brother and father).

In his book *No Sense of Place,* Meyrowitz offers impressions and anecdotes to support his claims of media portrayals of adult-like children. On the surface, the claims seem valid. It is important, however, to test these ideas systematically. Scholars have had interesting success investigating the portrayal of television families (Comstock and Strzyzewski 5; Heintz 7) and children's reactions to TV families (Brown, Austin, and Roberts 12; Dorr, Kovaric, and Doubleday 377; Newcomb and Collins 417), but relatively few studies have looked specifically at the child members of these television families since it is the family unit or the parents which are most often the focus.

Method
Procedures and Sample

The sampling frame of programs included all family-based situation comedies which aired Monday through Sunday between the hours of 8:00 P.M. and 10:00 P.M. which had a *child as a main character* who appeared to be 17 or younger. Family situation comedies were chosen as the types of shows that might inform children about themselves because, as Heintz and others have found, these are some of children's favorite and most frequently watched programs (5).

Two weeks of programs were sampled—one in January 1990 and one in March 1990. This sampling procedure resulted in 19 prime time, network situation comedies which could be systematically analyzed for their portrayals of children. Because two weeks of programs were selected, three programs had two episodes in the sample. Included in the nineteen programs were long-standing favorites such as *Growing Pains* and *The Cosby Show* as well as newly introduced (and subsequently canceled) programs like *Uncle Buck, Grand,* and *Parenthood.*

Child characters were coded and analyzed if they appeared to fall between the ages of 0 and 17, totaling 59 characters from the 19 programs. From them, demographics were examined, including the gender, race and approximate age of the child characters. More central to this study were the analyses of the *interactions* TV children have with other characters. Interactions were analyzed if at least one of the interactants was a child and if the interaction lasted more than five seconds. In these analyses two questions were asked. First, *what is the type of interaction?* Type of interaction ranged from talking to pleasing to manipulating (see Table 1). Every attempt was made to make the coding scheme exhaustive and mutually exclusive and each of the 200 interactions that were coded did have a dominant theme which fit the scheme. Second, I asked: *what is the tone of the interaction?* Interactions were coded as "positive," "negative," or "neutral" (see Table 2).

Findings and Discussion
The Demographics of the Children

A total of 59 individual child characters were examined. Of these 59, 42 percent were boys and 58 percent were girls. This is a fairly uneven gender distribution, with girls being somewhat overrepresented in this sample of programs.

The overall mean age for the child characters was 12.1. Boys tended to be slightly older than the mean—they averaged 12.6—and girls tended to be slightly younger—averaging 11.7 (though this difference was not statistically significant).

The majority of the child characters in this sample were white: 81 percent. Another 19 percent were African-American. It is a black and white world—mainly white—in which non-black minority children are virtually invisible. A sharp segregation also exists between the child characters. White and black children rarely mix on television. There are a few exceptions—*The Cosby Show,* for example—but even here the closest friends are same-race characters.

Interactions Involving Child Characters

A second level of analysis involved examining interactions that child characters have with other children and with adults (see Table 1). In this sample, children were significantly more likely to have interactions with adults than with other children. While children interacted with adults 68 percent of the time, only 32 percent of the coded interactions involved two or more children.

The interactions were also coded as "positive," "negative," or "neutral." In this sample, 41 percent of the interactions were "neutral," 34 percent were "negative" and 25 percent were "positive" (see Table 2). These interactions were broken down more carefully to examine the interactions children had with other children and the interactions children had with adults. In this study, interactions between adults and children were significantly more likely to be positive than those between children. Almost 30 percent of adult/child interactions were positive while only 13.4 percent of the child/child interactions were. Expectedly then, interactions between children were more likely to be negative. Forty-three percent of all child/child interactions were negative while only 29.7 percent of the adult/child interactions were negative. Neutral interactions transpired equally across different character interactions. Thus, children on television are portrayed as having more positive and harmonious relationships with adults than with peers or siblings.

Apart from the tone of the interactions, types of interactions involving child characters were examined (see Table 2). The most common interaction children have with adults, and also with other children, is talking or bantering (22.6 percent and 38.1 percent, respectively). When children are with adults, they are also likely to be directed by them (a parent telling a child what to do). This occurred 16.8 percent of the time. The third most frequent type of interaction was advice-giving (11.7 percent). This will be explored more fully below.

When children interact with one another, if they are not neutrally talking or bantering (38.1 percent of the time), then they are likely to be fighting (23.8 percent of the time). Children also nurtured and shared feelings with one another, but these types of interactions were much less frequent (7.9 percent and 6.3 percent, respectively).

The key question which the study has sought to answer is whether or not Meyrowitz's theory of the mediated child-like adult and adult-like child has become manifested in the family situation comedy of the 1990s. For this study, interactions between adults and children which were classified as nurturing, confiding, advice-giving, di-

TABLE 1
TYPES OF INTERACTIONS INVOLVING CHILDREN

	Adult/Child	Child/Child
Talking/Bantering	22.6% (n = 31)	38.1% (n = 24)
Joking/Wisecracking	9.5% (n = 13)	3.2% (n = 2)
Nurturing	8.0% (n = 11)	7.9% (n = 5)
Confiding	5.8% (n = 8)	4.8% (n = 3)
Fighting	5.8% (n = 8)	23.8% (n = 15)
Advising	11.7% (n = 16)	4.8% (n = 3)
Precociousness	5.8% (n = 8)	4.8% (n = 3)
Silence	0.8% (n = 1)	—
Emoting (sharing pleasant feelings)	3.6% (n = 5)	6.3% (n = 4)
Pleasing	3.6% (n = 5)	—
Directing	16.8% (n = 23)	6.3% (n = 4)
Judging	1.6% (n = 2)	—
Manipulating	4.4% (n = 6)	—
Totals	100% (n = 137)	100% (n = 63)

recting and manipulating were examined for *directionality*. That is, who is doing the nurturing, advising, and confiding: is it the adults or children? (See Table 3.) These data indicate that it is always the adults who nurture and direct children (100 percent). But these data also indicate that adults are more likely to confide in children (62.5 percent) than children are to confide in adults (37.5 percent). For example, in the episode of *Grand* which was examined, the mother in the program confided in her 15-year-old

TABLE 2
TONE OF INTERACTIONS

Characters	Tone			
	Positive	Negative	Neutral	
Adult/Child	29.7%	29.7%	40.6%	
	(n = 38)	(n = 38)	(n = 52)	
Child/Child	13.4%	43.3%	43.3%	
	(n = 8)	(n = 26)	(n = 26)	
Total 100%	24.5%	34.0%	41.5%	
	(n = 46)	(n = 64)	(n = 78)	(n = 188)*

*Totals do not add up to 200 as 12 interactions could not be coded under these categories.
Contingency Table Analysis yields significant results at the .05 level (chi square = 6.81, df = 2).

TABLE 3
DIRECTIONALITY OF KEY INTERACTIONS

	Child to Adult	Adult to Child
Nurturing	100%	0%
	(n = 11)	(n = 0)
Confiding	62.5%	37.5%
	(n = 5)	(n = 3)
Advice-giving	68.7%	31.3%
	(n = 11)	(n = 5)
Directing	78.3%	21.7%
	(n = 18)	(n = 5)
Manipulating	33.3%	66.7%
	(n = 2)	(n = 4)
Totals	100%	100%
	(n = 47)	(n = 17)

*Contingency Table Analysis yields significant results at the .05 level (chi square = 9.78, df = 3).

daughter about the problems she was having with her ex-husband (the 15-year-old daughter's father). Moreover, one-third (33.3 percent) of all advice given in these television programs is given by children to adults. One episode of *Growing Pains* showed both the mother and the father of the Seaver family turning to their children (Mike and Carol) for advice about how to discipline their third child (Ben). Thus, television's children are often portrayed as "parenting" their parents. They give advice and act as confidants in many of the interactions they have with adults. Finally, when one TV character is shown manipulating another (getting another character to do something without being aware of it), two-thirds of the time it is the child manipulating the adult. For example, the episode of *Just the Ten of Us* analyzed for this study showed the youngest daughter of the family manipulating both of her parents into delaying the Sunday dinner. She was stalling so that her brother could return with a replacement for the set of china she and her brother had broken the week earlier. The stalling game went on for many hours, apparently without the parents' awareness that she was "up to something."

Conclusions

Meyrowitz may be correct in his belief that Americans are witnessing a reversal of the roles of adults and children (231). Nowhere is this more clear than on the television programs Americans watch every evening. This study indicates that not only are television's children having more conversations with adults than they are with other children, but the interactions they are having with adults are more likely to be positive while the interactions they have with other children are more likely to be negative. Moreover, these characters and interactions have taken on peculiar qualities. Children on television are often shown as precocious, manipulative, and adult-like in their maturity and sensitivity. Adults on television often assume the less mature role in their interactions with children, asking children for advice or entrusting them with their problems and secrets. Thus, the situations set up by television's writers involve a two-way street with adults regressing and children progressing into behaviors uncharacteristic of their equivalent age-related behaviors in reality.

But does this mean that the children who view the programs will become less childlike as a result? There is evidence that younger children who see characters in realistic contexts (such as family life) believe the characters to be more realistic (Dorr 217). Thus, it is possible that children are being socialized to beliefs about who counts, how to behave, and how to relate to adults. On another level, long-term and consistent images of children may ultimately become integrated into our beliefs about the nature of childhood. Furthermore, adults who watch family situation comedies may be learning how to parent, how to behave, and what types of information to disclose through the parent-child interactions they observe on television. While they are certainly more likely to bring critical viewing skills to the programs they view than children, they, too, may be influenced over the long term by the consistency of the relationships they witness.

Certainly this study is preliminary and in need of more data over a larger time frame. For example, it would be very interesting to see if the image of the child and the interactions children have on television have changed significantly in the past five decades. It is also important to examine what effects, if any, these portrayals have on the adults and children who watch them. We cannot correlate effects from a content analysis such as this. Television's examples are potent and consistent for adults and children but they are not the only sources of information regarding the relationships adults and children have with each other. However, given the concerns our society holds regarding the welfare and well-being of children, this area of research is an important one and worthy of future investigation.

Works Cited

Aries, P. *Centuries of Childhood: A Social History of Family Life.* New York: Vintage, 1962.

Beales, R. "In Search of the Historical Child: Miniature Adulthood in Colonial New England." In *Growing Up in America: Children in Historical Perspective.* Ed. N. Hines and J. Hawes, Chicago: University of Illinois Press, 1985, pp. 7–26.

Brown, G.; E. Austin; and D. Roberts. "Real Families' versus 'Television Families': Children's Perception of Realism in *The Cosby Show.*" Paper presented to the Mass Communication Division of the International Communication Association Annual Conference, New Orleans: May 1988.

Comstock, J. and K. Strzyzewski. "Interpersonal Interaction on Television: Family Conflict and Jealousy on Prime Time." *Journal of Broadcasting and Electronic Media* 34 (1990), pp. 263–82.

Dally, A. *Inventing Motherhood: The Consequences of an Ideal.* New York: Shocken, 1983.

Dorr, A. "No Shortcuts to Judging Reality." *Children's Understanding of Television: Research on Attention and Comprehension.* Ed. J. Bryant and D. Anderson. New York: Academic, 1983.

Dorr, A.; P. Kovaric; and C. Doubleday. "Age and Content Influences on Children's Perceptions of the Realism of Television Families." *Journal of Broadcasting and Electronic Media* 34 (1990), pp. 377–97.

Goodman, P. *Growing Up Absurd: Problems of Youth in Organized Systems.* New York: Random, 1960.

Heintz, K. "Children's Favorite Television Families." Paper presented to the Mass Communication Division of the Speech Communication Association Conference, Chicago: November 1990.

Meyrowitz, J. *No Sense of Place: The Impact of Electronic Media on Social Behavior.* New York: Oxford University Press, 1985.

Newcomb, A. and W. A. Collins. "Children's Comprehension of Family Role Portrayals in Televised Drama: Effects of Socioeconomic Status, Ethnicity, and Age." *Developmental Psychology* 15 (1979), pp. 417–23.

Postman, N. *The Disappearance of Childhood.* New York: Dell, 1982.

Weiss, N. P. "Mother, the Invention of Necessity: Dr. Benjamin Spock's *Baby and Child Care.*" In *Growing Up in America: Children in Historical Perspective.* Ed. N. Hines and J. Hawes, Chicago: University of Illinois Press, 1985, pp. 283–304.

Winn, W. *Children without Childhood.* New York: Pantheon, 1983.

Does Attack Advertising Demobilize the Electorate?*

Stephen Ansolabehere
Massachusetts Institute of Technology

Shanto Iyengar, Adam Simon, and Nicholas Valentino
University of California, Los Angeles

We address the effects of negative campaign advertising on turnout. Using a unique experimental design in which advertising tone is manipulated within the identical audiovisual context, we find that exposure to negative advertisements dropped intentions to vote by 5%. We then replicate this result through an aggregate-level analysis of turnout and campaign tone in the 1992 Senate elections. Finally, we show that the demobilizing effects of negative campaigns are accompanied by a weakened sense of political efficacy. Voters who watch negative advertisements become more cynical about the responsiveness of public officials and the electoral process.

It is generally taken for granted that political campaigns boost citizens' involvement—their interest in the election, awareness of and information about current issues, and sense that individual opinions matter. Since Lazarsfeld's pioneering work (Berelson, Lazarsfeld, and McPhee 1954; Lazarsfeld, Berelson, and Gaudet 1948), it has been thought that campaign activity in connection with recurring elections enables parties and candidates to mobilize their likely constituents and "recharge" their partisan sentiments. Voter turnout is thus considered to increase directly with "the level of political stimulation to which the electorate is subjected" (Campbell et al. 1966, 42; Patterson and Caldeira 1983).

The argument that campaigns are inherently "stimulating" experiences can be questioned on a variety of grounds. American campaigns have changed dramatically since the 1940s and 1950s (see Ansolabehere et al. 1993). It is generally accepted that television has undermined the traditional importance of party organizations, because it permits "direct" communication between candidates and the voters (see Bartels 1988; Polsby 1983; Wattenberg 1984, 1991). All forms of broadcasting, from network newscasts to talk show programs, have become potent tools in the hands of campaign operatives, consultants, and fund-raisers. In particular, paid political advertisements have become an essential form of campaign communication. In 1990, for example, candidates spent more on televised advertising than any other form of campaign communication (Ansolabehere and Gerber 1993).

Stephen Ansolabehere is assistant professor of political science, Massachusetts Institute of Technology, Cambridge, MA 02139.

Shanto Iyengar is professor of and Adam Simon and Nicholas Valentino are doctoral candidates in political science, University of California–Los Angeles, Los Angeles, CA 90024-1472.

Source: American Political Science Review 88:4 (December 1994), pp. 829–38. Copyright © 1994 by the American Political Science Association. Reprinted with permission of the author and the American Political Science Association.

We are now beginning to realize that the advent of television has also radically changed the nature and tone of campaign discourse. Today more than ever, the entire electoral process rewards candidates whose skills are rhetorical, rather than substantive (Jamieson 1992) and whose private lives and electoral viability, rather than party ties, policy positions, and governmental experience, can withstand media scrutiny (see Brady and Johnston 1987; Lichter, Amundson, and Noyes 1988; Sabato 1991). Campaigns have also turned increasingly hostile and ugly. More often than not, candidates criticize, discredit, or belittle their opponents rather than promoting their own ideas and programs. In the 1988 and 1990 campaigns, a survey of campaign advertising carried out by the *National Journal* found that attack advertisements had become the norm rather than the exception (Hagstrom and Guskind 1988, 1992).

Given the considerable changes in electoral strategy and the emergence of negative advertising as a staple of contemporary campaigns, it is certainly time to question whether campaigns are bound to stimulate citizen involvement in the electoral process. To be sure, there has been no shortage of hand wringing and outrage over the depths to which candidates have sunk, the viciousness and stridency of their rhetoric, and the lack of any systematic accountability for the accuracy of the claims made by the candidates (see Bode 1992; Dionne 1991; Rosen and Taylor 1992). However, as noted by a recent Congressional Research Service survey, there is little evidence concerning the effects of attack advertising on voters and the electoral process (see Neale 1991).

A handful of studies have considered the relationship between campaign advertising and political participation, with inconsistent results. Garramone and her colleagues (1990) found that exposure to negative advertisements did not depress measures of political participation. This study, however, utilized student participants and the candidates featured in the advertisements were fictitious. In addition, participants watched the advertisements in a classroom setting. In contrast to this study, an experiment reported by Basil, Schooler, and Reeves (1991) found that negative advertisements reduced positive attitudes toward both candidates in the race, thereby indirectly reducing political involvement. This study, however, was not conducted during an ongoing campaign and utilized a tiny sample, and the participants could not vote for the target candidates. Finally, Thorson, Christ, and Caywood (1991) reported no differences in voting intention between college students exposed to positive and negative advertisements.

We assert that campaigns can be either mobilizing or demobilizing events, *depending upon the nature of the messages they generate.* Using an experimental design that manipulates advertising tone while holding all other features of the advertisements constant, we demonstrate that exposure to attack advertising in and of itself significantly decreases voter engagement and participation. We then reproduce this result by demonstrating that turnout in the 1992 Senate campaigns was significantly reduced in states where the tone of the campaign was relatively negative. Finally, we address three possible explanations for the demobilizing effects of negative campaigns.

EXPERIMENTAL DESIGN

There is a vast literature, both correlational and experimental, concerning the effects of televised advertisements (though not specifically negative advertisements) on public opinion (for a detailed review, see Kosterman 1991). This literature, however, is plagued by significant methodological shortcomings. The limitations of the opinion survey as a basis for identifying the effects of mass communications have been well documented (see Bartels 1993; Hovland 1959). Most importantly, surveys cannot reliably assess exposure to campaign advertising. Nor is most of the existing experimental work fully valid. The typical experimental study, by relying on fictitious candidates as the "target" stimuli, becomes divorced from the real world of campaigns. Previous experimental studies thus shed little evidence on the interplay between voters' existing information and preferences and their reception of campaign advertisements. When experimental work has focused on real candidates and their advertisements, it is difficult to capture the effects of particular characteristics of advertising because the manipulation confounds several such characteristics (Ansolabehere and Iyengar 1991; Garramone 1985; Pfau and Kenski 1989). That is, a Clinton spot and Bush spot differ in any number of features (the accompanying visuals, background sound, the voice of the announcer, etc.) in addition to the content of the message. Thus there are many possible explanations for differences in voters' reactions to these spots.

To overcome the limitations of previous research, we developed a rigorous but realistic experimental design for assessing the effects of advertising tone or valence[1] on public opinion and voting. Our studies all took place during ongoing political campaigns (the 1990 California gubernatorial race, the 1992 California Senate races, and the 1993 Los Angeles mayoral race) and featured "real" candidates who were in fact advertising heavily on television and "real" voters (rather than college sophomores) who on election day would have to choose between the candidates whose advertisements they watched. Our experimental manipulations were professionally produced and could not (unless the viewer were a political consultant) be distinguished from the flurry of advertisements confronting the typical voter. In addition, our manipulation was unobtrusive; we embedded the experimental advertisement into a 15-minute local newscast.

The most distinctive feature of our design is its ability to capture the casual effects of a particular feature of campaign advertisement—in this case, advertising tone or valence. The advertisements that we produced were identical in all respects but tone and the candidate sponsoring the advertisement. In the 1992 California Senate primaries, for example, viewers watched a 30-second advertisement that either promoted or attacked on the general trait of "integrity." The visuals featured a panoramic view of the Capitol Building, the camera then zooming in to a closeup of an unoccupied desk inside a Senate office. In the "positive" treatments (using the example of candidate Dianne Feinstein), the text read by the announcer was as follows:

> For over 200 years the United States Senate has shaped the future of America and the world. Today, California needs honesty, compassion, and a voice for all the people in the U.S. Senate. As mayor of San Francisco, Dianne Feinstein *proposed* new government ethics rules. She *rejected* large campaign contributions from special interests. And Dianne Feinstein *supported* tougher penalties on savings-and-loan crooks.
> California *needs* Dianne Feinstein in the U.S. Senate.

In the "negative" version of this Feinstein spot, the text was modified as follows:

For over 200 years the United States Senate has shaped the future of America and the world. Today, California needs honesty, compassion, and a voice for all the people in the U.S. Senate. As state controller, Gray Davis *opposed* new government ethics rules. He *accepted* large campaign contributions from special interests. And Gray Davis *opposed* tougher penalties on savings-and-loan crooks.

California *can't afford a politician* like Gray Davis in the U.S. Senate.

By holding the visual elements constant and by using the same announcer, we were able to limit differences between the conditions to differences in tone.[2] With appropriate modifications to the wording, the identical pair of advertisements was also shown on behalf of Feinstein's primary opponent, Controller Gray Davis, and for the various candidates contesting the other Senate primaries.

In short, our experimental manipulation enabled us to establish a much tighter degree of control over the tone of campaign advertising than had been possible in previous research. Since the advertisements watched by viewers were identical in all other respects and because we randomly assigned participants to experimental conditions, any differences between conditions may be attributed only to the tone of the political advertisement (see Rubin 1974).

The Campaign Context

Our experiments spanned a variety of campaigns, including the 1990 California gubernatorial election, both of the state's 1992 U.S. Senate races, and the 1993 mayoral election in Los Angeles. In the case of the senatorial campaigns, we examined three of the four primaries and both general election campaigns. The campaigns we examined were all characterized by extensive broadcast advertising and, in most cases, by frequent use of negative or attack advertising.

We used the same design for all of the campaigns under investigation. That is, we manipulated advertising valence within the identical audiovisual framework. The content of the experimental advertisement, however, varied across campaigns. In general, the experimental advertisements focused on issues or themes that were particularly salient in the various campaigns. In the 1990 gubernatorial race, we created advertisements that dealt with the issues of crime and pollution. In the positive conditions, the sponsoring candidate was presented as "tough" on crime and a protector of the environment. In the negative versions, the opponent was depicted as "soft" on crime and indifferent to the quality of the environment. (Samples of the text and accompanying visuals of the experimental manipulations are provided in Appendix A.)

The experimental advertisements for the 1993 Senate primaries dealt with either the candidates' personal integrity or competence. In the case of integrity (discussed in the given examples), the advertisement described the candidate as either honest and a supporter of campaign reform or as dishonest and an opponent of reform. In the case of competence, the advertisement asked voters to consider the sponsor's "ability, determination, and leadership" (or the absence of these characteristics in the opponent).

During the Senate general election campaign, we shifted the focus of the advertisements to the issue of unemployment. The condition of the state's economy and the significant loss of jobs (unemployment had reached 10% in September) were the overriding issues in both races. All four candidates aired advertisements promising to reverse the state's economic decline. Our treatment advertisements depicted the sponsor or opponent as an advocate or critic of government-subsidized job training and industrial modernization programs.

Finally, one of our studies concerned the nonpartisan election for mayor of Los Angeles between Richard Riordan and Michael Woo. Here, the manipulation dealt with the candidates' integrity and discussed the degree to which the candidates' campaign promises to increase job opportunities and reform city government were consistent with their past actions.

In summary, our experimental advertisements dealt with a variety of campaigns and themes. In all cases, however, the advertisements corresponded to the actual focus of campaigns. In their content, the experimental advertisements closely reflected the advertisements aired by the candidates.

Subjects and Procedure

We recruited subjects by multiple methods including advertisements placed in local newspapers, flyers distributed in shopping malls and other public venues, announcements in employer newsletters, and by calling names from voter registration lists. Subjects were promised payment of $15 for participation in an hour-long study of "selective perception" of local news programs.

Although the "sample" was obviously nonrandom, our participants resembled the composition of the greater Los Angeles area. Across all the experiments, 56% of the participants were male, 53% were white, 26% were black, 12% were Hispanic, and 10% were Asian. The median age was 34. Forty-nine percent of the participants claimed affiliation with the Democratic party, 24% were Republicans, and 21% were independents. Forty-four percent were college graduates, with the balance being evenly divided between high school graduates and individuals with some college.[3]

The experiments were conducted at two separate locations: West Los Angeles and Costa Mesa (Orange County). The former is a heavily Democratic area, while the latter, an affluent suburb of Los Angeles, is predominantly Republican. The experimental facilities in both locations were identical—a three-room office suite consisting of two viewing rooms and a separate room for completion of questionnaires (in addition to a reception area). The viewing rooms were furnished casually with sofas and easy chairs. Participants could browse through newspapers and magazines and snack on cookies and coffee.

When participants telephoned the facility they were scheduled for a particular time period of their choice. Experimental sessions were available from 10:00 A.M. to 8:00 P.M., Monday through Saturday. The typical session consisted of two to three participants.

On arrival, subjects were given an instruction sheet informing them that the study concerned selective perception of local newscasts. They then completed a short pretest questionnaire concerning their social background, media activities, and political interest. Following completion of the pretest, participants were taken to a viewing room, where, depending upon the condition to which they had been assigned,[4] they watched a 15-minute (complete with commercials) videotape recording of a recent local newscast (described to participants as having been selected at random).

The experimental or "treatment" advertisement was inserted into the first commercial break midway through the tape. The political spot was shown always in the middle position in a three-advertisement break. As described, the advertisements in the various conditions were identical in all respects except for the factors of valence and source.

Following completion of the videotape, participants completed a lengthy posttest questionnaire tapping their beliefs and opinions on a wide range of campaign issues. Of course, we also ascertained participants' voting intentions and general level of involvement in the campaign. On completion of the posttest, participants were debriefed and paid.

ANALYSIS AND RESULTS

We shall limit our analyses to the effects of negative advertising on intention to vote. In our posttest questionnaire, we ascertained whether participants were registered to vote. Using registration as a filter, we then asked, "Looking forward to the November election, do you intend to vote?" (In the case of the primary election study, the question was worded accordingly.) We identified "likely voters" as those who were both registered and who stated their intention of voting.[5]

In analyzing our experimental data, we pooled the gubernatorial study, the various senatorial studies, and the mayoral study into a single data set. While the effects of attack advertising are tempered by campaign-specific constraints, including the background of the candidates and the specific content of their advertising, we are especially interested in the average effect, if any, of advertising valence.[6] Moreover, pooling the separate studies makes it possible to obtain reliable estimates of the demobilizing effects of attack advertising.

After pooling, we compared the percentage of viewers classified as likely voters among participants who watched the positive and negative versions of the experimental advertisements. The demobilization hypothesis predicts the exposure to negative advertising will lower the percentage of likely voters. Among those who watched a positive advertisement, 64% intended to vote. Among participants who saw a product advertisement instead of a political one, 61% intended to vote. Among participants who were exposed to the negative versions of the campaign advertisement, only 58% were likely to vote. A one-way analysis of variance yielded an F-statistic of 2.2, significant at the .11 level.[7]

The decision to vote depends upon aspects of the campaign other than advertising valence. In addition, some people are more likely to vote than others, regardless of the nature of the campaign. To capture these contextual and dispositional effects on turnout, we regressed intention to vote (using a logistic regression) on advertising tone and a set of dummy variables corresponding to specific elections, as well as various indicators of individual differences. Because the positive and negative advertisements exerted symmetric effects on voting intention, we specified advertising tone as a trichotomy corresponding to positive advertisement (+1), no political advertisement (0), and negative advertisement (–1). The individual difference variables included the frequency with which people said they followed public affairs, prior voting history, the "match" between viewers' and the candidates' gender and party identification, age, race, and education. This multivariate analysis, in essence, estimates the independent effects of the campaign advertising stimulus on voting intention above and beyond campaign-specific influences and personal predispositions.

Table 1 presents the results of two logistic regressions corresponding to a full model (with all control variables included) and a restricted model (with nonsignificant controls excluded). The baseline (constant) in this specification represents the 1993 Los Angeles mayoral race. Off-year local elections tend to be characterized by low levels of citizen involvement. Not surprisingly, the 1990 gubernatorial, the 1992 Senate primary, and the 1992 Senate general elections all registered higher turnout.

The individual difference factor with the greatest ability to discriminate between likely and unlikely voters, as expected, was prior voting history. Participants who reported voting in the 1988 election were much more likely to be classified as likely voters in 1992–93 than those who reported not having voted. Partisans, those with higher levels of political interest, the more educated, and whites were also characterized by significantly higher levels of voting intention.

From our perspective, the most important result in Table 1 is the effect of advertising tone on voting intentions. In both equations, a one-sided t-test showed that advertising tone significantly (at the .05 level) affected turnout. Converting the logistic coefficient on advertising tone into a linear probability shows that those participants exposed to the negative version of the advertisement were 2.5% less likely to vote than those exposed to no political advertisement. Conversely, the positive version of the advertisement increased voting intention by 2.5 percentage points. In short, the initial estimate of the demobilization effect survived the multiple controls.

Overall, the experimental results demonstrate that exposure to negative (as opposed to positive) advertising depresses intention to vote by 5%. Considering the scope of our experimental manipulation (a single 30-second advertisements embedded in a 15-minute newscast) and the variety of campaigns examined, these effects seem remarkable. Despite our best efforts at experimental realism, it is possible that the effect has been magnified by some aspect of the research design. It is important, therefore, to place the experimental findings in the context of the world of actual campaigns.

Replicating the Experimental Results

To reconstruct our experimental framework in the real world, we measured the tone of the campaign in each of the 34 states holding a Senate election in 1992. Senate campaigns are especially appropriate for our purposes because the candidates rely heavily on advertising (Ansolabehere and Gerber 1993). Moreover, four of our seven experiments focused on Senate campaigns.

TABLE 1
LOGISTIC REGRESSION ESTIMATES OF THE EFFECT OF TONE ON INTENTIONS
TO VOTE IN THE 1990, 1992, AND 1993 EXPERIMENTS

	Model	
Variable	Full	Restricted
Constant	−.212	−.230
	(.331)	(.331)
Advertising tone[a]	.110	.114
	(.055)	(.036)
Experiments		
1990 gubernatorial	.434	.477
	(.203)	(.195)
1992 primary	.404	.335
	(.179)	(.168)
1992 general election	1.221	.778
	(.208)	(.138)
1988 turnout	1.748	1.614
	(.141)	(.128)
Follow government affairs	.497	.501
	(.059)	(.058)
Independent	−1.112	−1.122
	(.108)	(.108)
Same party	−.028	—
	(.087)	
Same gender	−.033	—
	(.117)	
Age	.002	—
(.004)		
Education	.100	.129
	(.068)	(.058)
Female	.034	—
	(.119)	
White	.348	.353
	(.131)	(.128)
Log likelihood	−905.5	−906.7
Percent correctly predicted	78.2	78.1

Note: Entries are logit coefficients with standard errors in parentheses.
N = 1,655.
[a]Coded 1 for positive ad, 0 for control ad, −1 for negative ad.

Our indicator of campaign tone was based on a systematic content analysis of news coverage of the various Senate races. We searched through the NEXIS and DATA-TIMES databases for all newspaper and newsmagazine articles bearing on the Senate campaigns in general and the candidates' advertisements in particular. This search yielded a total of over 2,500 articles ranging from a high of 1,000 on the Feinstein–Seymour contest in California to a low of 28 in the case of the Idaho race. Based on a reading of the news coverage, campaigns were classified into one of three categories: generally positive in tone (scored 1); mixed (scored 0); and generally negative in tone (scored –1). The classification scheme is described in Appendix B, along with each state's tone score.

As our indicator of turnout, we simply computed the votes cast for U.S. Senate and divided by the state's voting-age population. In addition to turnout, we also examined ballot *roll-off* in the Senate elections. For each relevant state, we subtracted the total number of votes cast for senator from the total cast for president and divided by the latter. The roll-off indicator has two distinct advantages. First, roll-off is a campaign-specific effect indicating the degree to which people who were sufficiently motivated to vote in the presidential election chose to abstain in the Senate race. Second, because roll-off uses the presidential vote as a baseline, it adjusts for a variety of state-related differences (e.g., demographic factors, political culture, and party competition), which affect the level of voting turnout.[8]

Turnout in senatorial elections depends upon a variety of influences in addition to the tone of the campaign. These include the competitiveness of the race, the volume (or "decibel level") of the campaign, and the electorate's sense of civic duty. (For a thorough discussion, see Rosenstone and Hansen 1993.) Our measure of the volume of the campaign was the level of campaign spending by incumbents and challengers (measured in logarithms). Competitiveness or closeness was measured by the squared difference between the Republican and Democratic shares of the total vote. Lastly, to incorporate differences in civic duty and other relevant orientations, we also controlled for per capita income, turnout in the 1988 presidential election, percentage college-educated, region (South, non-South), and the census form mail-back rate.[9]

Having compiled the turnout, roll-off, and campaign tone indicators, we proceeded to replicate the experimental results. Table 2 presents the results from the full and restricted multiple regression analyses of turnout and roll-off. Following the analysis of the experimental data, the tone variable was specified as a trichotomy (negative tone = –1, mixed = 0, positive tone = 1). This specification measures the deviation in turnout and roll-off of the positive and negative campaign tone categories from the mixed-tone category.[10]

Do Senate races characterized by relatively negative campaigns have lower turnout and higher roll-off rates than races in which the campaign is more positive in tone? For both turnout and roll-off, we found significant effects of campaign tone. Negative campaigns decreased turnout by 2%. (This also means that positive campaigns boosted turnout by 2%, for a total difference of 4%.) Negative campaigns also increased ballot roll-off by 1.2% and vice versa. Since the demobilization hypothesis is directional, we resorted to one-tailed tests (i.e., negative campaigns decrease turnout and increase roll-off, while positive campaigns increase turnout and decrease roll-off). The t-statistics for this hypothesis were 3.64 for turnout and –2.26 for roll-off, both significant at the .05 level.[11]

The use of both experimental and nonexperimental methods to measure the very same naturally occurring phenomena is highly unusual in the social sciences. It is even more unusual if both methods yield equivalent results. In our study, the aggregate-level analysis of turnout and roll-out in the 1992 Senate elections and the experimental studies of negative advertising converge: negative campaigns tend to demobilize the electorate.

TABLE 2

REGRESSION ESTIMATES OF THE EFFECT OF TONE ON TURNOUT AND ROLL-OFF IN THE 1992 SENATE ELECTIONS

Independent Variable	Turnout[a]		Roll-off[b]	
	Full Model	Restricted	Full Model	Restricted
Constant	−.294	−.295	.157	.160
	(.171)	(.124)	(.173)	(.040)
Campaign tone[c]	.020	.021	−.011	−.012
	(.006)	(.006)	(.006)	(.006)
1988 turnout	.660	.571	.046	—
	(.101)	(.090)	(.102)	
Per capita income	.010	—	.048	.049
	(.027)		(.027)	(.019)
Mail-back rate	.337	.340	−.058	—
	(.149)	(.125)	(.151)	
Southern state	.048	.047	−.014	−.016
	(.015)	(.013)	(.016)	(.013)
% College-educated	.120	.172	−.215	−.247
	(.099)	(.076)	(.100)	(.067)
Log challenger $	.001	—	−.011	−.010
	(.005)		(.005)	(.004)
Log incumbent $	.013	.011	−.004	—
	(.007)	(.006)	(.007)	
Open seat	.011	—	−.008	—
	(.012)		(.012)	
(Non)closeness	−.053	−.068	.058	.069
	(.048)	(.039)	(.046)	(.037)
R^2	.94	.94	.67	.64
SS residuals	.0099	.0102	.101	.0112

Note: Entries are multiple regression coefficients with standard errors in parentheses. N = 34.
[a]Total Votes for Senate Voting-Age Population.
[b](Total Votes for President − Total Votes for Senate)/(Total Votes for President).
[c]1 = positive tone, 0 = mixed tone, −1 = negative tone.

Psychological Correlates

That attack advertisements discourage people from voting raises questions about the psychological underpinnings of this effect. One possibility is that partisanship mediates the effects of attack advertisements on turnout. It is generally thought that campaign messages resonate especially strongly among supporters or proponents of the source of the message. Campaigns thus have the effect of reinforcing or crystallizing existing partisan loyalties. Extending this argument to attack advertising implies the obverse. That is, the intention to vote among supporters of the candidate airing the negative advertisement will be unchanged, since the message provides no reasons to vote for their candidate. On the other hand, voting intention should be weakened among supporters of the candidate who is attacked, since the message provides these partisans with reasons not to vote for their candidate.

If attack advertisements demobilize on a partisan basis, we should find a significant interaction effect between advertising valence and viewers' party identification. We thus reestimated the logistic regression presented in Table 1, this time including the appropriate interaction (valence × same party). The results revealed that the interaction term was nonsignificant and had the wrong sign.[12] Partisanship does not mediate the demobilizing effects of attack advertising; supporters of the source and target candidates are not affected differently.

An alternative account of the demobilization effect is that attack advertising generates blanket negativity toward both candidates. According to this "plague-on-both-your-houses" explanation, voters not only become more critical of the target of the attack but turn against the sponsor as well (for some evidence of this effect, see Basil, Schooler, and Reeves 1991). We investigated this possibility by examining participants' evaluations of the personal traits of both the sponsor and the target of the attack advertisements.[13] Our results indicated that attack advertisements generally "work." That is, ratings of the target were generally less positive after participants watched the attack. Ratings of the sponsor, however, were generally unaffected, suggesting that participants did not penalize candidates for airing negative messages.[14]

The fact that attack advertisements do not demobilize on a partisan basis and do not induce negativity toward *both* candidates suggests a third explanation for demobilization. Negative advertising may affect voting intent by conveying cues not about the candidates but about the nature of political campaigns and the political influence of ordinary citizens. Perhaps the act of attacking another candidate in a 30-second advertisement denigrates the entire process.

To explore this possibility, we measured our participants' sense of political efficacy—their beliefs in the responsiveness of public officials and electoral institutions to popular will. We used four questions, coded the responses to each as either efficacious (1) or inefficacious (0) and computed the average response to all four items.[15] Among viewers who were exposed to the positive versions of the campaign advertisement, the mean efficacy score was .24. The mean was no different (.23) among participants in the control group. In the case of viewers who were exposed to the negative versions of the advertisement, the mean dropped to .19. The F-statistic from the one-way analysis of variance was significant at the .02 level.[16] In short, exposure to campaign attacks makes voters disenchanted with the business of politics as usual.

In summary, we have considered three possible explanations for the demobilizing effects of attack advertisements: partisan demobilization, a plague-on-both-houses effect, and general cynicism. Our evidence points toward the third. Among our experimental participants, exposure to attack advertising significantly weakened confidence in the responsiveness of electoral institutions and public officials. As campaigns become more negative and cynical, so does the electorate.

CONCLUSION

Taken together, our studies demonstrate that attack advertising extracts a toll on electoral participation. In the experiments, voting intention dropped by 5% when participants were shown an attack advertisement in place of a positive advertisement. Our aggregate-level replication of the experimental results suggests that Senate turnout in 1992 was roughly 4% lower when the candidates waged relatively negative campaigns. Since the scope of the experimental manipulations never exceeded a single advertisement, our estimates of the demobilizing effects of campaign attacks may be conservative. Over the course of two or three weeks of sustained negative advertising, the flight of voters can be more substantial.

The effects of attack advertising on the decision to vote have significant implications for our understanding of the impact of campaigns on electoral outcomes. Voter withdrawal in response to negative advertising also raises questions concerning the legitimate and fair uses of broadcast advertising.[17]

The most important implication of these results is that in the era of media campaigns, *both* surges and declines in turnout can be generated by high-intensity campaigns. Candidates with sufficient resources can, through the use of negative messages, keep voters away from the polls. Campaigns are not inherently mobilizing forces, and the secular decline in presidential and midterm voter turnout since 1960 (for evidence, see Rosenstone and Hansen 1993) may be attributed, in part, to the increasingly negative tone of national campaigns.

Finally, this research raises normative questions concerning the trade-off between the right to political expression and the right to vote. Should candidates be free to use advertising techniques that have the effect of reducing levels of voter turnout? In the case of publicly financed presidential campaigns, is it legitimate for candidates to use public funds in ways that are likely to discourage voting? How do we weigh the public interest in free political expression against the competing public interest in widespread public participation? When, if ever, should politicians' expression be restrained or subjected to incentives to modify its form or content?

In other areas of public communication, allegations of "antisocial" effects have prompted extensive analysis and debate. In some areas, the outcome has been governmental regulation. Thus the tobacco companies have been banned from using the airwaves for certain forms of commercial speech and are required to include mandated health warnings in their print advertisements. Direct regulation of political speech, which is at the core of the values protected by the First Amendment, is probably both impossible as a matter of law and undesirable as a matter of policy. The classic remedy in this society for injurious speech is simply "more speech." However, there is precedent in the law governing the broadcast media requiring that "equal time" be given to the targets of certain "personal attacks" (see Ferris and Leahy 1990). Possibly, new regulations governing the broadcast media ensuring that the targets of attack advertisements have reasonable opportunity to respond (regardless of their own financial resources) should be considered. Ohio and other states are currently experimenting with "truth in political advertising" guidelines designed to make candidates think twice before resorting to false or misleading advertising. However, approaches that simply ensure that there will be "more speech" miss the essential point raised by this research, which is that negative advertising impacts adversely on voting; remedies that can only multiply the number of negative advertisements will exacerbate, rather than address, the essential problem.

The more realistic approach to influencing the tone of campaign advertising rests on voluntary or incentive-based restraints. There have been several instances in which public controversy over the content of entertainment programming has prodded the networks, local stations, or record companies to withdraw the program in question. Similar reasoning is embodied in legislation pending in Congress that seeks to reform campaign advertising. (For a discussion of recent legislative efforts, see O'Neill 1992.) One bill would impose a double standard on advertising rates under which only "positive" advertisements would be entitled to the "lowest unit rate" rule. Other suggestions include the so-called in-person rule, under which the candidates would be required to deliver their attack statements in person (on camera).

A third set of suggestions for reform addresses the use of media "monitoring." In the aftermath of the 1988 campaign, the press decided to scrutinize the candidates' paid messages (in the form of "ad watches," "truth boxes," and the like). Anticipation of critical news coverage may deter candidates from relying heavily on attack messages. To this point, however, there is no reliable evidence concerning the effects of these monitoring effects on voter response to advertising.

We do not yet understand the implications of these various approaches. Some would certainly raise objections from civil libertarians, others would be objectionable to those concerned with political competitiveness. As in the case of campaign finance reform, broadcast advertising reform may work to benefit those in office at the expense of challengers. Although providing incentives for campaigns to air "positive" messages provides no assurance that these messages will be more substantive, verifiable, or honest, they would, at least, be less likely to deter voting. While the case for broadcast advertising reform has yet to be made, the relationship between negative advertising and voting suggests that these issues are worth further research and discussion.

APPENDIX A: SAMPLES OF EXPERIMENTAL ADVERTISEMENTS

The wording and visuals used in two of our studies appear below. The changes associated with the negative versions of the advertisements are given in parentheses.

1990 Gubernatorial Study: Crime

Text. It's happening right now in your neighborhood. A generation of youth slowly dying. _____ is (is not) the candidate who intends to stop this tragedy and preserve California's future. As mayor of _____ , _____ added (reduced the number of) police officers, constructed (blocked) new jails, and fought hard against drugs (opposed drug education programs). The result: major crime rates fell (increased) by 12%. His (her) record won the endorsement (was condemned by) the California Association of Police Chiefs. They know _____ will push for (will oppose) tougher sentencing and strengthen (weaken) our state's justice system.

Visuals. Schoolchildren on playground; addict injecting heroin; body bag being removed from crime scene; police officers outside courthouse; interior of prison cell; candidate logo.

1992 Senate Study: Unemployment

Text. Since 1990, California has lost two-and-a-half million jobs. The state now has the highest unemployment rate in the nation. California needs elected officials who will end the recession. _____ will work (has done nothing) to bring jobs back to our state. As a U.S. Senator, _____ will introduce legislation (_____ opposes legislation) to increase funding for job training programs and to give California companies incentives to modernize and expand their factories and plants. California needs (can't afford) _____ in the U.S. Senate.

Visuals. Closed factory; graph showing state's unemployment rate; lines at unemployment office; picture of candidate (opponent); factory workers assembling planes; workers on construction site; candidate logo.

APPENDIX B: CLASSIFICATION OF 1992 SENATE CAMPAIGNS ACCORDING TO ADVERTISING TONE

We examined a subset of the NEXIS and DATATIMES databases that contained full-text reproductions of articles from more than 30 major daily newspapers and five politically oriented magazines (e.g., the *Cook Political Report,* the *Roll Call,* and the *Hotline*). A separate search was conducted for all 34 senatorial campaigns. The search was designed to access all articles about the campaign printed after the primary and before the general election. When the search produced more than 150 articles (as was the case for seven races), then a further search command focusing on campaigns advertising was added. This procedure elicited a total of 2,573 articles.

Each article was read by a graduate student coder who specifically looked for discussion of campaign tone. The coder followed a strict scheme in order to place each race into one of the three campaign-tone categories. If a majority of the tone-related references to a campaign were negative (e.g., it was characterized as being nasty, dirty, or vicious and provided specific examples of negative attacks from each of the race's candidates), the race was coded as negative. If at least three articles specifically mentioned that one of the Senate candidate's was deliberately refraining from making a negative response to the opponent's attacks and no later article contradicted this information, then the race was coded as mixed. Finally, when the news coverage yielded no discernible information about negative campaign tone, the race was coded as positive.

We validated our news-based classification scheme by asking two major political consultants (David Hill, Republican, and Mark Mellman, Democrat) to rate each of the Senate campaigns on the same three-point scale. The consultants disagreed with our classification in only one instance (Kentucky), and we deferred to their expertise. (The analysis is unchanged if Kentucky is eliminated from the analysis.) Each state's tone score is shown in the following list:

Negative Tone	Mixed Tone	Positive Tone
Arkansas	Alabama	Alaska
California	Arizona	Hawaii
(6-yr. seat)	Florida	Idaho
California	Illinois	Iowa
(2-yr. seat)	Missouri	Kansas
Colorado	Oklahoma	Maryland
Connecticut		Nevada
Georgia		North Dakota
Indiana		South Dakota
Kentucky		Utah
Louisiana		Vermont
New Hampshire		Wisconsin
New York		
North Carolina		
Ohio		
Oregon		
Pennsylvania		
South Carolina		
Washington		

(Note that the California 6-year seat was contested between Boxer and Herschenson and the 2-year seat, between Feinstein and Seymour, and that the Louisiana general election was uncontested.)

NOTES

This research was supported by generous grants from the John and Mary R. Markle Foundation, the National Science Foundation, and the University of California. We are indebted to Kelley Carlin, Diana Estrada, Travis Dixon, Terri Hall, Mikel Healy, Clark Hoover, Victoria Mitchell, Erin O'Neal, Raza Syed, and Sharmaine Vidanage for superb research assistance.

1 We use these terms interchangeably to describe whether the advertisement, or the campaign as a whole, focuses on a candidate's positive aspects or on the opponent's liabilities and faults.

2 In addition to minimizing the visual differences in the advertisement, we also used identical logos, in which the sponsoring candidate's name appeared in large red letters against a brown backdrop.

3 Using a weighted average of Los Angeles and Orange counties as the baseline, the demographics for our sample match closely for age (median of 34 versus 31), gender (44% vs. 51% male), race (52% vs. 47% white), and partisanship (49% identifying Democratic vs. 47% registration). Our participants deviated in the local area in two respects: 26% of our participants were African-American (compared to 10% in Los Angeles and Orange counties), and 44% were college graduates (compared to 24% for the local area).

4 Random assignment of participants to experimental conditions was used throughout. The use of random assignment assures (subject to the rules of probability) that differences in the dependent variable can be attributed only to the experimental manipulation (see Campbell and Stanley 1969, 25). We took the additional precaution of controlling for a number of background variables considered predictive of participation, including partisanship, prior voting history, age, and education.

5 Responses to the two questions were generally cumulative; that is, few people who said they were not registered indicated an intention to vote. These respondents were classified as unlikely voters.

6 For a more detailed analysis of the effects of advertising valence in specific campaigns, see Ansolabehere, Iyengar, and Valentino 1993.

7 The number of cases was 1,716. Since the F-statistic is nondirectional, that is a conservative test of the demobilization hypothesis.

8 The average roll-off in the 1992 Senate elections (rounded to the nearest thousand) was 127,000, with a maximum of 609,000 and a minimum of –13,000. In percentage terms, roll-off average 4.9% with a range of –1.8% to 11.6%.

9 The Bureau of the Census mails forms to every resident in each state. The mail-back rate is the fraction of forms that are completed and returned.

10 A simple F-test revealed that the symmetry restriction was justified.

11 There are a variety of other interesting results in this analysis, but since we are especially interested in the effects of campaign tone, we set them aside for future consideration.

12 These results are available from the authors.

13 Participants rated the candidates' intelligence, honesty, compassion, leadership, toughness, arrogance, weakness, and deviousness. We formed an index by subtracting the number of negative ratings from the number of positive ratings.

14 These results are available from the authors.

15 The questions asked participants to agree or disagree with the following statements: (1) "Generally speaking, those who get elected to public office keep in touch with the people in their constituencies"; (2) "In this country, politics works for the benefits of a few special interests, rather than the public good"; (3) "Most politicians are willing to tackle the real problems facing America"; (4) "Having elections makes government responsive to the views of the people."

16 The F-statistic was 4.0, with 1,716 cases.

17 It is possible, of course, that negative advertising also exerts prosocial effects not tapped by our studies. For instance, there is some evidence that negative advertisements allow voters to differentiate more readily between candidates' issue positions, thus facilitating "issue voting" (see Garramone et al. 1990; Patterson and McClure 1976).

REFERENCES

Ansolabehere, Stephen, and Alan Gerber. N.d. "The Mismeasure of Campaign Spending." *Journal of Politics*. Forthcoming.

Ansolabehere, Stephen, and Shanto Iyengar. 1991. "The Electoral Effects of Issues and Attacks in Campaign Advertising." Presented at the annual meeting of the American Political Science Association, Washington, DC.

Ansolabehere, Stephen; Shanto Iyengar; and Nick Valentino. 1993. "The Effects of Campaign Advertising on Voter Turnout." University of California, Los Angeles. Typescript.

Bartels, Larry M. 1988. *Presidential Primaries and the Dynamics of Public Choice*. Princeton, NJ: Princeton University Press.

Bartels, Larry M. 1993. "Messages Received: The Political Impact of Media Exposure." *American Political Science Review* 87, pp. 267–85.

Basil, Michael, Caroline Schooler, and Byron Reeves. 1991. "Positive and Negative Political Advertising: Effectiveness of Advertisements and Perceptions of Candidates." In *Television and Political Advertising,* vol. 1, *Psychological Processes,* ed. Frank Biocca. Hillsdale, NJ: Erlbaum.

Berelson, Bernard, Paul Lazarsfeld, and William McPhee. 1954. *Voting: A Study of Opinion Formation in a Presidential Campaign.* Chicago: The University of Chicago Press.

Bode, Kenneth. 1992. "Pull the Plug, Empower the Voters." *Quill* 80, pp. 10–14.

Brady, Henry, and Richard Johnson. 1987. "What's the Primary Message: Horse Race or Issue Journalism?" In *Media and Momentum,* ed. Gary R. Orren and Nelson W. Polsby, Chatham: Chatham House.

Campbell, Angus et al. 1966. *Elections and the Political Order.* New York: Wiley.

Campbell, Donald T., and Julian C. Stanley. 1969. *Experimental and Quasi-Experimental Designs for Research.* Chicago: Rand-McNally.

Dionne, E. J., Jr. 1991. *Why Americans Hate Politics.* New York: Simon & Schuster.

Ferris, Charles, and Terrance Leahy. 1990. "Red Lions, Tigers, and Bears: Broadcast Contest Regulation and the First Amendment." *Catholic University Law Review* 38, p. 309.

Garramone, Gina M. 1985. "Effects of Negative Political Advertising: The Roles of Sponsor and Rebuttal." *Journal of Broadcasting and Electronic Media* 29, pp. 147–59.

Garramone, Gina M.; Charles K. Atkin; Bruce E. Pinkleton; and Richard T. Cole. 1990. "Effects of Negative Advertising on the Political Process." *Journal of Broadcasting and Electronic Media* 34, pp. 299–311.

Hagstrom, Jerry, and Robert Guskind. 1988. "In the Gutter." *National Journal,* 5 November, pp. 2782–90.

Hagstrom, Jerry, and Robert Guskind. 1992. "Airborne Attacks." *National Journal,* 31 October, pp. 2477–82.

Hovland, Carl. 1959. "Reconciling Conflicting Results from Survey and Experimental Studies of Attitude Change." *American Psychologist* 14, pp. 8–17.

Jamieson, Kathleen H. 1992. *Dirty Politics: Deception, Distraction, and Democracy.* New York: Oxford University Press.

Kosterman, Richard J. 1991. "Political Spot Advertising and Routes to Persuasion: The Role of Symbolic Content." Ph.D. diss. University of California, Los Angeles.

Lazarsfeld, Paul; Bernard Berelson; and Hazel Gaudet. 1948. *The People's Choice.* 2nd ed. New York: Columbia University Press.

Lichter, S. Robert; Daniel Amundson; and Richard Noyes. 1988. *The Video Campaign.* Washington: American Enterprise Institute.

Neale, Thomas. 1991. *Negative Campaigning in National Politics: An Overview.* Report No. 91-775 GOV. Washington: Congressional Research Service.

O'Neill, Robert M. 1992. "Regulating Speech To Cleanse Political Campaigns." *Capitol University Law Review* 21, pp. 575–91.

Patterson, Samuel, and Gregory Caldeira. 1993. "Getting Out the Vote: Participation in Gubernatorial Campaigns." *American Political Science Review* 77, pp. 675–89.

Patterson, Thomas, and Robert McClure. 1976. *The Unseeing Eye: The Myth of Television Power in National Politics.* New York: Putnam.

Pfau, Michael, and Henry C. Kenski. 1990. *Attack Politics: Strategy and Defense.* New York: Praeger.

Polsby, Nelson W. 1983. *Consequences of Party Reform.* New York: Oxford University Press.

Rosen, J., and Paul Taylor. 1992. *The New News and the Old News: The Press and Politics in the 1990s.* New York: Brookings Institution.

Rosenstone, Steven, and Mark Hansen. 1993. *Mobilization, Participation, and Democracy in America.* New York: Macmillan.

Rubin, Donald. 1974. "Estimating Causal Effects in Randomized and Non-Randomized Studies." *Journal of Educational Psychology* 66, pp. 688–701.

Sabato, Larry. 1991. *Feeding Frenzy: How Attack Journalism Has Transformed American Politics.* New York: The Free Press.

Thorson, Esther, William G. Christ, and Clarke Caywood. 1991. "Effects of Issue-Image Strategies, Attack and Support Appeals, Music, and Visual Content in Political Commercials." *Journal of Broadcasting and Electronic Media* 35, pp. 465–86.

Wattenberg, Martin P. 1984. *Decline of American Political Parties, 1952–1980.* Cambridge, MA: Harvard University Press.

Wattenberg, Martin P. 1991. *The Rise of Candidate-Centered Politics: Presidential Elections of the 1980s.* Cambridge, MA: Harvard University Press.

A FINAL WORD

We're done! As a final word we would like to ignore, for the moment, all the specific details and focus our attention on what this book is about: helping readers of research defend themselves from inadequate, incomplete, and incompetent research. The tactic we used to achieve this goal has been to concern ourselves with error and its possible occurrence in a given piece of research. The tactic we think is a good one, and hopefully will stand you in good stead throughout your professional career.

But the tactic, like any tactic, does not guarantee that the goal will be achieved. Some studies containing errors will report correct findings, and some studies without error will be wrong. As a final reminder of this important caution, we repeat the "fallacist's fallacy,"* which consists of any of the following false propositions:

1 *An argument which is structurally fallacious in some respect is therefore structurally false in all respects.*

2 *An argument which is structurally false in some respect, or even in every respect, is therefore substantively false in its conclusion.*

3 *The appearance of a fallacy in an argument is an external sign of its author's depravity.*

4 *Sound thinking is merely thinking which is not fallacious.*

5 *Fallacies exist independent of particular purposes and assumptions.*

Thus, there is no certain road to truth. A careful examination of research will provide evidence as to the factual accuracy and generalization of the findings, but it is not proof. As readers we need to increase our tolerance of uncertainty and whenever possible search for truth among the patterns of similarity in numerous studies.

*The "fallacist's fallacy" is from D. H Fischer, *Historians' Fallacies*. New York: Harper & Row, 1970, p. 305.

NOTES

CHAPTER 1

SOURCES OF INFORMATION

Our eight examples of the inadequacy of social science research came from the following sources; they are listed in the same order here as used in the text. You might wish to evaluate those evaluations.

1 E. Wandt (Ed.). *A Cross-Section of Educational Research.* New York: McKay, 1965, pp. 1–7.

2 D. H. Fischer. *Historians' Fallacies: Toward a Logic of Historical Thought.* New York: Harper & Row, 1970, p. 305.

3 L. Wolins. "Responsibility for Raw Data." *American Psychologist* 17 (1962), pp. 657–58.

4 O. Morgenstern. *On the Accuracy of Economic Statistics,* 2nd ed. Princeton, NJ: Princeton University Press, 1963.

5 A. Tversky and D. Kahneman. "Belief in the Law of Small Numbers." *Psychological Bulletin* 76 (1971), pp. 105–10.

6 B. Rensberger. "Fraud in Research Is a Rising Problem in Science." *The New York Times,* January 23, 1977, p. 44.

7 The study of spreadsheet errors was conducted by Raymond Panko and Richard Halverson, Jr. of the University of Hawaii in Honolulu. The findings were reported in *Harvard Business Review,* September–October 1996, pp. 10–11.

8 R. Rennie, quoted in *The New York Times,* February 16, 1988, p. C11.

CHAPTER 2

SOURCE OF INFORMATION

The poem by Piet Hein was reprinted by permission of the author. Copyright PHI, Copenhagen, Doubleday, New York. All rights reserved.

CHAPTER 3

SOURCES OF INFORMATION

The study of people's reactions to the Princeton-Dartmouth football game was reported by Albert H. Hastorf and Hadley Cantril, "They Saw a Game: A Case Study," *Journal of Abnormal and Social Psychology* 49 (1954), pp. 129–34.

We can't find the citation for the study of how inaccurately researchers reported a "scuffle" in a lecture hall, but many such studies have been conducted. One is reported by M. C. Otto, "Testimony and Human Nature," *Journal of Criminal Law and Criminology* 9 (1919), pp. 98–104. We would appreciate the citation for the study we mentioned.

The study of anti-Oriental feeling was reported by R. T. LaPiere, "Attitudes vs. Actions," *Social Forces* 13 (1934), pp. 230–37.

Additional details about one adult's reaction to gaining sight after being blind from birth is given in R. L. Gregory, *Eye and Brain,* 2nd ed. New York: McGraw-Hill, 1973, pp. 194–98.

Two studies of what people see when two pictures are shown simultaneously were reported by Hans H. Toch and Richard Schulte, "Readiness to Perceive Violence as a Result of Police Training," *British Journal of Psychology* 52 (1961), pp. 389–93, and James W. Bagby, "A Cross-Cultural Study of Perceptual Predominance in Binocular Rivalry," *Journal of Abnormal and Social Psychology* 54 (1957), pp. 331–34.

The study of seven normal people entering mental hospitals were reported by D. L. Rosenhan, "On Being Sane in Insane Places," *Science* 179 (1973), pp. 250–58. Heisenberg's uncertainty principle is discussed in the book by George Gamow that is suggested in For Further Reading.

Studies of how teacher's expectations affect students are described in Robert Rosenthal and Lenore Jacobsen, *Pygmalion in the Classroom: Teacher Expectation and Pupil's Intellectual Development.* New York: Holt, 1968.

CHAPTER 4

SOURCES OF INFORMATION

The study of the effect of words on estimates of the speed of a car was reported by Elizabeth Loftus, "Reconstructing Memory: The Incredible Eyewitness," *Psychology Today* 8 (December 1974), pp. 117–19.

The lecture by Dr. Fox has been reported in several journals. One of these descriptions is by D. H. Naftulin et al., "The Doctor Fox Lecture: A Paradigm of Educational Seduction," *Journal of Medical Education* 48 (July 1973), pp. 630–35.

Dishonesty in science is discussed by Salvador E. Luria, "What Makes a Scientist Cheat," *Prism* (May 1975).

The full discussion of factifuging is referenced as a Further Reading.

CHAPTER 5

SOURCES OF INFORMATION

Studies of high status communicators are in Chapter 6 of Marvin Karlins and Herbert I. Abelson, *Persuasion,* 2nd ed. New York: Springer, 1970.

A thorough discussion of closed systems of beliefs (or closed-mindedness) can be found in Milton Rokeach, *The Open and Closed Mind.* New York: Basic Books, 1960.

CHAPTER 6

[1]These potential biases have been called (1) the evaluation apprehension effect, (2) the expectancy effect, and (3) the social desirability effect.

[2]"The power of these effects is hard to overstate. A rule of thumb is that 30 percent of patients in the placebo half of a drug trial . . . will experience an improvement in symptoms" (N. Wade, *New York Times Magazine,* 1/7/96, p. 16)

SOURCES OF INFORMATION

The nature of volunteer subjects is discussed in Robert Rosenthal and Ralph L. Rosnow, *The Volunteer Subject.* New York: Wiley, 1975.

The studies that discovered the "Hawthorne effect" are described in F. J. Roethlisberger and W. J. Dickson, *Management and the Worker.* Cambridge, MA: Harvard University Press, 1939 (republished in 1970).

CHAPTER 7

[1]In this example, we have been considering the noise that occurs when something is measured or weighed. Measurement error per se is discussed in Chapter 9 under the topic of reliability. Noise, however, is a broader topic than reliability because noise can be introduced into a study even if the measuring instruments are perfectly reliable.

CHAPTER 8

[1]Of course, strongly held beliefs about what "should" occur in a study may increase the possibility that expectancy effects (see Chapter 3) will bias the research results.

CHAPTER 10

[1]Methodological arguments for accuracy and generality are frequently all that is possible in research settings that require lengthy observations. Arguments based on replications would require agreement among several researchers who independently observed the same phenomenon—clearly a much more expensive approach.

[2]To minimize the computations, all the percentiles in this chapter are calculated this way. Actually, a more standard (but also more complicated) way to compute percentiles would give the top score a percentile of 87.5.

CHAPTER 11

[1]Researchers use this idea of prediction to help define what they mean by a relationship: two variables are related if you can use one of them to predict the other one better than you could have done without knowledge of the first one. For example, you probably can more accurately predict the weight of people if you know how tall they are.

While your predictions wouldn't be perfect, you would do a better job if you knew their heights than if you didn't know anything about them. Similarly, knowing the heights of people would allow you to predict their weights better than if all you knew was their political preferences. The reason height predicts better is that height and weight are related, but political preference and weight are probably not.

[2]Relationships are usually described in the following terms: (a) How strong are they? The stronger the relationship, the more accurately you can predict one variable from another. (b) What direction are they? Positive relationships are those where high values on one variable tend to match up with high values on the other variable (such as found in the relationship between height and weight), while negative relationships match up high scores on one variable with low scores on the other. (c) Are the variables causally related, as in the example of study habits causing high or low grades, or are they not causal, such as in the relationship between height and weight?

[3]This number is the Pearson correlation coefficient. It is very commonly used to quantify the amount of (linear) relationship. When it is a positive number it means that the relationship is positive—higher values on one variable are associated with higher values on the other. When it is a negative number it means that the relationship is negative or inverse—higher values on one variable are associated with lower values on the

other. The Pearson statistic can range from −1.00 through +1.00. Most values of this statistic are between 0.00 (meaning no relationship) and +1.00 (a perfect positive relationship) or −1.00 (a perfect negative relationship).

[4]Researchers have a name for this type of erroneous reasoning; it's called the "ecological fallacy."

[5]In this extreme case, since the weight has no freedom to vary, it really wouldn't be a variable. With no freedom, it will always have the same value of 110.235 pounds, and hence it would be better described as a "constant."

CHAPTER 12

[1]More precisely, (B) would be an independent variable.

[2]The word "people" is used as a convenience. What we are saying here about studies of people also applies to studies of groups, tribes, and organizations, as well as individuals.

[3]This rival explanation is called "regression toward the mean" because its apparent effect is to move (or regress) scores from either or both ends of a set of scores toward the average (or mean) of those scores.

[4]While doing this removes a potential source of rival explanation, it also seriously weakens a methodological argument for the generality of the findings, because they will then be based on people who are clearly different from the people who began the study—people more like those found in other classrooms. More about the generality of findings is presented in Chapter 14.

[5]We should not confuse this with random sampling; see Chapter 14.

[6]For very large samples (1,000 or more) we should be able to be reasonably confident that randomization will work. For very small samples (under 25) we have good reason to be concerned. But for the sample size of most studies we can't be sure that randomization will have made the groups reasonably equal.

[7]Called an "instrumentation effect."

[8]In Chapter 11, we would have analyzed rival explanations in terms of "third variables."

CHAPTER 13

[1]This is one major use of statistical inference in the social sciences. Another, equally important, use of statistics is discussed in Chapter 14.

[2]This assumption that the two drugs are equally effective is, in statistics, called the "null hypothesis."

SOURCE OF INFORMATION

"A Modern-Day Parable" was reprinted by permission of the publisher and author, G. M. Gillmore, "A Modern-Day Parable," *The American Psychologist* 26, March 1971, p. 314. Copyright 1971 by the American Psychological Association.

CHAPTER 14

SOURCE OF INFORMATION

The newspaper article about saccharin testing on rats was from the Seattle *Post-Intelligencer,* March 15, 1977. Reprinted by permission of United Press International.

[1]For the sake of brevity, in this chapter we will use the word people throughout as the generic name for what or who is being studied. It may actually be people, but it can also be groups of people (committees, organizations, nations), objects, animals, time periods, etc. It is used synonymously with what social researchers call "units," "cases," or "observations."

[2]We chose to use hair length in this example because we felt it to be an obviously irrelevant factor insofar as teaching is concerned. However, choosing nonessential differences isn't as easy as it seems. One of our reviewers suggested that "the prevailing hair styles for males at a given point in time may be related to prevailing views about good teaching. Thus, the 'long hairs' of the 60s also argued for unstructured, student-centered classes; whereas a prevailing short-hair style might signal a more structured, teacher-centered preference."

[3]Random sampling should not be confused with random assignment (see Chapter 12). Both use random procedures to remove biases, but their purposes are different. In random sampling the researcher is strengthening a methodological argument for generality; in random assignment the researcher is strengthening a methodological argument for factual accuracy.

[4]To be a bit more precise, this rule of thumb applies when the population is large in comparison with the size of the sample. But when the sample size forms a reasonable portion of the population (certainly by the time the sample is 25 percent of the population), the actual size of the sample does matter.

[5]To statisticians these are far from equivalent statements, but for our purposes they can be considered so.

[6]That is, if the poll were repeated many times, and each time it was repeated a 95 percent confidence interval was computed, the researchers would be right in their conclusions in 95 percent of those polls.

CHAPTER 15

These two ways of being wrong when making a decision are related to what researchers call Type I and Type II errors. An error of the first type occurs when the decision maker thinks the evidence is strong enough to take action—but the decision maker is wrong because the evidence is misleading, no action is justified. The second type of error occurs when the decision maker believes there is not enough evidence to justify doing something; the decision maker is wrong in this case because there really is enough evidence to take action.

SOURCES OF INFORMATION

The study of the introduction of programmed instruction into Pittsburgh city schools was adopted from Everett M. Rogers and Floyd Shoemaker, *Communication of Innovations,* 2nd ed. New York: The Free Press, 1971, p. 329. They adopted it from Richard O. Carlson, "Strategies for Educational Change: Some Needed Research on Diffusion of Innovations," a paper presented at the Conference on Strategies for Educational Change, Washington, D.C., U.S. Office of Education, 1965.

The study of the marketing recommendations by students and managers was adopted from Gerald Zaltman and Philip C. Burger. *Marketing Research.* Hinsdale, IL: Dryden, 1975, p. 563.

CHAPTER 16

SOURCES OF INFORMATION

T. R. Black. *Evaluating Social Science Research.* Thousand Oaks, CA: Sage Publications, 1993.

J. R. Fraenkel and N. E. Wallen. *How to Design and Evaluate Research in Education.* New York: McGraw-Hill, 1993.

E. R. Girden. *Evaluating Research Articles from Start to Finish.* Thousand Oaks, CA: Sage Publications, 1996.

P. C. Stern and L. Kalof. *Evaluating Social Science Research,* 2nd ed. New York: Oxford University Press, 1996.

GLOSSARY

Each term in this glossary is followed by a brief definition. In general, terms are defined according to their most common usage. This means that, occasionally, a precise distinction between closely related terms will be blurred or ignored. Terminology does differ in different disciplines; we have tried to compensate for this somewhat by using terms synonymously. (For example, see "data matrix.")

When another term in the glossary is used in a definition, it appears in italics. Following many definitions are "pointers" to additional information about the term. (These pointers are enclosed in brackets.) For example, following the definition of "validity" you will find [*reliability,* Chapter 9].

Pointers in lowercase italics (e.g., *reliability*) refer to other terms in the glossary that are strongly associated with the original term, but are not used in the definition of that term. Pointers such as "Chapter 9" refer to chapters that discuss the original term.

At the end of the glossary we have listed a few textbooks that include introductory-level discussions of most of the terms.

accuracy   In the social sciences, frequently used synonymously with *validity* and thus refers to the absence of both *bias* and *noise*. In the physical sciences, sometimes restricted to meaning the absence of bias only. [*precision*]

action research   Research in which the decision maker using the results of the research takes part. [*applied research, basic research, policy research*]

after-only design   A *research design* characterized by measuring the *dependent variable* once, after the *independent variable* (or *treatment*) took place or occurred. Also called a "posttest-only design." [*before-after design*]

alpha   The probability of incorrectly rejecting the *null hypothesis* with a *significance test;* the probability of making a *Type I error.* [*p value, level of significance, beta,* Chapter 13]

alternative hypothesis   The *hypothesis* that the researcher would like to be able to accept if the *null hypothesis* is rejected with a *significance test.* [Chapter 13]

analysis of covariance   A *significance test* to determine whether significant differences among *group means* exist if the effects of *extraneous variables* are held constant by statistical means.

analysis of variance   (Also known as AOV or ANOVA.) A *significance test* most commonly used in the social sciences to determine whether significant differences exist among the *means* of a number of *treatment groups.*

antecedent variable   A variable in a *causal model* that precedes other variables. [*consequent variable, intervening variable*]

applied research   Research carried out to discover new knowledge that has immediate applicability. [*action research, basic research, policy research*]

area sampling   A method of *random sampling* using geographical areas.

area under curve   An area under the curve of a *probability distribution.*

artifact   An error, usually a *bias,* caused by something the researcher does or something about the research situation.

association   (Also known as relationship.) The state of being related or dependent. Two variables are *associated* if knowledge of one variable permits a better prediction of the value of the second variable than could be obtained without knowledge of the first. Often the association between two variables can be noticed by the pattern in the two sets of *scores:* if the rows of the *data matrix* are rearranged so that the scores for one of the variables in question are in increasing order, then a positive relationship or association exists if the scores on the second variable also tend to increase. A negative association would exist if the second set of scores decreased as the first set increased. There are many ways to quantify the degree of association between two (or more) variables; these are called *measures of association.* [Chapter 11]

asymmetrical measures of association   *Measures of association* that distinguish between the *independent* and *dependent variables* so that the degree of *association* between two variables depends upon which variable is independent and which is dependent. If the roles of the variables were reversed, a different degree of association would be calculated. [*symmetrical measures of association*]

attribute   A property or characteristic of something, as opposed to the thing itself.

attribute variable   A variable that cannot be experimentally manipulated; an *attribute* of the individuals under study.

average   A measure of *central tendency* (the middle) of a set of scores. Usually, it is synonymous with the *mean.* [Chapter 10]

axiom   A statement assumed to be true for the purposes of further deductions.

b   A nonstandardized *regression coefficient.* [*beta weight*]

bar graph   (Also known as a histogram.) A visual representation of a *frequency distribution* where the height of each bar represents the *frequency* or percentage of a *level* of the *variable.* It includes the same information as a *frequency polygon.*

basic research   Research carried out to discover new knowledge with relatively little concern for the applicability of that knowledge. [*action research, applied research, policy research*]

Bayesian statistics   A branch of statistics in which the probabilities obtained from data are affected by the researcher's prior estimates of those probabilities.

before-and-after design   An *experimental design* in which *subjects* are measured on a given *variable* both before and after the *independent variable* (or *treatment*) is administered or *manipulated.*

before-after design   A *research design* characterized by measuring the *dependent variable* twice—both before and after the *independent variable* (or *treatment*) took place or occurred. Also called a "pretest-posttest design." [*after-only design*]

behavioral research   *Empirically* based research carried out in one of the behavioral sciences; research that involves measuring or observing human or animal behavior.

beta   The probability of failing to reject the *null hypothesis* when it should be rejected (i.e., when it's false) with a *significance test;* the probability of making a *Type II error.* [*alpha, p value*]

beta weight   A *standardized regression coefficient.* [*curvilinear regression, linear regression, b*]

between-group differences   Differences between *treatment groups* (or between treatment and *control groups*), usually between their *group means.* [*within-group differences*]

bias   An error that is always in the same direction. A bias in statistics is the degree to which the average of an infinite number of determinations of a statistical value, such as the *mean,* fails to equal the corresponding *parameter* (e.g., the *population* mean). [*noise,* Chapter 6]

binomial sampling distribution   A *sampling distribution* based on the results of two alternative outcomes such as yes-no answers or the male-female *attribute.*

biserial correlation   A *measure of association* between one *continuous variable* and one *dichotomous variable.*

bivariate analysis   An analysis of the *relationship* between two *variables.* [*multivariate analysis, univariate analysis*]

blind   The condition of not knowing which *treatment* is being administered or was administered to a given *subject.* The term can apply to anyone associated with a research project including subjects. [*double blind*]

blocking variable   A *variable* used to divide *subjects* into homogeneous subgroups to form a *related group design.*

bridging variable   A *variable* used to determine if the *independent variable* is having an effect when the *dependent variable* cannot be measured for a long time after *treatment.*

C (Pearson's)   (Also known as the contingency coefficient.) A *symmetrical measure of association* between two *categorized variables.*

canonical correlation   A technique for determining a way of combining a group of *predictor variables* and a way of combining a group of *criterion variables* such that the *correlation* between the two combinations is a maximum.

case   Each instance of the *unit of analysis* under study is a case; often synonymous with *observation* or *subject.* When the unit of analysis is the individual, each person is a case. When the unit of analysis is the organization, each organization is a case. [*data matrix*]

case study   An analysis and explication of a single situation or single *case* often using *qualitative* methods.

categorized variable   A *variable* having categorical, or *nominal level,* values. [*continuous variable*]

causal modeling   Procedures whose purpose is to identify causal links among several *variables.* [*causality*]

causality   The concept that some phenomena cause other phenomena. [*causal modeling,* Chapters 11 and 12]

ceiling effect   The concentration of *scores* toward the high end of a measuring *scale* because of restraints on the highest value the scores can assume. [*floor effect*]

census   A *survey* of an entire *population.*

central tendency   The middle of a *distribution of scores.* The *mean, median,* and *mode* are all measures of central tendency. [Chapter 10]

chi square test   (Also known as Pearson's chi square test of independence.) A *significance test* often used in the social sciences to determine if two *categorized variables* are related.

closed questions   Questions that have fixed alternative answers for a *respondent* to choose from. [*open questionnaire items*]

cluster sampling   A method of *random sampling* in stages. In the first stage, clusters are chosen that contain groups of *units* or *subjects.* In the last stage, the individual units are chosen from the clusters. There may be two, three, or more stages in a cluster sampling plan (e.g., first select census tracts, then blocks within those tracts, then households within those blocks, then people within those households). [Chapter 14]

cohort study   A type of *longitudinal study* of a group of people in which data or observations may be collected from different members of the group at the various measurement periods. [*panel study*]

coding   The process of assigning a value for a *variable* to a case. For instance, a coder might decide, based on the way a *respondent* to a *survey* describes his job, that he is a "blue collar worker" for the variable "type of occupation." Or, the variable "sex" might be coded numerically using "1" for female and "2" for male.

coefficient of concordance   A *measure of association* among several sets of *rankings.*

coefficient of determination   The *multiple correlation coefficient, R, squared.* It is interpreted as the percent of variation of the *dependent variable* accounted for by the *independent variables* in the *multiple regression equation.*

common factor variance   *Variance* shared by two or more *variables.*

commonality   The percent of *variance* of a given *variable* that is accounted for by the derived *factors* obtained from a *factor analysis.*

comparison group   See *control group.*

compensatory equalization of treatment effect   A possible *bias* due to the reluctance of administrators to tolerate unequal *treatments* which are needed to test the effects of a given *independent variable.*

compensatory rivalry effect   A possible *bias* due to competition among *treatment groups.*

completion rate   See *response rate.*

conceptual definition   (Also known as constitutive definition.) A definition of a *construct* based on other constructs. [*operational definition*]

concurrent validity   One of several ways to assess the *validity* of a *measure.* It is a type of *criterion validity* based on the ability of the *variable* in question to predict another variable, both variables being measured at the same time.

confidence interval   A range of values within which there is a specified probability that the *population parameter* will exist, over all possible *samples.* The specified probability is called the *confidence level.* A confidence interval is a type of *interval estimate.* [Chapter 14]

confidence level   If the process of estimating a *parameter* from a *sample statistic* were repeated many times, the confidence level would be the percent of the obtained *confidence intervals* which contain the parameter (i.e., which are correct).

confounded effect   The combined effects of *independent variables* and *extraneous variables* on the *dependent variable.*

consequent variable   A *variable* in a *causal model* that follows other variables. [*antecedent variable, intervening variable*]

constitutive definition   See *conceptual definition.*

construct   A concept or idea used in research; often used synonymously with *variable.*

construct validity   A general approach to determine whether a *measuring instrument* is measuring what it should be measuring. It is based on the degree of agreement between the *measurements* in question and other measurements known to be *valid.* The degree of agreement is most simply ascertained by an appropriate *measure of association.* In the absence of measurements known to be valid various methods are used to ascertain both *convergent* and *discriminate validity*—for instance, *multitrait-multimethod* analysis. [Chapter 9]

contamination   The effect of *extraneous variables* on the *dependent variable.*

content analysis   Any of several methods used in the analysis of various forms of verbal communication such as documents and news stories.

content validity   A general approach to determine the *validity* of a *measuring instrument* based on the apparent reasonableness of the measuring procedure or the content of the instrument. *Face validity* and *sampling validity* are types of content validity.

contingency coefficient   See *C (Pearson's).*

contingency table   See *cross-tabulation.*

continuous variable   A *variable* that can take on any value within a given range. [*categorized variable*]

control   In *research design,* control is the concern for *biases,* especially their treatment and prevention. In data analysis, control is the attempt to "remove the effect" of one or more *variables* in order to increase understanding about the other variables in the analysis. [*elaboration model,* Chapter 12]

control group   (Also known as comparison group.) In a study made up of several different *treatment groups,* the control group is the one against which the others are compared. Often the control group does not receive any *treatment.* [Chapter 12]

control variable   A *blocking variable, test variable,* or a variable whose effects are lessened or removed statistically. [*elaboration model*]

convergent validity   One of several ways to assess the *construct validity* of a *measure;* often used with *discriminant validity.* It is based on the degree to which two or more different measuring procedures "converge" or measure the same thing.

correlated group design   See *related group design.*

correlation   In informal usage, correlation is often used as a synonym for *association,* though there is a technical distinction between these terms. Correlation is also used to stand for a particular *measure of association, Pearson's r.* [Chapter 11]

correlational research   Research conducted so that *relationships* between *variables* can be examined, but none of the variables can be considered a *treatment* or an intervention in the lives of the subjects. [*experiment*]

covariable   An additional *variable* used in the *analysis of covariance* either to increase the *precision* of the analysis, or to have its effects removed statistically, or both.

covariance   Used alone, the covariance is an inadequate *measure of association* between two *variables.* It is often an important component in statistical formulas.

Cramer's V   See *V (Cramer's).*

criterion validity   A general approach to determine the *validity* of a *measure* based on the accuracy with which the *variable* in question can predict the *criterion variable. Concurrent validity* and *predictive validity* are types of criterion validity.

criterion variable   See *dependent variable.*

cross-sectional study   A study conducted at only one point in time, in contrast to a *longitudinal survey.*

cross-tabulation   (Also known as a contingency table.) A table or set of tables which show the number or percent of *observations* (i.e., *frequencies*) existing at every combination of the *levels* of two or more *variables*. Each table has rows representing the values of one variable and columns representing the values of another variable.

cross-validation   A method for determining if a *regression model* is *generalizable*.

cumulative scale   A *scale* in which each response statement has an increasing amount of the attitude or reaction being measured. A *Guttman scale* is a commonly used type of cumulative scale.

curve fitting   The process of finding a straight line or curve that best fits a set of data plotted on a graph.

curvilinear regression   A statistical procedure that fits a curve to a set of data. The curve summarizes the *relationship* between one or more *predictor variables* and a *dependent variable*. [*linear regression*]

D_{yx}(Somer's)   An *asymmetrical measure of association* based on *ranks*.

data matrix   A rectangular arrangement of data. Each row represents a single individual (*case, subject, unit,* or *observation*). Each column represents a different *variable* or *measure*. The body of the data matrix contains *scores,* values, or *measures*.

decile   One of ten points representing an increment of 10 percent of the *scores* in the data. For instance, the third decile is that value or score such that 30 percent of the *cases* fall below it (i.e., have lower scores). [*median, quartile, percentile,* Chapter 10]

degrees of freedom   A number (usually based on the number of *observations* in a set of data) used in the calculation of many *significance tests*.

Delphi study   A study in which a number of people (usually experts) are asked to make predictions about future events, are later furnished with group results of the predictions, and are then asked for revised predictions. This process may go through several iterations until the group arrives at relative agreement.

demand characteristics   All cues about the study (whether given formally by the researcher, or conjectured by the *subjects,* or learned from the grapevine) that affect subjects' beliefs about what is expected of them. A possible source of *bias* because subjects may try to do what they think is expected of them. [Chapter 6]

demographic variable   An *attribute variable* of a person; usually a variable that classifies people into social groupings. Common demographic variables are age, sex, social class, religion, ethnicity, and marital status.

demoralization effect   A possible *bias* due to the resentment of the group not receiving the *treatment*.

dependent variable   (Also known as the criterion, outcome, predicted, or response variable.) The *variable* that is thought to be affected by an *independent variable*.

descriptive research   Research carried out to describe a given phenomenon, but not to formally draw inferences about a *population*.

descriptive statistics   Statistics that summarize a set of data; inferences from the data to a larger *population* are not made. *Univariate* statistics summarize the values of a single *variable* often in terms of *central tendency* and *dispersion*. Measures of *skewness* and *kurtosis* are also univariate descriptive statistics. Univariate data may be summarized graphically in a *historian* or in a *frequency polygon*. *Bivariate* descriptive statistics summarize the *association* between variables: is there an association and if so how large is it? For some types of variables, bivariate analyses can determine the direction (positive or negative) and the shape (e.g., linear) of the association. Bivariate data may also be summarized graphically in a *scatterplot*. Other common statistical procedures which can be used descriptively include *factor analysis, simple* or *multiple regression, canonical correlation,* and *discriminant analysis*. [*inferential statistics, statistic*]

dichotomous question   Questions that provide only two choices as possible answers.

dichotomous variable   A *variable* with only two possible values. Gender is a dichotomous variable. [*continuous variable*]

differential scale   A *scale* in which the responses provided have a known difference between them; thus each item does not count equally in the total score.

directive interviewing   An *interviewing* technique in which the interviewer has tight control over the questions asked or the topics discussed. [*nondirective interviewing*]

discrete variable   See *categorized variable.*

discriminant analysis   A method for determining a mathematical equation to predict an *observation's* value on a *discrete variable.*

discriminant validity   One of several ways to assess the *construct validity* of a *measure;* often used with *convergent validity.* It is based on the degree to which the *measuring instrument* can discriminate between the concept being measured and different concepts which are closely related to it.

dispersion   The amount of variation in set of *scores;* how far apart the scores are from one another. The *range, standard deviation,* and *variance* are a few of the commonly used measures of dispersion. [Chapter 10]

distorter variable   A *variable* that distorts a *relationship* among other variables.

distribution   See *frequency distribution, probability distribution,* and *sampling distribution.*

double-blind experiment   An *experiment* in which neither the *subjects* nor the researchers interacting with the subjects know which *treatment* is being administered to a given subject. [*blind,* Chapter 6]

dropout bias   See *mortality* effect.

dummy variable   A *variable* used to group other variables for the purpose of analysis.

ecological fallacy   The mistaken belief that *relationships* found at one level of analysis must also apply at another, usually lower, level of analysis. Suppose counties with high *median* incomes also tend to have a larger percentage of college-educated residents. It would be a mistake to automatically apply this statement about counties to people—that is, that college-educated residents earn more money.

ecological representativeness   A question of *generality* which asks how representative are aspects of the study other than the people or *units* (e.g., the conditions, researchers, *operational definitions*). [Chapter 14]

effect size   The amount of impact the *independent variables* have on the *dependent variable;* a measure of the strength of the *relationship* between the two types of variables. [Chapter 13]

elaboration model   A method for analyzing *associations* among *variables.* An association existing between two variables may be affected by a third variable, called a *test variable* or a *control variable.* To apply the elaboration model, the association is recomputed separately at each *level* of the test variable, thereby holding that variable constant. Three outcomes are possible: (1) if the separate associations equal the original association, the test variable is not a factor in the original association and the result is called a "replication"; (2) if, however, the separate associations become negligible or zero, the interpretation of the original association depends upon the nature of the test variable—it is either an *intervening* or an *antecedent variable.* If intervening, the original association is considered real and the test variable provides an "interpretation" of how the two variables are causally linked. With an antecedent test variable, the original association becomes *spurious* and the test variable is said to provide an "explanation" for the association; (3) if some, but not all, of the separate associations become negligible, the outcome is called "specification" (an *interaction*) because the test variable specifies the conditions for the association to exist.

empirical   Subject to critical evaluation through observation or *experiment* rather than through speculation or theorizing.

empirical data   Data collected using empirical methods.

empirical validity   The truth of statements as established by observation or *experiment*. [*criterion validity, validity*]

endogenous variable   A *variable* in a *causal model* or *path analysis* which is to be explained by the model; it is affected by other variables in the model. [*exogenous variable*]

equal appearing intervals   A method for forming *differential scales*.

error model   A way of thinking about truth in terms of what is left after all important distortions to truth have been eliminated or accounted for. The error model is based on the premise that looking at the world as non-scientists do is not a good way to learn something because of the many factors which can lead the observer to a faulty conclusion. Under the error model it is the job of the researcher to know potential distorting factors and to take them into account in the design and conduct of the study. The job of the evaluator of research is to detect factors that the research may have missed in the error-reduction process. The error model provides the basic rationale that underlies what we're doing in this book.

error term   A measure of error *variance* in a *criterion variable*. It is usually the denominator in the calculation of a *significance test* or a term in a statistical model (such as a *regression equation*).

error variance   *Variance* of the *dependent variable* not accounted for by the *independent variable* or variables. [*unexplained variance*]

eta   An *asymmetrical* measure of *linear* or *curvilinear association*. Eta squared is a PRE measure of *effect size* often used after the *analysis of variance*.

evaluation apprehension   A potential *bias* caused by *subjects* trying to look "good" or appear socially and psychologically well-adjusted. [Chapter 6]

evidence   Any information supplied by a researcher to support a *hypothesis* or assertion.

ex post facto research   A type of *experiment* in which the researcher has no *control* over the *independent variables*. Often the independent treatment variable occurred in the past, before the researcher considered doing the study. [*quasi-experiment, true experiment*]

exogenous variable   An *independent variable* in a *causal model* or *path analysis* which affects other *variables* but does not have other variables (in the model under consideration) influencing it. [*endogenous variable*]

expectancy effect   (Also known as experimenter expectancy effect or pygmalion effect.) A potential *bias* caused by the researcher's expectations being communicated to subjects. [Chapters 3 and 6]

experiment   In the social sciences a study is called an experiment if the *subjects* have been subjected to a *treatment* or a naturally occurring event, and the purpose of the study is to assess the effect of that treatment or event. Three general types of experiments have been identified: *true experiments, quasi-experiments,* and *ex post facto research*. [*correlational research*]

experimental design   A *research design* in which the criteria for an *experiment* are met. [*nonexperimental design*]

experimental group   A *treatment group* that receives a *level* of the *independent variable* which is of substantive interest, as contrasted with the *control group*. [Chapter 12]

experimental research   Research using *experiments*. [*nonexperimental research, quasi-experimental research,* Chapter 12]

experimenter expectancy effect   See *expectancy effect*.

explanation   One of the possible outcomes of the *elaboration model*.

exploratory research   Research conducted in order to get ideas of what to study in a more rigorous way.

external criteria   Criteria for the evaluation of social science research based on reader's prior knowledge about the subject matter. [*internal criteria,* Chapter 1]

external validity   The *generality* of research results. [*internal validity*]

extraneous variable   A potentially *biasing variable.*

F test   A *significance test* that measures the ratio of two *variances.* It is often used as a synonym for the *analysis of variance* because the F *distribution* is used in that procedure.

face validity   One of several ways to assess the *validity* of a *measure.* It is a type of content validity based on someone's judgment of the appropriateness of the *measuring instrument* or its content. For example, using a series of directive questions about a subject's feelings and thoughts may seem to be more immediately related to emotional well-being than would the subject's interpretation of an ambiguous inkblot; most people would say the series of questions has a greater degree of face validity than the inkblots.

factor   A *variable;* in *factor analysis,* an underlying or invented variable discovered by doing the factor analysis. [*latent variable*]

factor analysis   A method for determining a new set of *variables* (called *factors*) which underlie the variables actually measured, usually for the purpose of reducing the number of variables to a smaller number of factors.

factor loadings   The *correlations* between the *factors* and the *variables* they underlie in *factor analysis.*

factor scores   The *scores* that the *units* or *subjects* would have obtained if they were measured on the *factors* in *factor analysis.*

factorial design   A *research design* with at least two *independent variables;* each level of every variable occurs at each level of every other variable. Factorial designs are often analyzed by *analysis of variance.*

factual accuracy   The accuracy of findings as applied to what was actually studied without regard to their *generality.* [*internal validity,* Chapter 2]

field experiment   An *experiment* conducted in a non*laboratory* setting, usually the natural environment of the phenomenon under study.

field study   *Nonexperimental research* carried out in a non*laboratory* environment, usually the natural environment of the phenomenon under study.

findings   The results of a research study.

fixed factor   An *independent variable* whose *levels* have been specifically chosen by the researcher. [*random factor*]

floor effect   The concentration of *scores* toward the low end of a measuring *scale* because of constraints on the lowest value the scores can assume. [*ceiling effect*]

forced-choice scale   A *scale* in which the *subject* is forced to make a choice among equally likely items. It is also a method for forming a *differential scale.*

fourfold point correlation   A *measure of association* for two *dichotomous variables.*

frequency   A count of how often a given value of a *variable* occurs in a set of *scores.*

frequency distribution   A table that shows how frequently each value of a *variable* occurs in a set of *scores.*

frequency polygon   A graph summarizing the *scores* of a single *variable.* The horizontal axis of the graph represents the different values of the variable and the vertical axis represents the *frequency*—that is, the number of times each score occurs in this set of data. The points on the graph are connected by line segments. It includes the same information as a *bar graph.*

gamma (Goodman & Kruskal's) A *symmetrical measure of association* based on *ranks*.

generality (Also known as generalizability.) The extent to which research *findings* can be applied outside the specific research situation. [*external validity,* Chapters 2 and 14]

generalizability See *generality.*

Goodman & Kruskal's gamma See *gamma (Goodman & Kruskal's).*

Goodman & Kruskal's tau See *tau (Goodman & Kruskal's).*

goodness of fit test A *significance test* which compares the *frequency distribution* of the obtained data with a hypothetical frequency distribution to see how well they match.

group mean The *mean* of the *scores* of the *subjects* in a *treatment group.* [Chapter 10]

Guttman scaling A *scale* consisting of *rank* ordered statements to choose among. The scale is constructed so that a given response on one statement will imply a given response on the following statement, thus indicating that a single dimension or aspect is being measured. The Guttman scale is one kind of *cumulative scale* because each item reflects an interesting amount of the individual's attitude or reaction.

Guttman's lambda See *lambda (Guttman's).*

H (index of uncertainty) A measure of the uncertainty in the prediction of a *variable.* H can be used as a measure of *dispersion* for a single variable or as a *measure of association* for two variables.

halo effect A possible *bias* due to the tendency to rate an *attribute* of a person or object based on a general overall impression of that person or object. [Chapter 3]

Hawthorne effect A possible *bias* caused by the attention given *subjects* by the experimenters. [Chapter 6]

histogram See *bar graph.*

history effect A possible *bias* due to the action of *extraneous variables* which occurred prior to obtaining the *dependent variable scores.* [*local history effect,* Chapter 12]

homogeneity of variance Equality of *variances.*

hypothesis A conjectural statement. [*operational hypothesis, theoretical hypothesis*]

hypothesis testing A method of *statistical inference* that leads to the rejection or nonrejection of statistical *hypotheses.* [Chapter 13]

independence No *association;* no *relationship.*

independent group design Any of several *research designs* in which the *dependent variable scores* in a *treatment group* are not related to the dependent variable scores in any other group.

independent variable The *variable* thought to produce an effect on the *dependent variable.*

index The results of combining two or more *variables* into a single measure; sometimes used synonymously with *scale.*

inference The process of reasoning from particular to general statements.

inferential statistics See *statistical inference.*

informant A person who gives the researcher information about what is being studied (e.g., the native language or customs). [*respondent, subject*]

instrumentation effect A possible *bias* caused by the *measuring instruments* themselves, particularly if the instruments change from *pretest* to *posttest.* [Chapter 12]

interaction The joint effect of more than one *independent variable* on the *dependent variable,* as contrasted to the individual effects of the independent variables. [*main effect, specification*]

internal consistency A common method for ascertaining the *reliability* of paper-and-pencil *measuring instruments.* Under this approach the instrument is considered reliable if there is agreement in the responses to individual items. For example, an achievement test is said to be internally consistent if people who do well on half the test also do well on the other half. [*test-retest, Spearman-Brown formula*]

internal criteria Criteria for the evaluation of social science research based on an examination of the methods used. [*external criteria,* Chapter 1]

internal validity A consideration of whether the *independent variable* produced variation in the *dependent variable.* Thus, internal validity is a type of *factual accuracy.* [*external validity*]

interpretation One of the possible outcomes of the *elaboration model.*

interquartile range A measure of *dispersion;* the difference between the third *quartile* and the first quartile.

intersubjectivity The notion that different scientists who make the same observations or carry out the same experiment will arrive at the same conclusions.

interval estimate A range of values within which a *parameter* is estimated to lie. [*confidence interval*]

interval level of measurement The *level of measurement* that preserves the intervals between values. That is, equal differences on the measurement scale reflect equal differences in what is being measured.

intervening variable 1. A measurable variable used to indicate the values of unmeasurable *constructs.* 2. A *test variable* in a *causal model* that follows an *antecedent variable* but precedes a *consequent variable.* [*elaboration model*]

interview schedule The questions and instructions an interviewer uses in the conduct of an *interview.*

interviewing A method of data collection used in *survey research* and in *case studies.* There may be face-to-face meeting between the interviewer and the *respondent,* or it can take place over the telephone. [*mail survey, telephone survey*]

item analysis A method of establishing the *validity* of an *index* or the individual items on a test or *questionnaire.*

judgmental sampling A nonrandom sampling technique in which researchers use their knowledge of a *population* to select a *sample* for a given purpose.

Kendall's tau See *tau (Kendall's).*

Kruskal-Wallis test A *nonparametric significance test* of the difference between two or more *independent groups* based on *ranks.*

kurtosis A measure of how peaked a *frequency distribution* is. [*leptokurtic, mesokurtic, platykurtic*]

laboratory experiment An *experiment* that takes place in an environment that can be highly controlled.

lambda (Guttman's) A *measure of association* between two *categorized variables.* There is a *symmetrical* and an *asymmetrical* version of lambda; both have straightforward P.R.E. interpretations.

latent variable A *variable,* not directly observed, which is assumed to underlie or effect the response. [*factor*]

least squares criterion   A mathematical method of finding a line of best fit for a set of data; used in *linear* and *curvilinear regression.* [*curve fitting*]

leptokurtic   A sharply peaked *frequency distribution.* [*kurtosis*]

level   See *treatment level.*

level of measurement   A characteristic of *measurements.* The level of measurement refers to which numeric properties the data values have. The most commonly cited levels are *nominal, ordinal, interval,* and *ratio.*

level of significance   See *significance level.*

leveling variable   A *variable* used to form a *related group design.*

Likert scale   A type of *summated rating scale* consisting of responses such as "strongly agree," "agree," "disagree," and "strongly disagree." The *subject* is asked to choose the response that best reflects his or her reaction to a given statement.

linear regression   A statistical procedure which fits a straight line to a set of data. The line summarizes *relationships* between one or more *predictor variables* and a *dependent variable.* [*curve fitting, curvilinear regression, multiple regression, regression model, simple regression*]

local history effect   A *history effect* which occurs in only one of the *treatment groups.*

log-linear model   A mathematical model of the *association* between *variables* and of data arising from *cross-tabulations.*

longitudinal study   A study conducted over a period of time, although sometimes only at a few discrete points in time during the period. [*cross-sectional study*]

mail survey   A *survey* method in which *self-administered questionnaires* are sent to potential *respondents* through the mails. [*telephone survey, interviewing*]

main effect   The effect of an individual *independent variable* on the *dependent variable.* [*interaction*]

manipulated variable   An *independent variable* whose values are manipulated by the experimenter. For instance, an experimenter might give various amounts of reward to various *experimental groups.*

Mann-Whitney U test   A *nonparametric significance test* of differences between two *independent groups* based on *ranks.*

marginals   Row and column totals which appear, for instance, at the bottom and sides of a *cross-tabulation.*

matched-pairs design   A type of *related group design.*

matching   The process of pairing individuals in different *experimental groups* on the basis of another *variable* in order to control the potential extraneous effects of that variable or to increase the *precision* of the study, or both. Matching is used to produce a *related group design.*

maturation effect   A possible *bias* due to changes in the *subjects* between *measurements* which are due to reasons unrelated to the experimental *treatment.* [Chapter 12]

mean   A measure of *central tendency* (the middle) of a set of scores. The mean is frequently called the *average.* [*median, mode,* Chapter 10]

measure   See *measurement* and *data matrix.*

measurement   (Also known as a score or a measure.) 1. A value obtained from using a *measurement instrument.* 2. The process of obtaining those values.

measurement error   The degree to which the *measuring instrument* fails to measure the phenomenon under study; often used to refer only to *random errors.* [Chapter 9]

measures of association   *Descriptive statistics* which summarize the amount of *association* between two or more *variables.* There are many measures of association commonly used in the social sciences; some are included as separate items in this glossary. Most measures of association are constructed so that the maximum obtainable value is +1 (indicating the strongest possible association between the variables). The lowest possible obtainable value is usually either zero (no *relationship,* or *independence* between the variables) or –1 indicating the strongest possible negative relationship. Choosing the appropriate measure of association depends upon several considerations: whether there are two or more than two variables involved; whether the variables are *continuous* or *discrete;* whether the data values are numeric scores, *ranks,* or *frequencies;* whether a *symmetrical* or *asymmetrical measure of association* is appropriate; and whether it is important for the measure to have P.R.E. interpretation. [Chapter 11]

measuring instrument   A device, applied to the *subjects* or *observations,* which produces the data values for one or more *variables.* A *questionnaire* is a measuring instrument, so is a stopwatch, and so is an expert making judgments.

median   A measure of *central tendency* (the middle) of a set of scores; the point below which 50 percent of the scores in a set of data lie. [*mean, mode,* Chapter 10]

median test   A *nonparametric significance test* of the differences between two or more *independent groups* based on *frequencies.*

mesokurtic   A moderately peaked *frequency distribution.* [*kurtosis*]

meta-analysis   A type of non-empirical research that is based on the findings from many or most of the prior studies of the topic. Meta-analysis analyzes the existing studies to discover if any common trends or overall conclusions can be justified.

mode   A measure of *central tendency* (the middle) of a set of scores; the most frequently occurring value in a set of scores. [*mean, median,* Chapter 10]

model   A simplified description of a phenomenon, often in words, in pictures, or in symbols.

monomethod bias   A possible *bias* due to using a single method of administering stimuli to *subjects.* [*multitrait-multimethod*]

mono-operational bias   A possible *bias* due to having a single (and therefore limited) *measure* represent multiple *constructs.*

mortality effect   A possible *bias* due to having *subjects* drop out of the *experiment* in some systematic way. [Chapter 12]

multicollinearity   High intercorrelations among *independent variables.* If these *correlations* are too high, the stability of the results of some statistical analyses is weakened and the interpretation of the results will be unclear.

multidimensional scaling   A method of representing judgments of the *relationships* among stimuli as distances and then using those distances to calculate the corresponding location of the stimuli in multidimensional space.

multiple correlation coefficient   A *measure of association* (symbolized by R) between two or more *predictor variables* and a single *criterion variable.* [*coefficient of determination*]

multiple regression   A statistical procedure determining an equation which best predicts the *dependent variable* from two or more *predictor variables.*

multitrait-multimethod   A method of testing *construct validity* using the *correlations* among more than one *attribute* or trait and more than one method of *measurement.*

multivariate analysis   Statistical techniques involving more than one *dependent variable* in a single analysis. Sometimes the term multivariate is applied to statistical procedures that use more than two *variables* at once, regardless of whether those variables are *independent* or dependent. [*bivariate analysis, univariate analysis*]

naturalistic observation   A method of gathering data that involves making a detailed record of events as they occur in their natural setting while having as little effect as possible on those events.

negative skew   A frequency distribution whose scores are bunched up at the positive end of the scale; the "tail" of the distribution sticks out in the negative direction. [*skew*]

nesting   A *research design* in which some *levels* of one *independent variable* are contained within the levels of another independent variable. For example, a study may examine five social welfare agencies in two cities—two agencies in the first city and three in the second. This situation would be described as agencies nested within cities.

noise   (Also known as random error.) Error that is unpredictable in the short run; it can be in either direction and varies in magnitude. [*bias,* Chapter 7]

nominal level of measurement   The *level of measurement* at which numeric values represent only the inclusion in or exclusion from a category; the numbers do not have any numeric meaning, they are simply symbols which "name" each category. Sex and race are typically measured at the nominal level.

nondirective interviewing   *Interviewing* that attempts to give the *respondent* maximum latitude as to how questions will be answered. *Open questions* are usually used. [*directive interviewing*]

nonexperimental design   A *research design* in which it is impossible to control all *biases* and protect *internal validity.* [*experiment, experimental design*]

nonexperimental research   Research using *nonexperimental designs.* [*experiment, experimental research*]

nonparametric statistics   *Inferential statistical* procedures that make fewer or less restrictive assumptions about the underlying *populations.* Usually, these procedures are based on *frequencies* (i.e., how many *subjects* got each *score* or fell into each category) or *ranks.* [*parametric statistics*]

nonprobability sampling   Nonrandom sampling. [*random sampling*]

nonsampling error   Error in the data arising from a study which used some form of *survey research.* The error may be due to inadequacies in design, *questionnaire* construction, *interviewing,* data analysis, etc. Nonsampling error may contain *noise* or *biases* or both. It may exist even if the entire *population* was surveyed; thus, nonsampling error can be present if *sampling error* does not exist.

normal distribution   A mathematically defined, symmetrical, unimodal *distribution.* Many *variables* are approximately normally distributed, and many *inferential statistical* procedures require or make some assumptions about the normality of the scores.

null hypothesis   A *hypothesis* about *parameters* which is tested statistically. Usually the null hypothesis reflects no *relationship,* no difference, or the status quo of a phenomenon or relationship. [*alternative hypothesis, statistical inference,* Chapter 13]

objective tests   Tests that do not require researchers to make judgments. For instance, tests that involve counting and calculations (that all trained people can do in exactly the same way) are usually more objective than tests that require insight or "reading between the lines."

observation   Use synonymously with either *case* or *measurement.*

omega squared   A *proportionate reduction of error measure of effect size;* often used after a *t test* or the *analysis of variance.* It is interpretable as a percent of *variance* in the *dependent variable* accounted for through knowledge of the *independent variable.*

one-alternative test   (Also known as one-tailed test.) A *significance test* of a *null hypothesis* whose *alternative,* or region of rejection, lies in one tail of the *sampling distribution.*

one-way analysis of variance   (Also known as a one-way design.) An *analysis of variance* design with only one *independent variable*.

open questions   Questions that allow the *respondent* maximum latitude as to how to answer. For instance, "How do you feel about capital punishment?" [*closed questions*]

operational definition   A method of defining *variables* or *constructs* based on how they are *measured*. [*conceptual definition*, Chapter 8]

operational hypothesis   The specific *hypothesis* tested in a study.

ordinal level of measurement   The *level of measurement* at which order is preserved. That is, higher values on the measuring scale reflect more of what is being *measured*, but not how much more. Socioeconomic status is typically measured at the ordinal level.

organismic variable   An *attribute variable* when the *unit of analysis* is a person or a group of people.

orthogonal factors   *Factors* that are *independent* of each other in *factor analysis*.

outcome variable   See *dependent variable*.

outlier   A *measurement* very different in value from other measurements in the data set.

paired comparisons   1. Comparisons made in pairs, as between all possible pairs of groups. 2. A method for forming a *differential scale*.

panel study   A type of *longitudinal study:* the collection of data from the same *respondents* at several different points in time. [*cohort study*]

paradigm   A complex theoretical *model* that is used to explain phenomenon.

parameter   A numeric attribute of a *population*, such as the *mean* of the population. [*statistic*]

parametric statistics   *Inferential statistical* procedures which are based on certain required conditions in the underlying *populations*. [*nonparametric statistics*]

part correlation   (Also known as part r or semipartial r.) A *measure of association* that includes *control* for one or more related *variables*. The related variables are mathematically removed from one of the variables in the association.

partial correlation   (Also known as partial r.) A *measure of association* that includes *control* for one or more related *variables*. The related variables are mathematically removed from both of the variables in the association.

participant observation   A method of gathering data where the researcher becomes a participant in the events of interest in order to make observations and gain insights not available through other types of research.

path analysis   A graphic representation of the *relationship* between *variables* which, combined with *regression* analysis, allows the researcher to estimate the effects of some variables on other variables; often used to form *causal models*.

Pearson's chi square test of independence   See *chi square test*.

Pearson's product moment correlation   See *r* (*Pearson's*).

Pearson's r   See *r* (*Pearson's*).

percentile   A representation of a given *score* in terms of the percentage of scores lower than that score. [*decile, quartile*, Chapter 10]

phi coefficient   A *symmetrical measure of association* between two *categorized variables*.

pilot study   A study carried out on a small *sample* drawn from the *population* of interest in order to gain additional information or to check out procedures for use in the design and conduct of the main study.

placebo effect   A possible *bias* caused by a *subject's* expectations that a *treatment* will have an effect—even though the treatment should not have an effect (such as distilled water as a medication).

platykurtic distribution   A relatively flat *frequency distribution*. [*kurtosis*]

point-biserial correlation   A *measure of association* between one *continuous variable* and one *dichotomous variable*.

policy research   Research conducted to help formulate or evaluate policy, usually policy of government agencies. [*action research, applied research, basic research*]

pooling   A method of combining *error variances* in *inferential statistics*.

population   All possible *observations* or *units* which could be used in a study. [*sample*, Chapter 14]

positive skew   A *frequency distribution* whose scores are bunched up at the negative end of the scale. The "tail" of the distribution sticks out in the positive direction. [*skew*]

postanalysis of variance testing   *Significance testing* conducted following an *analysis of variance* to identify which *means* differ significantly.

posttest   *Measurement* of experimental *subjects* on a given *variable* after a *treatment* is given. [*pretest*]

posttest-only design   See *after-only design*.

power   The probability of correctly rejecting a *null hypothesis* which is in fact false.

P.R.E.   See *proportionate reduction in error*.

precision   The degree to which research results are free from *noise*. [*accuracy*]

predicted variable   The *variable* whose values are predicted from other variables. The term is synonymous with *dependent variable* but used when the researcher is engaged in *prediction*.

prediction   Using one or more *variables* to predict the value of another variable.

predictive validity   One of several ways to assess the *validity* of a *measure*. It is a type of *criterion validity* based on the ability of the *variable* in question to predict another variable that will be measured at a later time. [Chapter 9]

predictor variable   The *variable* used to predict another variable; often it is an *independent variable*.

pretest   1. *Measurement* of *subjects* on a given *variable* before the *independent variable treatments* are administered. 2. A *pilot study*. [*posttest*]

pretest-posttest design   See *before-after design*.

primary data   Data specifically collected for a given analysis. [*secondary analysis*]

principal factor solution   A method of obtaining a unique solution in a *factor analysis*.

probability distribution   A table or graph which pairs different possible values of a *variable* with their probabilities. A *sampling distribution* is an important type of probability distribution.

probability sampling   See *random sampling*.

product moment correlation   See *r (Pearson's)*.

proportionate reduction in error   (Also known as P.R.E.) The improvement in one's ability to predict values of one *variable* when knowledge of another variable is made available, expressed as a percentage.

proximate measures   Obtainable *measures* that are used as clues for the desired measures which will not be available for some time.

psychometrics   Methods for measuring psychological *variables*.

purposive sampling   See *judgmental sampling*.

***p* value**   See *significance level*.

Pygmalion effect   See *expectancy effect*.

Q sort   A method of *scaling* wherein *subjects* are asked to sort statements into a special number of discrete categories with the additional restriction that a certain number of statements must be placed in each category. The categories are ordered in some way, often along the agree-disagree continuum.

Q (Yule's)   A *symmetrical measure of association* for two *dichotomous variables.*

qualitative research   (Also known as qualitative analysis.) 1. Research methods that attempt to understand people or social entities from their own point of view. Qualitative "data" often take the form of description in natural language. 2. Research methods that make extensive use of *nominal level* data. [*field study, quantitative research*]

quantitative research   (Also known as quantitative analysis.) 1. Research methods that attempt to categorize and summarize *observations* numerically; a *measuring instrument* is used to help transform the observations into *scores.* 2. Research methods that make extensive use of *ordinal, interval,* or *ratio level* data. [*qualitative research*]

quartile   One of four data points each representing an increment of 25 percent of the scores in a data set. [*decile, median, percentile*]

quasi-experimental research   An *experiment* in which some, but not all, sources of potential *bias* are under the *control* of the experimenter; at least *random assignment* is usually missing. [*ex post facto research, true experiment*]

questionnaire   A list of questions to be asked of respondents either through an *interview* or through self-administration. [*self-administered questionnaire*]

quota sampling   A method of sampling which requires that a specified number of each identified subgroup of the *population* (e.g., blue-collar, males, under age 25) is included and the results from each subgroup are weighted to conform to the proportion of that subgroup in the population.

R   See *multiple correlation coefficient.*

r (Pearson's)   A measure of linear *association,* most commonly used with two *continuous variables.* It is a *symmetrical measure* and *r squared* has a straightforward P.R.E. interpretation.

R squared   See *coefficient of determination.*

r squared   *Pearson's r* squared is a *proportionate reduction of error measure* of *effect size.* It is interpreted as a percent of *variance* in the *independent variable* accounted for through knowledge of the *independent variable.*

random assignment   The process of assigning *subjects* to *treatment groups* at random such that each subject has an equal probability of being assigned to each treatment group. [Chapter 12]

random error   See *noise.*

random factor   An *independent variable* whose *treatment levels* were randomly selected from a *population* of treatment levels.

random sampling   A method of sampling in which every unit in the *population* has a known chance of being selected. [Chapter 14]

randomization   See *random assignment.*

randomized block design   A type of *related group design.*

range   A *measure* of *dispersion* equal to the value of the highest *score* minus the value of the lowest score in the data set.

rank   The rank of 1 indicates that the *observation* or *subject* with that rank has the highest *score,* or was judged the best. A rank score of 2 indicates second best, and so on. Rank data may be collected originally as ranks (e.g., experts may be asked to indicate which object or person is best, second best, etc.) or ranks can be derived directly from scores. If, for example, the scores of five subjects were 73, 14, 81, 82, and 76, then the rank scores for the five would be 4, 5, 2, 1, and 3. Rank data meets the requirements of *ordinal level of measurement.*

rating scale   A *scale* on which a *subject* assigns items into classes or assigns them numeric values. For example, in a study of language problems among emotionally disturbed children, the items might include: "doesn't talk, mumbles incoherently, uses words clearly, uses incomplete sentences, uses sentences correctly." The subject is then asked to place the person in question (usually it is the person completing the instrument, but it can be anyone known to that individual, or it can be a group, organization, or country) on the scale by identifying which item is closest to that person's belief or situation.

ratio level measurement   The *level of measurement* which has all the properties of the other levels of measurement plus a true zero point. That is, zero on the measuring scale corresponds to "none" of what is being measured. Time, age, income, and counts (e.g., number of errors) are typically measured at the ratio level.

raw scores   Values of data derived directly from the *measuring instrument.*

recruitment effect   See *selection effect.*

recursive model   A type of *causal* or *path model* which is relatively simple in its structure in that causal links go only in one direction.

regression   See *linear, curvilinear,* or *multiple regression.*

regression coefficient   A weight (or multiplier) of a *predictor variable* in *regression.* Regression coefficients are determined by applying the *least squares criterion* to the data. [*b, beta weight*]

regression model   A mathematical representation of the *relationship* between a *predicted variable* and one or more *predictor variables.* [*linear regression, curvilinear regression, multiple regression*]

regression toward the mean   A possible *bias* due to remeasuring individuals who were originally selected because they all had either extremely low or extremely high *scores.* Their *average* score on the second *measurement* will be closer to the mean of all the scores, even though there are no changes in the individuals between the two measurements. [Chapter 12]

related group design   (Also known as correlated group design.) Any of several *research designs* in which one or more additional *variables* (called *blocking, leveling,* or *matching* variables) are used to place the *dependent variable scores* in some arrangement so that the groups of these scores are related. One attraction of related group designs is that they can have more *precision* than *independent group* designs. *Matched-pairs designs, randomized block designs, treatment by levels designs,* and *repeated measures designs* are commonly used related group designs.

related group tests   *Significance tests* among groups that are *correlated* on some *variable.* Used on data arising from a *related group design.*

relationship   See *association.*

reliability   The extent to which a *measuring instrument* would give the same value if used over and over providing the *attribute* measured did not change. [*validity, internal consistency, test-retest,* Chapter 9]

reliability coefficient   A number, usually between zero and one, indicating the degree of *reliability* of a *measuring instrument.* A reliability coefficient can often be interpreted as a *measure of association* between a set of scores obtained at one time, and another set of scores obtained at another time; both sets of scores are from *measurements* of the same variable on the same subjects. [Chapter 9]

repeated measures design   An *experimental design* in which each *subject* or *unit* is tested under more than one *level* of the *independent variable;* a type of *related group design.*

replication   1. A repetition of a research investigation. 2. One possible outcome of the *elaboration model.*

research design   The strategy or plan of an *experiment,* often focusing on the *control* of possible *biases* and the scheduling of *treatments* and *measurements.* [Chapter 12]

residual   The portion of each *dependent variable score* which cannot be accounted for by the *independent variables.*

respondents   The person who answers the questions asked in an *interview* or on a *questionnaire*. [*informant, subject*]

response rate   (Also known as return rate or completion rate.) The percentage of people selected that actually take part in the study. For example, in a *mail survey*, the response rate may be calculated by dividing the number of returned questionnaires by the total number mailed.

response variable   See *dependent variable*.

retrospective case study   A *case study* of events that have occurred in the past. Usually information is obtained from institutional records.

return rate   See *response rate*.

rho (Spearman's)   A *symmetrical measure of association* based on *ranks*.

robustness   The ability of *significance tests* to work adequately when their underlying assumptions are violated.

rotated axes   The mathematical redefinition of the hypothetical *factors* (obtained from *factor analysis* or from several other *multivariate* statistical procedures) in order to fit the original data better or account for the data more economically.

sample   The subset of the *population* actually used in the research. [Chapter 14]

sample mean   The *mean* of a *sample*. [Chapter 10]

sampling bias   A potential *bias* caused by drawing a nonrepresentative *sample*.

sampling distribution   A type of *probability distribution* which pairs together each possible value of a *statistic* (such as a *mean*) with its probability of occurrence under the assumption that nothing but randomness was operating.

sampling error   The degree to which a *sample statistic* (e.g., the *mean*) fails to equal the *average* of an infinite number of determinations of this statistic from the same *population*. Sampling error is the result of *noise* from *random sampling*. [*nonsampling error*]

sampling frame   The actual list from which the *sample* is selected.

sampling validity   One of several ways to assess the *validity* of a *measure*. It is a type of *content validity* based on the degree to which the instrument or procedure measures all aspects of what should be measured.

scale   In the social sciences, a scale usually begins from a paper and pencil instrument which has been designed to measure beliefs, attitudes, or opinions. Usually, many questions, items, or statements are needed to ensure that the desired *concept* or attitude is being measured; one or two items would not tap all aspects of the concept. A large number of items, however, are troublesome to deal with. Scaling helps the researcher by identifying the "best" items to use and by specifying how to summarize the responses to all the items being used into a single numeric value for each individual. This value or *score* places the individual on the scale, and different individuals can be compared in terms of their attitudes or reactions by comparing their scores. While it is easy to develop a set of questions or items people can react to, it is often difficult to produce a scale that results in numeric values that have certain desired properties such as linearity, unidimensionality, and additivity. It is highly unlikely that any given scale has all these properties yet alone *validity* and *reliability*. Thus, researchers need to choose from among several common scale types the one that best meets their needs.

scalogram analysis   A method for determining if a *scale* meets the requirements of a *Guttman scale*.

scattergram   (Also known as a scatterplot.) A plot of points showing the *relationship* between two or more *variables*. Each observation contributes one "point" on the scattergram; the variables form the axes of the plot.

score   See *measurement*.

secondary analysis   An analysis of data originally collected for another purpose. [*primary data*]

selection effect   (Also known as recruitment effect.) A possible *bias* due to differences in treatment groups caused by faulty selection of *subjects* for the groups. [Chapter 6]

self-administered questionnaire   A *questionnaire* such as the kind used in a mail survey which does not need to be explained to *respondents* and which does not involve a researcher's asking the questions.

self-fulfilling prophecy   The idea that researchers' expectations can be communicated to *subjects* and that subjects may say or do things to meet those expectations. [*expectancy effect*]

semantic differential   A method of determining the connotative meaning of concepts or attitudinal reactions to them. Semantic differential *scales* consist of several bipolar adjectival pairs (e.g., good-bad) and a continuum between them of usually seven steps. All the adjective pairs are used in assessing an individual's reaction to a single topic or concept. The adjective pairs reflect several *independent* dimensions of one's attitude or reaction to the concept. The scoring within each dimension often consists of summing or averaging the responses to each of the adjective pairs, each pair contributing equally to the total.

semipartial r   See *part correlation*.

sign test   A *nonparametric significance test* of the difference between two *related groups*.

significance level   In a *significance test* the probability that the results could be due to chance if the *null hypothesis* is true. The lower the significance level, the stronger the evidence that the null hypothesis should be rejected. [*alpha*]

significance test   An inferential statistical procedure which uses statistical values to help determine whether or not the *null hypothesis* should be rejected.

simple regression   A statistical procedure for determining an equation that best predicts the *dependent variable* from a single *predictor variable*.

skew   Lack of symmetry in a *frequency distribution*. [*negative skew, positive skew*]

slope   The angle of a *regression* line through a set of data.

smallest space analysis   A graphical method for representing *associations* among *variables* in multidimensional space.

snowball sample   A type of *nonprobability sampling* in which each *respondent* identifies others to be included in the *sample*.

social desirability effect   A potential *bias* caused by *subjects* trying to say or do what they think they should. [Chapter 6]

sociogram   A method for graphically expressing *relationships* among the people in a group.

Spearman-Brown formula   A formula for correcting a *reliability coefficient*. *Internal consistency* measures of *reliability* are based on a shortened version (usually half) of the instrument which, if uncorrected, would produce a reliability coefficient that was too low.

Spearman's rank order correlation coefficient   See *rho (Spearman's)*.

Spearman's rho   See *rho (Spearman's)*.

specification   One of the possible outcomes of the *elaboration model*.

spurious correlation   Evidence of a *correlation* where no correlation actually exists or which disappears when a *test variable* is *controlled*. [*suppressor variable, elaboration model*]

standard deviation   A measure of *dispersion*.

standard error   The *standard deviation* of the *sampling distribution* of a given *statistic*.

standard error of the mean   The *standard deviation* of the *sampling distribution* of the *sample mean*.

standardized score   A *score* that has had the effects of *central tendency* and *dispersion* removed so that it can be used to make comparisons. A *z score* is a frequently used standardized score.

statistic   A numeric property of a *sample* such as the *mean* of the sample. [*parameter*]

statistical inference   (Also known as inferential statistics.) The process of estimating *parameters* from *statistics,* or the process of determining the amount of *random error* in the data and the probability of that random error having produced the obtained results. *Confidence intervals* and *significance tests* are the most frequently used forms of statistical inference in the social sciences.

statistical significance   The outcome (usually the desired outcome) of *significance tests* in which the results are shown to have a low probability (less than *alpha*) of being due to chance alone, thereby eliminating chance as a viable cause of the results. [Chapter 13]

stepwise regression   A *multiple regression* technique in which *predictor variables* are added to (or taken out of) the *regression model* one at a time according to specified criteria.

stochastic   Involving probabilities.

stratified sample   A *random sample* drawn from homogeneous subsets of a *population.* For example, subsamples might be drawn from nonethnic and ethnic subpopulations rather than from the city as a whole. [Chapter 14]

structural equations   Mathematical models (similar to *regression models*) which summarize the causal relationships in a *causal model* or *path analysis.* There will usually be one structural equation for each *endogenous variable* in the model.

structured interviewing   *Interviewing* in which both the format for asking questions and the exact phrasing of the questions are fixed; the interviewer has little, if any, flexibility in conducting the interview. [*unstructured interviewing*]

student's t   See *t test.*

subject   A term used to refer to the people being studied. [*informant, respondent*]

subject variable   An *attribute variable* when the *unit of analysis* is a *subject.*

successive intervals   A method for forming a *differential scale.*

sum of squares   The sum of squared deviations of *scores* from their *group mean.*

summated ratings scale   A *scale* in which the numeric value obtained from each response statement or item is added to form the total *score* for an individual. A *Likert scale* is a commonly used type of summated rating scale.

suppressor variable   A *variable,* which if uncontrolled, acts to lower the *association* between two other variables. That is, if that variable is controlled for (as in *partial correlation*), the association between the two variables will be higher. [*elaboration model*]

survey research   A method of studying the characteristics of large groups of people or other units by examining *variables* measured on all the people (as in a *census*) or on a *sample* of those people. [Chapter 14]

symmetrical measures of association   *Measures of association* that do not distinguish between *independent* and *dependent variables.* If the roles of the variables were reversed, the degree of association calculated would be the same. [*asymmetrical measures of association*]

systematic error   See *bias.*

T (Tschuprow's)   A *symmetrical measure of association* between two *categorized variables.*

t test   A *significance test* most commonly used to determine if the *means* of two groups are different.

tau (Goodman & Kruskal's)   An *asymmetrical measure of association* for two *categorized variables.* Tau has a straightforward P.R.E. interpretation.

tau (Kendall's)   There are three different versions of Kendall's tau; all are *symmetrical measures of association* based on *ranks.*

telephone survey   A *survey* conducted by telephone. [*mail survey, interviewing*]

test statistic   The *statistic* that is tested in *statistical inference.* Test statistics such as t, F, or chi square do not have as much commonsensical meaning as do other statistics (e.g., the *mean* and *standard deviation*).

test variable   (Also known as a *control variable.*) A *variable* which may affect the degree of *association* or the interpretation of the association between two other variables. [*elaboration model*]

testing effect   A possible *bias* due to the effect of the testing or measuring process itself. [Chapter 12]

test-retest   A method for assessing the *reliability* of a *measuring instrument* based on repeated uses of it. If a *measurement* is repeated on the same people or objects and the two sets of *scores* are highly *correlated,* the measurement procedure has a high test-retest reliability. [*internal consistency,* Chapter 9]

tetrachoric r   A *measure of association* between two *dichotomous variables.*

theoretical hypothesis   A more general *hypothesis* within a theoretical framework.

time series analysis   A *quasi-experimental design* in which *measurements* are taken periodically over time.

total variance   The *variance* of all the *scores* in a study.

trait   Some property or quality, usually of a person.

treatment   See *treatment level.*

treatment by levels design   A *related group design.*

treatment groups   Groups of *subjects* in *experimental* research each of which receives one *level* of the *independent variable;* sometimes used synonymously with *experimental groups.*

treatment level   A value of an *independent variable* in *experimental research.* For example, if the treatment is drug dosage, the treatment levels might be 0 milligrams, 10 milligrams, and 20 milligrams. If the treatment is a therapeutic procedure, the treatment levels might be different types of therapy.

trend study   A study of changes in *variables* over time.

true experiment   An *experiment* in which the researcher has a high degree of *control* over possible sources of *bias* and uses *random assignment.*

Tschuprow's T   See *T (Tschuprow's).*

two-alternative test   (Also known as a two-tailed test.) A *significance test* of the *null hypothesis* whose *alternatives,* or regions of rejection, lie in both tails of the *sampling distribution.* [*one-alternative test*]

two-way analysis of variance   (Also known as a two-way design.) An *analysis of variance* with two *independent variables;* often, but not necessarily, a *factorial design.* [*one-way analysis of variance*]

Type I error   Incorrectly rejecting a true *null hypothesis.*

Type II error   Failing to reject the *null hypothesis* when it should be rejected (i.e., it is false).

U test   See *Mann-Whitney U test.*

uncertainty measure   See *H (index of uncertainty).*

unexplained variance   *Dependent variables variance* not accounted for by the *independent variables;* the variance of the *residuals.* [*error variance, variance accounted for*]

unit of analysis   The things being studied such as individuals, organizations, classrooms, etc. [*case*]

univariate analysis   An analysis of each *variable* in a study, one at a time. [*bivariate analysis, multivariate analysis*]

universe   Often, but not always, used synonymously with *population.*

unobtrusive measures   Methods of data collection that do not affect or impinge upon the objects being studied. [Chapter 12]

unstructured interviewing   *Interviewing* in which both the format for asking questions and the exact phrasing of the questions to be asked are flexible. [*structured interviewing*]

V (Cramer's)   A *symmetrical measure of association* between two *categorized variables.*

validity   How well a *measuring instrument* measures the phenomenon under investigation. Major classes of validity include *construct validity, content validity,* and *criterion validity.* [*reliability,* Chapter 9]

variable   An *attribute* or property of a person, group, or object that can be measured; the resulting *measures* are capable of assuming different values. [Chapter 11]

variance   A measure of *dispersion.*

variance accounted for   *Variance* that one *variable* has in common with other variables and is therefore considered to be accounted for by them. [*unexplained variance*]

Wilcoxin test for signed ranks   A *nonparametric significance test* of the difference between two *related groups* based on *ranks.*

wild score   See *outlier.*

within-group differences   Variability among *scores* within a *treatment group;* usually thought to indicate *random error.* [*between-group differences*]

Yule's Q   See Q (Yule's).

Z score   A specific type of *standardized score.*

BIBLIOGRAPHY

The following textbooks include introductory-level discussions of most of the terms in the glossary. Of course, numerous others could have been listed. We chose those which we have found especially helpful and which are likely to be readily available.

Babbie, Earl. *The Practice of Social Research,* 7th ed. Belmont, CA: Wadsworth, 1995.

Isaac, Stephen and William B. Michael. *Handbook in Research and Evaluation: A Collection of Principles, Methods, and Strategies Useful in the Planning, Design, and Evaluation of Studies in Education and the Behavioral Sciences,* 3rd ed. San Diego, CA: Educational and Industrial Testing Services, 1995.

Kerlinger, Fred N. *Foundations of Behavioral Research,* 3rd ed. New York: Holt, Rinehart & Winston, 1986.

Krathwohl, David R. *Methods of Educational and Social Science Research: An Integrative Approach.* New York: Longman, 1993.

Maxwell, Joseph A. *Qualitative Research Design: An Interactive Approach.* Thousand Oaks, CA: Sage Publications, 1996.

Pedhazur, Elazar J. and L. P. Schmelken. *Measurement, Design, and Analysis: An Integrated Approach.* Hillsdale, NJ: Erlbaum, 1991.

INDEX